THE WALL STREET JOURNAL.

NATIONAL
BUSINESS
EMPLOYMENT
WEEKLY

D0674957

GUIDE TO
SELF-EMPLOYMENT

THE NATIONAL BUSINESS EMPLOYMENT WEEKLY
PREMIER GUIDES SERIES

Resumes,   ISBN #0-471-31029-8 cloth;
                             ISBN #0-471-31028-X paper

Interviewing,   ISBN #0-471-31024-7 cloth;
                             ISBN #0-471-31025-5 paper

Networking,   ISBN #0-471-31026-3 cloth;
                             ISBN #0-471-31027-1 paper

Jobs Rated Almanac,   ISBN #0-471-05495-X paper

Cover Letters,   ISBN #0-471-10671-2 cloth;
                             ISBN #0-471-10672-0 paper

Love Your Work,   ISBN #0-471-11956-3 paper

Self-Employment,   ISBN #0-471-10918-5 paper

THE WALL STREET JOURNAL.

NATIONAL
BUSINESS
EMPLOYMENT
WEEKLY

GUIDE TO
SELF-EMPLOYMENT

A Round-up of Career Alternatives
Ranging from
Consulting & Professional Temping
to Starting or Buying a Business

David Lord

John Wiley & Sons, Inc.

New York • Chichester • Brisbane • Toronto • Singapore

Copyright © 1996 by National Business Employment Weekly
Published by John Wiley & Sons, Inc.

Library of Congress Cataloging-in-Publication Data:

National business employment weekly guide to self-employment /
   National business employment weekly book.
       p.   cm. — (The National business employment weekly premier
  guides series)
   Includes bibliographical references.
   ISBN 0-471-10918-5 (pbk. : alk. paper)
   1. New business enterprises.   2. Self-employed.
  3. Entrepreneurship.   I. National business employment weekly.
  II. Series.
  HD62.5.N365   1996
  658'.041—dc20   95-51321

10   9   8   7   6   5   4   3   2   1

Foreword

When David Lord and I first discussed this book, he was happily employed by a New Hampshire publishing and consulting firm. In the months that followed, David decided to take the leap and start a consulting firm of his own. The lessons he learned—combined with the wonderful advice he researched and reported—have led to the creation of a truly helpful book.

The Guide to Self-Employment covers every meaningful aspect of launching a consulting practice, starting a company from scratch, buying a business or franchise and accepting temporary executive positions. It's also designed to help you analyze your strengths and weaknesses, as well as your ability to thrive as an entrepreneur.

What makes David's advice especially compelling are the many case studies of others who have tread these paths successfully in recent years. By following their examples, you can avoid common mistakes and emulate strategies that appeal to your working style.

Also helpful are the many quizzes and self-exams that allow you to compare your talents and experiences with those of effective small-business owners and consultants. As the high new-business failure rate proves, not everyone is cut out to run his or her own operations. This book will help you determine whether you'd be more satisfied and productive as a sole proprietor or working under a corporate umbrella.

TONY LEE
Editor
National Business Employment Weekly

Acknowledgments

This book would never have been possible without the heroic efforts of NBEW Editor Tony Lee, whose patience, professionalism and always-uplifting spirit are obvious to all who work with him. Thank you beyond words, Tony.

Also right there as I struggled to gain momentum in the early going was my good friend and life-enrichment advisor Lonny Brown, who contributed mightily to "Getting Started" (Chapter 9) in the sections on electronic networking, time management and mind-body issues and who helped me scour great books for the bon mots featured throughout the text.

Career management wizard Judith Koblentz gave me more leads than a magic wand. Kit Kammer contributed hugely to my understanding of assessment (and, therefore, myself). Byron Reimus, Nick Gardiner and the Friends of Sam powered me continuously with their encouragement. Tony Anthony chipped in with several welcome improvements as the text neared completion. And thanks to Tom Cheney for his wonderful cartoons.

I'm grateful to Tom Kearney and all the great newswriters at *The Keene Sentinel* with whom I learned my craft, to Jim Kennedy and everyone at Kennedy Publications, who showed me the ropes of consulting and career management, and to my clients, who've made it possible for me to reach yet another level of career achievement.

Above all I thank—and dedicate this book to—Mother, Dad, Susie, Caitlin, Travis and Guthrie, for all your love and support as I not only wrote, but began to live, the life described here.

About the Author

David A. Lord is a writer on management consulting, executive search and career management and a consultant to firms in those fields and their clients.

He consults with search and consulting firms on issues related to growth: alliances and acquisitions, recruitment of professional staff and marketing of professional services. He also consults with corporations on their use of management consulting and executive search. Mr. Lord is a frequently quoted observer of the consulting and recruitment market and a speaker to professional and partner groups on trends in consulting, search and career management.

Mr. Lord is co-author of *Executive Search in the Americas,* published in 1995 by The Economist Intelligence Unit, and editor of *The Journal of Executive Search Consulting,* published by the Association of Executive Search Consultants. He was editor of Kennedy Publications, a leading independent source of information on consulting and executive search, from 1987 to 1995. There, he wrote and edited *Consultants News* and *Executive Recruiter News* and coordinated publication of market studies and special reports on related issues.

Mr. Lord is a native of New Hampshire and holds a bachelor's degree in psychology from the College of William & Mary in Williamsburg, Virginia. He has 18 years of experience in journalism and has received several awards for newswriting. He is a director of the New England Foundation for the Humanities and lives with his wife, Susan, and their three children in Harrisville, New Hampshire.

Contents

2 Is a Self-Directed Career for You?   23

3 Choosing a Path   45

4 Starting a Business   69

THE WALL STREET JOURNAL.

GUIDE TO
SELF-EMPLOYMENT

Introduction

A new vision of the workforce is emerging so quickly and pervasively that we're all scrambling to see whether our futures are safe.

Unfortunately, if you think of your future as something apart from yourself—your "lot in life" that's based on uncontrollable factors in your past—then your future may well be in doubt.

If you think that your career is at the mercy of economic shifts, corporate restructurings, population trends or to-be-expected outbursts of a "mid-life crisis," then your future isn't just in doubt, it's in danger.

But if you see your career as expressing an outlook on the world that squarely reflects your interests, which you can shape daily because you know the kind of person you want to be, then the future is as bright and exciting as ever.

Woody Guthrie is one of my heroes because he believed in this philosophy as strongly as anyone I've ever known or read about. His most famous song, "This Land Is Your Land," sounds like a straightforward, uplifting message of gratitude about the great goodness of America. But it's actually a protest against complacency. (It's not often understood that way partly because a couple of hard-hitting verses were left out of the school song-books we grew up with.) "This Land Is Your Land" cries out against the attitude that you have nothing to fear because God

1

> We have never worked harder and have never enjoyed work more, because, with rare exceptions, the work was significant, self-directed, constructive and therefore interesting.
>
> —Helen and Scott Nearing in *Living the Good Life*

(i.e., all forces beyond our control) will take care of the future for you.

Guthrie wrote "This Land Is Your Land" while traveling across America during a time when "God Bless America," written by Irving Berlin and sung by Kate Smith, was the number-one song of the day. It was being played incessantly on the radio and resonated in the hearts and minds of Americans everywhere. While Guthrie loved the country as much as anyone, it bothered him greatly that people might come to believe that only God and fate would determine their futures. So he wrote a song that originally carried the angry punch line, "God blessed America for me." In other words, "for me to do something about." Later, he crossed out that line and made it, "This land was made for you and me," less defiant, but a powerful statement that takes responsibility for the future.

Your future—your career—isn't at the mercy of the next wave of corporate change. It's for you to do something about, and this book is based on that point of view.

When National Business Employment Weekly editor Tony Lee asked me to write this book, I was happily and successfully employed as the editor of a small publishing company specializing in business information. But I was beginning to feel that I needed to become more active in determining my future there—or elsewhere. Researching the concept of self-directed careers reinforced this feeling. But I still didn't really think I had to be an entrepreneur to be happy until, facing an opportunity to make a long-term commitment to a role that offered little management authority, I concluded that I liked my chances better on my own.

In early 1995, I left my job to start my own writing and consulting practice and have written this book during the early months of getting my new business off the ground. I don't really recommend this as a scheduling strategy, but, in talking to others who've made the jump, there's no such thing as a perfectly peaceful time or way to do it. Today, more than six months later, I have no regrets; my business is going very well and the future not only looks bright, but appears to be something I can influence more than ever. My self-directed career is always under construction and includes many (potential) detours. It's more a journey than a destination, and well worth taking (in my brief experience so far).

As I considered the rather frightening possibility of going "entrepreneurial," I found comfort in career thinker William Bridges' reminder that "jobs" didn't really exist until very recently in the world's history—since the Industrial Revolution. An awful lot of valuable work got done before there was such a thing as a "permanent" or regular job. Now, we can hope that even more will get done as "jobs" begin to fade.

These days, instead of a job, I have work that comes in the form of projects. In this regard, I'm accumulating what one friend, executive recruiter Bill Dubbs of Williams Executive Search in Minneapolis, calls "career currency." Job titles are one form of career currency, but today's labor market shows this kind of currency slipping steadily against the kind that's backed by projects rather than positions.

Today's best resumes emphasize what's been accomplished rather than where you were in the company hierarchy. And while more and more jobs within organizations are offering a project orientation, self-employment provides the opportunity to be completely project-focused. Bill notes that career currency increases in value in proportion to the size of each project you undertake. In my work, for example, writing a book—a consuming single project that takes many months—offers the potential of adding much more to my career currency, if I do it well, than a few magazine articles. For a carpenter, building a house makes a greater long-term contribution to career equity than a series of remodeling projects. I like Bill's analogy. It keeps my eyes on the big picture.

Why be like me?

Are you just like me? Not necessarily. There are several reasons why you may be considering alternatives to being on a company payroll full-time:

☆ You've "lost" your job (or your job has lost you).

☆ You've been aiming at self-employment for years and are finally reaching the point where you can make the leap.

   ☆ You want to pursue something for which there's no available organizational vehicle.

   ☆ You want to buy someone else's business.

   ☆ You simply want a new work pattern, perhaps because of changes in your personal life.

More people are facing these choices. Literally millions of jobs have been eliminated from the world's largest corporations in the past 15 years, and many of those displaced by staff cuts are continuing their careers (and changing them, too) through project-based or contingent work. That's what we mean by self-employment: all the variations of work styles that go beyond being on someone else's "permanent" payroll.

Job Bank U.S.A. chairman Peter D. Weddle says one of three workers today now fills a contingent position, and he estimates that temporary employment will outrun "permanent" work by as early as the year 2000.

In fact, this shift has much more to do with attitude than with tangible numbers of "permanent" and "contingent" workers, and the ever-more-debatable distinction between the two. Being self-directed is a state of mind that can occur within organizations as well as outside it.

Gary Grappo, a Florida-based careers writer and former human resources executive, often asks groups he speaks to, "How many people here work for someone else's company?" Most hands go up. "And how many of you work for yourselves?" Only a few hands go up. "Most of you are wrong," Gary says. "We all work for ourselves."

"I don't know where I got the idea that I work for myself first," he says, "but it has always made me a better performer on the job. My expectations for myself have always been higher than my employers'. It has a lot to do with self-esteem. I've never liked thinking I'm somebody else's slave, so by thinking that I work for myself, I've been able to come up with enough self-esteem to get great promotions or create my own opportunities. Many people are working and waiting for the manager to say, 'We'll pay you more if you'll do more.' They never think of saying to the manager, 'Look what I could be doing for you. How about it?'"

Therefore, while the information in this book is aimed mainly at budding entrepreneurs, my thesis is that these concepts

There are only a few times in organization life when he can wrench destiny into his own hands—and if he does not fight then, he will make a surrender that will mock him. But when is that time? Will he know the time when he sees it? By what standards is he to judge? He does feel an obligation to the group; he does sense moral constraints on his free will. If he goes against the group, is he being courageous—or just stubborn? Helpful—or selfish? Is he, as he so often wonders, right after all? It is in the resolution of a multitude of such dilemmas, I submit, that the real issue of individualism lies today.

—William H. Whyte, Jr. in *The Organization Man*

could be put to perfectly good use within organizations. In fact, I'd encourage you to consider this as a possible career strategy. Look at what's happening in today's corporate world:

☆ Virtually everyone agrees that loyalty to employers, at least in large corporations, has disappeared along with numerous jobs. This is seen most dramatically within large organizations—such as IBM Corp.—that had never, ever let people go. While we may have a sense of loss over the end of employer-employee loyalty (realizing that many still-rebellious Baby Boomers never saw much in the 30-years-for-a-gold-watch routine), we're beginning to get a glimpse of what's next: a more open, honest working relationship. For the employee, this is where self-directedness can begin.

☆ In a landmark article in the *Harvard Business Review* (July–August 1994), Robert H. Waterman, Judith A. Waterman and Betsy A. Collard forecast "a new covenant under which the employer and the employee share responsibility for maintaining—even enhancing—the individual's employability inside *and outside* the company." The idea of betrayal, felt by workers losing their jobs and by organizations losing workers they wanted to keep, has got to go, the authors said.

☆ Instead, "companies must shift from using and then harvesting employees to constantly renewing them." The authors found several organizations claiming to have instituted this new attitude, including Apple Computer Inc. and Sun Microsystems. AT&T has a program in which employees, during periods of underutilization, are placed in jobs at other companies. There they may gain skills (or build more career currency) that will later make them even more valuable to AT&T. What may have sounded like pie-in-the-sky theory just a couple of years ago is beginning to happen.

So whether you work for an organization and want to apply concepts of self-directedness there, are considering going on your own, or have already made the jump, I hope you find profit in the following pages. In sum, it's a bit like *Where's Waldo?* (the fellow you try to find hidden in a big complex drawing). Can you see yourself in this picture? If not, keep looking. You are there. Find yourself!

Where We Aren't Going

Now let me tell you what this book isn't about. It's not the next career theory book (see Resources for a few very good ones). It's not *the answer* to your career crisis, if you're in one (see Resources again). Instead, it's as practical as it can be about what you really need to know as you pursue a self-directed career.

Well, okay, I hope there are a few glimmers of "the answer" in here somewhere, but the focus is on information: what you need to know to get going. I've found, and perhaps you share this view, that dreaming and planning become much more fun when you're doing. I have a note on my office wall that says "Action Prompts Thought" (not the other way around). That is, your thinking improves as soon as you begin to do something, even if it appears to be unrelated to what you're really trying to accomplish. It can even be a small step that you aren't sure will really lead anywhere.

Therefore, after painting the big picture in some detail ("New Economy, New You"), I'll devote just one chapter to the question, "Is a Self-Directed Career for You?" The focus is a hands-on evaluation of the pluses and minuses of advancing your career through an entrepreneurial approach.

In particular, I'll look, with you in mind, at the practicality of the options: starting your own business, buying a business, buying a franchise, consulting, contracting and temping. I'll end with an information-packed piece on the practical issues you'll face when getting started. This book was made for you and me.

1

New Economy, New You

These are the headlines of our times: "So Long, Organization Man"; "Find Your Own Road"; "The Rapidly Vanishing American Job"; "A World Without Jobs?"; "The End of the Job"; "Taking Care of Business—Without Leaving the House"; "Business Startups on the Rise Again."

Companies are slashing their payrolls and turning to outsiders to run larger pieces of their operations. As a result, nearly 35 million Americans now work from home, many as consultants and freelance contributors for their former employers. About seven million of them are telecommuters, doing their jobs via electronic links to the office.

Who in the working world is untouched by these trends? Literally everyone knows someone who has lost a job or launched an entrepreneurial venture, or both, due to change—be it change at work or change at home (or both). Change at work includes downsizing and all of its (often euphemistic) relatives: reengineering, restructuring, productivity improvement and automation. Change at home is about what's really important: a new emphasis on personal well-being, family life, self-expression and making a difference for loved ones and society.

Corporations and individuals, for these quite different reasons, want people to take the reins of their careers. The confluence of these two sweeping trends is overwhelming the workforce and its employers, and we're all affected.

"There used to be an unwritten contract between top managers and workers: If you made a good effort to do your job, you could count on having that job as long as the firm stayed in business," says U.S. Labor Secretary Robert Reich. "Today, that implicit contract is being abandoned at an ever-faster pace. Even reasonably healthy companies are cutting their payrolls."

At the same time, these "reasonably healthy" organizations, challenged to do more with fewer people, are redefining their approach: They're focusing on the organization's core competencies, but broadening the roles of individuals within these specialties so that multidisciplined teams can be formed for critical project-oriented work. Routine tasks are outsourced, contributing to another entrepreneurial phenomenon: developing contracted services relationships (see Chapter 8).

This is what work theorist William Bridges means by the "end of the job." In fact, it's the end of an attitude about jobs, from both the employers' and employees' point of view. Today, rather than "getting" or "keeping" a job, we all are responsible for finding customers for our work. Being successful means being good at figuring out how to meet someone's or some group's wants or needs.

Career counselors and outplacement pundits have tried to define this new phenomenon with terms such as "empowerment" and "living a new paradigm." There's a simpler way to define it. We all—no matter where or for whom we work—have self-directed careers. We can control the direction of our careers. It doesn't matter whether we're approaching our 30th year with the same employer, or running a one-person operation from our basements.

Has It Really Come to This?

The attitude that our careers are self-directed didn't develop overnight. How we got here tells us a lot about why most of us feel the way we do now. Madelyn Hochstein, president of Daniel Yankelovich Group, a leading research organization on social and economic trends, describes three stages of economic perception since World War II.

As Hochstein sees it, the Great Depression and World War II made such an impact on our perceptions of how things were going that an attitude she calls "I don't quite believe it" prevailed for nearly 20 years after the war, even though the era was marked by extraordinary economic growth and global leadership for the United States. By 1959, 70 percent of all households in America were classified as middle-class.

The "I don't quite believe it" agenda included a strong role for government in protecting the economic interests of its citizens, through funding for college education, opportunities for veterans and low-interest home mortgages. In business, government's role was viewed as including investments in promising industries and functional specialties.

On the job, employees were resolute in seeking advancement through loyalty and hard work. Corporations, in turn, showed concern for employees' long-term income needs. The idea of seniority emerged. Pension and healthcare benefits arrived.

Okay, I Believe It!

Eventually—in the mid-1960s—people, companies and government got comfortable with prosperity. They entered the era Hochstein calls unbridled optimism: "It will never end." It created a whole new attitude about work and jobs. Instead of focusing on getting a good job that paid well, young people were looking for "a job that's right for me." "Is this what I really want to do with my life?"

Suddenly there was a social agenda. We switched from wanting government to invest in business to seeing business as a villain. "Environmentalism, consumerism and the regulatory response threw corporations for a loop," Hochstein notes.

Eventually, companies responded by mirroring the new attitude, becoming statesmanlike in service to several constituencies: employees and the community, as well as shareholders.

I hold that man is in the right who is most closely in league with the future.

—Henrik Ibsen

It became the age of instant gratification. As Hochstein puts it, "If, economically, everything is always going to be okay, and there's always going to be another good job out there for me, I can indulge myself now." Credit cards appeared. Conformity gave way to what Hochstein labels "a sense of personal relative morality: You do your thing, I'll do my thing . . . Whatever works for you is okay."

Women entered the workforce in unprecedented numbers, and Hochstein points out that the movement was a social revolution, not an economic one. It was led not by poor women who simply needed the money, but by affluent, well-educated women responding to new options—options that followed the notion of entitlement in a strong economy.

Soon we began to feel that just showing up for work over time made us valued employees, deserving rewards beyond money. "Employee satisfaction" became a buzzword and thoughts about what was expected of companies—as well as workers—expanded greatly. The unwritten employment contract became very complicated.

Hitting the Roof

Now, Hochstein says, "Stage three has jolted us into another complete shift in psychology about affluence and growth: belief in an economic ceiling." Though it began for some corporations and certainly for blue-collar workers way back in the late 1970s and early 1980s, the full effect of the change didn't hit senior management until the stock market crash of 1987. "Now, it's clear to everyone, and we're going to be in it for a while despite (improved) economic conditions," Hochstein says.

Hochstein says the third phase should be called, "It's really rough out there." There's now a sense that economic well-being is in doubt, even if you're well off. Yankelovich Group research shows that optimism about the economy has dropped more among wealthier and managerial-class Americans than among any other group in our society.

They probably pick this up at work: Companies have accepted limits to growth dictated by what's seen as unrelenting downward pressure on profits from global competition, consumer demand for value, the rising cost of health care and what's generally perceived to be a slower growing economy. And, Hochstein says, "perception is much more powerful than reality."

She cites five trends in business today that are "ripping away at the unwritten contract" between employers and employees:

1. A dramatic shift in the goals of the corporation, from having several constituencies (employees, community, shareholders) to just one: shareholder value.

2. Success strategies that are built on cost-cutting. Not only are staffs continually shrinking, but benefits are being reduced for those who remain.

3. A policy of expendability instead of corporate paternalism and statesmanship. Long-term income growth for employees is no longer a priority.

4. But at the same time, an emphasis on employee initiative, dedication, leadership and commitment is growing. Empowerment also means responsibility.

5. The bottom line is a distinctly mixed message that shakes out to this: The contract is broken. Managers no longer believe their jobs are for life, or that they'll be rewarded for expanding their skills.

As a result, work is no longer the emotional center of life, even for senior managers. "The psychic rewards of work are disappearing," Hochstein says. She projects that by the year 2000, we'll have created a group of over-workers, adapting and accepting the new rules—18 hours a day, seven days a week. "They'll become the 'have-technology-will-travel' crowd," Hochstein says. "They'll have adapted because they're frightened." The other group is disenchanted, angry. "They'll ultimately drop out and become part of the great new thrust of entrepreneurism."

Is That You?

Do you see yourself in this picture? "Having your own business is the passion of America in the 1990s," Hochstein observes. "Ask any 10 adults anywhere (I do this regularly) and you'll find at least half have a business on the side or are totally out on their own. We're all setting up home offices and starting some kind of alternative form of income."

Saving to start a new business is now the fourth most popular item on people's wish list, according to CNW Marketing in Bandon, Oregon, which measures national attitudes on such issues. CNW's wish list is historically led by (1) new clothes, (2) a

> The unspoken factor behind the entrepreneurial boom is that working for most companies is so demeaning to the human spirit that many talented people are forced out the door.
>
> —John Naisbitt in *Reinventing the Corporation*

vacation and (3) remodeling the kitchen. Brand new in fourth place is starting or buying a business, having jumped from eighth place in 1994 (leapfrogging golf equipment, health clubs, antiques and home electronics). Just 10 years earlier, in 1984, starting or buying a business was a distant 15th, behind new cars, home furnishings, boats, artwork, investments and gourmet food and wine!

Along with the passion for being in business, however, is a move away from material glamour. "Today, it's how you live your life that counts, not what you own," Hochstein says. "Ten years ago, it was a Mercedes or BMW. Today, it's a sport utility vehicle. But it's not about functionality. It's about 'I'm a regular guy, I want control over my life, my time, my money.' The idea of self-reliance is incredibly important today. Also, there's an emphasis on family, better relationships and a home-centered lifestyle. There's a terrible fear of crime. We're looking for emotional and spiritual rewards," she says.

Together, these trends have triggered a phenomenal rise in self-employment and self-directed careers. It suits the needs of downsizing corporations and plays to the new priorities of individuals, including many who might not have chosen entrepreneurism but, when pushed into it, find they like being on their own and can succeed.

Art Spinella of CNW Marketing says basic interest in starting and buying businesses has existed in America for many years, and is blossoming now for two reasons. First, advancements in technology are really taking hold in a way that makes it possible for people to start successful businesses for a relatively small investment. Second, while we've been reading about a transformation to a service economy for years, people are finally realizing that they don't have to manufacture something to start a business. There are great opportunities in service- or information-based businesses, and even product-based enterprises that combine product development and sales can be launched as a relatively modest operation without making a huge investment in manufacturing.

Hochstein highlights this part of the new picture: Our burst of individual enterprise isn't aimed at building something big. "It's really about simply having something of my own." While it might be scary, with less income protection if not less income, it's less scary than waiting for the next restructuring.

"In fact, self-employment is so hot we've begun to notice that people in corporations now admire the ones who are out. The status is with the people who are on their own," Hochstein says.

And those who have been let go are looking farther afield than ever for the next opportunity. A recent Gallup Poll showed that many people being laid off don't want another job in their field. Instead, 14 percent want time off to think and rest; 13 percent would like to start their own businesses; 9 percent want jobs in another field; 7 percent plan to return to school, and 4 percent will retire.

Meanwhile, society is struggling to take it all in. Some see significant backlash ahead. Author Jeremy Rifkin, writing in *Utne Reader* (May–June, 1995), argues that automation's rapidly rising elimination of jobs could wreak socioeconomic havoc. He predicts massive retaliation by disenfranchised workers that would "make the summer of 1968 or the Los Angeles uprising of 1993 look like hootenannies," in the words of journalist Eric Utne.

Still a Stigma in Change

While that may be an extreme view and an unlikely scenario, it would be a mistake to underestimate the intensity and scope of change in the workplace and, therefore, in worker attitudes. It's tough on everyone, even those who choose, for all kinds of positive reasons, to go into business for themselves.

Before I resigned after eight years at a small business publishing company to begin my own business, I knew intellectually that—as good a move as this was going to be for me—it wouldn't be all positive. There would be hard feelings. I would face challenges that might intimidate or discourage me. Some people might even say, "Gee, I guess David couldn't cut it after all"—untrue as that may have been.

> Individual professionals and executives will have to learn that they must take responsibility for placing themselves—both within their organization and outside of it. This means above all that they must know their strengths.
>
> —Peter F. Drucker

I think we should all be prepared for a cycle of emotions amid a major change, whether it's in response to a stunningly unexpected firing or a fortune-seeking step forward. "The more I work with people going through this," says Connecticut career management consultant Judith Koblentz, "the more I'm convinced that there's a prescribed emotional process that happens regardless of how and why you came to this change point in your work life." Part of that is a lingering feeling of failure in your previous role.

The fact that our rather unforgiving culture waits in judgment over whether we move forward or back in making a change has another interesting effect: It makes us care more about what we think and less about what the world thinks. And that, as it turns out, is a darned good thing.

Fine-Tuning the Big Picture

This, then, is the context for your interest—and mine—in self-directed careers. The force behind the trend is both within us and a newly integral part of the business environment. In the big picture, "the backbone of the industrial age is disintegrating, much more rapidly than expected," says veteran executive recruiter Herman Smith in Toronto. "The large organizations that dominated the past no longer dominate the future. All evidence suggests that by the year 2000, many organizations either will not exist or will be substantially different from the way they are now."

The ways in which they'll be substantially different offer many opportunities to flexible, self-directed workers. Increasingly, organizations are looking for independent providers of goods—and, especially, services—who can help them meet their customers' needs without having to employ more people. Further, technology is creating many new ways for this to be practical as well, and to help you specialize further because you can draw upon a global market for whom to do your special thing.

But there will also be significant demands. Smith sees these factors as necessary for individuals in the New Economy:

- ☆ Computer literacy.
- ☆ A willingness to undergo ongoing retraining (if you're starting a business on your own, this means learning and doing a ton of new stuff immediately).
- ☆ The ability to determine which skills are needed to remain competitively employable.
- ☆ Better-than-average knowledge of the job market (even if you're self-employed).
- ☆ The ability and desire to continuously market your skills and services.
- ☆ Excellence in listening and speaking, including interviewing skills that will be called upon regularly—far more often than the traditional "every few years and only between jobs."
- ☆ Fluency in a second language.
- ☆ Negotiation skills.
- ☆ Knowledge of business, tax law and money management.

Any History of Motion Sickness?

If this all sounds intimidating, Smith reminds us that self-employment is hardly new. In 1900, half of all U.S. citizens were self-employed. By 1977, the figure had fallen to 7 percent.

For any of us to be truly free—if we are to learn to soar in this changing world—we must first be willing to be responsible for our lives.

—David McNally in *Even Eagles Need a Push*

Today, it's double that, but still less than one-third of the turn-of-the-century rate.

And to the extent that those who are individually self-employed interact with small business, they're tapping into the clear leader of growth in the economy today. Small businesses account for about 70 percent of all U.S. job growth, according to the Bureau of Labor Statistics.

We All Work for Somebody

It may become more and more difficult to define self-employment. We generally think in terms of being self-directed, which includes both owners of businesses as well as those who occasionally (or even regularly) have "employers" (as opposed to clients or customers). But the lines between self-employment and small business will likely get even fuzzier as more entrepreneurs adopt a business plan that states: "Rather than have employees, I'll joint-venture with other individuals and organizations to carry out projects that are bigger than my own abilities." (By the way, this is my own business plan, and it seems to resonate loudly with many entrepreneurs.)

What will this make a 21st-century satellite photo of employment patterns look like? The Academy for Advanced and Strategic Studies in Washington, D.C., says workforce 2000 will look like this:

☆ 35% will be a "core career cadre" of executives, managers, professional, technical, operations, production and administrative personnel.

☆ 15% will be "contract specialists," providing professional, technical and producer services.

☆ 25% will be "core contingent workers" who are career-committed, part-time, intermittent and flex-place staffers.

☆ 25% will be "component and support suppliers," including teams handling custodial, maintenance, security, food services, printing and other supplies and services.

Self-directed careers will be possible in each of the last three categories, plus the entrepreneurial members of the first group. You and I are little bits of a very big picture!

Your Career as a Small Business

How can we see ourselves more clearly in this big picture? Several leading observers of the world of work recommend this approach: Treat your career as if it were a little business, whether you work for someone else or not.

Great idea, if you have business management experience. But many of us who've put in a bunch of years being creative within the confines of job descriptions that made few demands on our management savvy may feel a bit out of touch with today's best practices. (Subsequent chapters include plenty of nuts and bolts on this, but I bring the subject up now as a way of putting our topic—your self-directed career—in the context of the New Economy.)

With our working lives at stake, how about a quick primer? How can we apply the most powerful management ideas to our career-businesses?

It's an interesting exercise. In preparing for *Fortune* magazine's 40th ranking (and first reworking) of its 500 largest U.S. corporations, writer Brian Dumaine searched recent decades of business history for management ideas that have outlasted fads and trends and appear to be of timeless value. He found five:

1. *Management is a practice*—that is, management is more than just a hierarchy of people who manage other people; it's a vehicle for shaping an organization to meet objectives determined by the ownership.

2. *People are a resource*—and therefore shouldn't be considered a cost. While this seems to fly in the face of the apparently permanent trend toward leaner organizational structures, it also reflects greater empowerment and autonomy of workers, which makes them an even more valuable resource.

3. *Marketing and innovation are the key functions of a business*—in other words, the customer is king.

4. *Discover what you do well*—another way of saying strategic planning really works.

5. *Quality pays for itself*—that is, when you choose among doing something well, fastest or least expensively, the first choice is likely to be the most profitable.

Suppose we consider how each of these givens of good management can be applied to a self-directed career?

1. *Management is a practice.*

This seems to say that building a self-directed career is a potentially more sophisticated move than simply hanging out a shingle and hiring people to execute your business idea. The structure of your self-directed career can actually take on a variety of shapes (start a business, buy a business, obtain a franchise, be a consultant, work on contract, form alliances, etc.) Therefore, it's important to craft and refine your structure to assure its consistent effectiveness and compatibility with your career objectives.

2. *People are a resource.*

Ah, the joys of networking, especially in seeking input as you develop your career and business objectives! The challenge for many entrepreneurial types is to be sufficiently good listeners to hear all that helpful feedback.

3. *Marketing and innovation are the key functions of a business.*

This reminds us as individuals that prospective customers or clients in our self-directed careers will determine—at least as much as our own abilities and efforts—our success. We must look carefully at what the market really needs, not just what we want to do. A big part of that is creating innovative ways to serve an existing market.

4. *Discover what you do well.*

I'd even put this ahead of marketing and innovation, because it's of little use to know what the market wants if you're unable to provide it. Strategic planning is a well-documented founding principle of successful careers, as well as businesses. Yet, obvious as it is, we can benefit from a reminder that business strategy must continuously be revisited, and so should our ideas about what we do well as individuals. Self-directedness in our careers has a way of bringing strengths and weaknesses into sharp focus, and creating capabilities with each new project. Keep an eye on what you do well and be ready to revise your opinions as you see yourself face new challenges.

5. *Quality pays for itself.*

Ongoing incremental improvements in our personal performance will reap increasing rewards. Why not apply the business model to our self-directed careers by finding things to measure about how well we do our work, establishing steps toward a lofty goal and putting ourselves to the test regularly in pursuit of those goals? Specifically, we should ask our clients and customers how we're doing on a regular basis.

The New You

So how does one become an overnight success at a self-directed career in the New Economy? Based on everything we now know about how we got here, and what we can conclude are the essential skills of managing your career as a business, we can distill it down to three: attitude, skills and creativity in finding customers for your work.

Under attitude comes adaptability. Byron Reimus, a communications consultant and thoughtful participant in the trend toward self-directed careers, sees the tearing up of the unwritten contract playing out this way for individuals: Unless we're self-directed, we've lost control of our careers. Before, we were able to forecast a career path to whatever extent we were willing to commit to a particular job or series of jobs based on tenure. There was justice; we were rewarded for years of duty. Now, in place of justice, we have ambiguity.

"The trick is getting comfortable with the ambiguity," he says, "which applies both to those with traditional jobs and those with self-directed careers." Without flexibility and adaptability, our loss of control will produce more stress—already high and manifesting itself regularly in frightening incidents of workplace violence.

Reimus notes that those who choose a self-directed path simply accelerate the process of facing up to the new ambiguity—willing to risk next month's income on whether you can meet customers' needs head on.

Under skills comes self-knowledge and professional development. Discover what you do well. Then base your career moves on a solid understanding of your abilities and how they might grow in a variety of new situations. We'll address this fully in Chapter 2, "Is a Self-Directed Career for You?"

The third essential element of success in the New Economy is marketing—developing a creative approach to how your abilities can be applied in the marketplace. Who are your best potential customers and how can you bring them the greatest imaginable value? We'll get into this in Chapter 3, "Choosing a Path," followed by in-depth looks in the succeeding chapters at each of several paths.

"From the endangered desk of Franklin R. Peabody . . ."

2

Is a Self-Directed Career for You?

All set for a self-directed career? Are you sure? I'll tell you why I ask. Consider what occurred on my fourth official day of business on my own, a day not unlike the many days that followed. (You could also consider this to be my sixth official day by counting the weekend, which, immediately and apparently forever, has become part of my work week, indistinguishable from family life.)

Anders the carpenter and I have just installed the "window of opportunity" that leads to my office upstairs. This may be the highlight of the day, or the most productive thing that happens. Nothing else is going right. The FedEx man didn't leave an important package this morning because I was in the cellar with the plumber and didn't hear him at the door. I can't find the WordPerfect manual amid the mess downstairs. Piles of books and displaced household treasures are cordoned off by temporary phone lines, which lead to some phones, but not to the two cordless look-alikes—one for business and one for the family. We haven't yet learned one phone's ring from another, so when one goes off, everyone runs. Eventually, we all reach the bottom of the stairs just before realizing with relief that it was the fax machine. No action necessary, or possible: It's a note from my printer to say he can't read the diskette that carries the design of my long-awaited business cards and stationery. Now, what was I talking about?

Are you sure this is for you? I was sure it was for me, but I also couldn't imagine the hundreds of tiny challenges awaiting me as I made my move (and forevermore). I spent a good chunk of a recent morning trying to print envelopes successfully on the laser printer. It can be done! Was it on my list of projects that would take hours? No way.

"Even with the most meticulous planning, it's normal to feel overwhelmed at first by the minutiae of commerce, both in the start-up phase and after your business is established," says Bill Radin, author of *Breakaway Careers* (Hawthorne, NJ: Career Press, 1994).

You may feel, as I did, that you're not too important to attend to all the details of your work—to make the computer do what you need, keep track of expenses, balance the checkbook, clean the toilet—whatever. But being willing is only the beginning. In fact, these innumerable little projects take loads of time just when you're dying to get going on the substance of your work.

Or is there some avoidance going on here? Hmmm . . . I do have a need to have systems in place for my resources to be well-organized and accessible around me, before I set fingers to keyboard on the creative part of my work. Am I using all the minutiae of getting a new business started to help fend off moments (hours, weeks, years) of truth when the rubber better meet the road, when I really have to produce, on my own, without a net, no colleagues with whom to commiserate, my whole new career riding on doing well right out of the gate?

The Eight Stages of Entrepreneurship must include one for the quiet wave of panic that ebbs into the late afternoon, when few of the day's goals have been met, while others have surfaced anew—when the kids are home from school and everyone else's activity seems to be peaking except mine—when almost all seems lost.

Stop, Reflect and Go

That's the time to take a deep breath and remember what a self-directed career is all about. It's about learning, meeting big and little challenges head on, stretching your capabilities in ways both courageous and, sometimes, menial. You make the coffee as well as the money—and the mistakes are all yours, too!

"This is a way of life," Tim DeMello, founder of Wall Street Games in New York City, told *Inc.* magazine. "It's not a job, it's not a career, it's a way of life. I started a business for the sense of accomplishment, period."

Traditional jobs offer fewer opportunities to truly stretch personal capabilities in learning, decision-making and meeting unexpected challenges. Self-directed workers get into this kind of hot water every day, and learn how to stay cool and become good swimmers very quickly. But the water is deep. It involves confronting yourself in entirely new ways.

Byron Reimus, the communications consultant we met in Chapter 1, believes the self-directed career removes the last shred of distinction between our professional and personal lives, and therefore puts into sharp focus our unproductive or even counterproductive behavior patterns that are less obvious—or somehow written off—when our lives are separated into personal and professional categories.

The self-directed career, he observes, forces the complete integration of the personal with the professional, highlighting problems in either camp. For example, full support from your spouse is often cited as a key ingredient of entrepreneurial success. But the issue might better be described as full and successful handling of all your personal blessings, challenges and shortcomings whatever their source. For the self-directed, it doesn't matter anymore whether the issue is personal or professional. Both parts of your life are equally important for success and equally affected by weakness or failings.

A Florida woman tells a very personal story that goes beyond careers and illustrates how personal issues are ever-present: "Twelve years ago, I was in an unhappy marriage where I recall accusing my then-husband of not making me happy (for all sorts of reasons). It never occurred to me that not being happy might be my problem. I've matured a lot since then and have come to realize that I alone am responsible for my own happiness. One should expect to be treated with love, kindness and respect by loved ones, but happiness must come from within one's self. If I could give others a little advice from my years of struggling, I would say to get out a sheet of paper and write down everything you can think of that you feel would bring you happiness. These things do not have to be drastic: One thing I do for myself is to try to take a half-hour walk after dinner each evening all by myself . . . A year ago, I returned to college just for the fun and enjoyment of learning!"

The bright side here, as usual, is opportunity: every day's promise of a chance to improve and even excel, personally and professionally. True, not everything on the list gets done, and it's even easier for the unexpected to overrun you when you're on your own. But I like the quality of the items on the list. Each one has the potential to measurably contribute to success—even cleaning the house and home office for the next visitor!

How Many People Go Through This?

"Everyone I work with, to one degree or another, considers a self-directed career," says Connecticut career management consultant Judith Koblentz. "How many of them pursue it? Perhaps one-fourth." Other consultants cite similar statistics.

There's the dream, and there's reality. You may have always wanted to open an antique store in an old New England town or trot the globe as a travel writer, but have commitments that would make such a move "impossible," or perhaps unwise. This often has to do with setting priorities, and if your career isn't number one, fine; no one said it had to be. This rakes out about half the field.

Those who are left need a little extra fire in the belly to make the change. They're ready to make, or at least risk, sacrifices in other parts of their lives in order to chase that dream.

Others go one step farther because they're motivated by external forces: They've lost a job and have to find something new, they're following a relocating spouse, they've plateaued in their jobs and can't bear another day at work, or they lay claim to another of a thousand different, good reasons.

Sometimes, more than one external force combine to prompt a change. "If the situation hadn't been impossible where I was working, I wouldn't have done this," says an independent management consultant in New England. "I'm very good at working for other people. But my company wasn't growing and didn't seem interested in moving aggressively to change that. I

> Work and leisure are complementary parts of the same process. They cannot be separated without destroying the joy of work or the bliss of leisure.
>
> —E.F. Schumacher in *Small Is Beautiful*

knew I could make it on my own and had a feeling I'd really enjoy making the effort."

The final step in the thought process cuts the group in half again: Can I really handle the change? This includes: Will my business plan work? Could I work effectively at home? Will I have credibility in my new role?

Many of the answers here depend on how big a jump is being made from a role in which you have experience. If your current work is solid and relevant to your prospective role, it's easier. But things become more challenging when, frankly, you haven't set the world on fire in your current role, or you seek to take a big step toward a role in which you have little direct experience.

In a close call, don't underestimate your ability to transfer skills and learn new ones if you're highly motivated. "Search firms pigeonhole people," complains Koblentz. "It's not about a job, it's about a person, finding a career that's an expression of who they are."

What Forces Are at Work?

As you consider a self-directed career, look again at the internal and external factors in your situation and plans. Internal motivations for a self-directed career include:

☆ You've always wanted to be in business for yourself.

☆ You want to work on your own schedule.

☆ You want to take a chance on a potentially lucrative business opportunity.

External motivations might be:

☆ You've lost your job or had your salary cut.

☆ You're blocked from further advancement in your present job.

☆ Your spouse has taken a job in a new location.

Ideally, in an honest self-appraisal, there's a fit. If you've lost your job and are considering starting your own business, becoming a consultant, or whatever, you must make sure that it coincides with the most basic internal motivation you'll need: truly wanting to be in business for yourself.

Career information specialist Kathryn Diggs of Farmington, Michigan, created such a fit when she started her own business. The primary motivation was external: a need to relocate to Farmington to care for her parents. Therefore, "I had three criteria," Kathryn recalls. "First, I wanted to base my work on knowledge I'd already gained since I wanted to stay in my field. Second, it had to be something I could do with virtually no regular schedule, so I could be available at all times to provide care and transportation to my parents. Third, it had to be a business that could be moved anywhere as circumstances change. I don't want to live in Farmington forever." She met these criteria by launching a newsletter, *Career Savvy*.

Sometimes it's possible to find the fit simply by doing exactly what you did before but for yourself instead of someone else. Reid Robbins was a court reporter who, due to a bout with cancer, was unable to keep to a schedule. So he started his own court reporting and transcription business from his home in Philadelphia, employing others as needed, especially to gather tapes and deliver transcripts. It's working. In three years, his business has grown from revenues of about $5,000 per month to between $50,000 and $80,000 per month.

"I didn't really work toward going out on my own," says Reid. But he responded well to the situation that made it necessary.

On the other hand, if you find yourself primarily motivated internally—you know that you want to "do your own thing"—are the external factors cooperating sufficiently? Do you have support from your family?

Earl Robinson wanted to stay in Phoenix. At 29, with a business degree from Wharton and several years of experience in financial reporting and auditing at Ford and Citibank, Earl had moved to Arizona with his new bride to accept an opportunity with Envirotest, an environmental testing company. The future looked fabulous: Envirotest's revenues had skyrocketed from $10 million in 1991 to $90 million in 1993 and were projected to hit $250 million in 1995—until the congressional election of 1994 changed government policy and stifled the market for Envirotest's services. Soon Earl and about 20 other hotshots who'd been recruited from Fortune 50 organizations were unemployed.

There was no shortage of opportunity for Earl. He could easily have returned to New York or Detroit and landed another corporate post. But Earl and his wife loved Phoenix and wanted to stay. So he teamed up with four other colleagues from Envirotest and formed two companies: Emily Christopher Associates, a management consulting practice aimed at growing $2 million companies into $10 million companies through better operations and financial management; and Constant Communications, which sells pagers and air time for pagers, which Robinson said offers 70 percent gross margins and is growing rapidly. (During our interview, Earl received a call that told him Emily Christopher had won its first big contract: a $200,000 job for the City of Phoenix.)

Earl's new efforts show a good balance between the external and internal forces driving his career: He picked a secondary market for his skills but played to his functional strength: finance. He loves his new setup: "In management of a large organization, you spend a lot of time worrying about someone else's money. In a smaller company, you worry about the employees and their families. But on your own, you just have to worry about yourself, and concentrate on doing what you do best."

How Well Do You Know Yourself?

When you pin your future on doing what you do best, on your own, you'd better make sure you know your talents. To this end, many career programs begin with a solid self-assessment. Most career advisers suggest you get right to your skills, using devices such as the flower diagram in Richard Bolles' classic book, *What Color Is Your Parachute?* (Berkeley, CA: Ten Speed Press, 1996) But it may also help to learn more about your personality; many job counselors rely on the Myers-Briggs test, or some variation on it, as a tool for this task.

In general, the world of career planning has moved away from psychological-based counseling toward the business of building a winning job campaign or business plan. But there's much to be learned about attitude, as well as personality, by taking a test administered by a trained consultant.

Katherine "Kit" Kammer of Kammer Associates in Atlanta is such a consultant. Kit has 23 years of experience in career and outplacement counseling and recommended the Birkman Advanced Report. It combines a look at aspects of your personality, not unlike Myers-Briggs, with your vocational interests (and shows interesting interplay between the two).

So, for a couple of hours one quiet afternoon, I answered the 173 questions that comprise the Birkman test. I was "up" for it, confident that the picture of me that emerged would be someone I could identify with and be proud.

The Birkman test reinforced much that I knew about myself—interests in music, literature and social service; a low-key, orderly, open and flexible style; a need for a creative atmosphere and a tendency to be self-protective under stress.

But there were also a few surprises. It showed me having interests in sales I never knew existed (and, strikingly for me, among the occupations for which I was found well-suited were furniture sales and marketing—my father's career—and the ministry, which is what my mother had quietly always wished for me to do). Kit's interpretation and application of the results to my current career options also gave me great insight. Soon, I began actively exploring a self-directed career and the test was a not-insignificant factor in the thought processes that led to my move. To say that it gave me confidence is an oversimplification; it pointed out some weaknesses, too. But it clearly showed that I projected a positive attitude about my skills and career opportunities.

I notice that's what I've reflected on the most in the six months since I took the test: that my attitude is everything and that the experience of learning more about myself bolstered my attitude. Taking the test made more tangible the personal skills

ARE YOU ENTREPRENEURIAL?

1. An entrepreneur is most commonly the _____ child in the family.
   a. oldest
   b. middle
   c. youngest
   d. doesn't matter

2. An entrepreneur is most commonly _____.
   a. married
   b. single
   c. widowed
   d. doesn't matter

3. An entrepreneur is most typically a _____.
   a. man
   b. woman
   c. either

4. An individual's first entrepreneurial activity usually begins at what age?
   a. teens
   b. twenties
   c. thirties
   d. forties
   e. fifties

5. Usually an individual's entrepreneurial tendency first appears evident at which of these stages?
   a. teens
   b. twenties
   c. thirties
   d. forties
   e. fifties

6. Typically, an entrepreneur has achieved the following educational attainment before beginning a first serious business venture.
   a. grammar school
   b. high school diploma
   c. bachelor's degree
   d. master's degree
   e. doctor's degree

7. An entrepreneur's primary motivation for starting a business is:
   a. to make money
   b. can't work for anyone else
   c. to be famous
   d. as an outlet for unused energy

8. The primary motivation for the entrepreneur's high ego and need for achievement is based on a close relationship with his or her:
   a. spouse
   b. mother
   c. father
   d. children

Continued

Continued

9. An entrepreneur moves which of these items from business to business:
   a. desk
   b. chair
   c. all office furniture
   d. none of these items

10. To be successful in an entrepreneurial venture you need an over-abundance of:
    a. money
    b. luck
    c. hard work
    d. good ideas

11. Entrepreneurs and venture capitalists are:
    a. cordial friends
    b. best of friends
    c. in secret conflict

12. A successful entrepreneur relies on which of these groups for critical management advice?
    a. internal management team
    b. external management professionals
    c. financial sources
    d. no one

13. Entrepreneurs are best as:
    a. managers
    b. venture capitalists
    c. planners
    d. doers

14. Entrepreneurs are:
    a. high-risk rollers (big gamblers)
    b. moderate risk-takers (realistic gamblers)
    c. small risk-takers (take few chances)
    d. doesn't matter

15. The only necessary and sufficient ingredient for starting a business is:
    a. money
    b. a customer
    c. product
    d. an idea

required to advance my career and gave me a model for presenting myself. Looking back, it was a first run at my self-directed career.

There's no specific "entrepreneur" profile in the Birkman test, but I could conclude from the results that Dr. Birkman would be neither shocked nor too concerned if I went into business for myself.

Some career psychologists do measure entrepreneurism, however, and we include here a very good test by Joseph R. Mancuso, founder and president of the Center of Entrepreneurial Management in New York City. Complete the test on pp. 31–32, then review the analysis of answers that follows.

Answers

Mancuso explains that when reviewing your score, don't be unnecessarily harsh on yourself and underestimate the worth of your answer versus the explanation given. "Who's to say we both can't be right?" I agree, and have added my thoughts to his analysis throughout.

1. There's no doubt about this answer. All independent studies agree that entrepreneurs are high achievers and that first-born children are the highest achievers. While about 40 percent of the population are first-born children, about 60 percent to 70 percent of entrepreneurs are first-born. However, a later-born child who is much younger than the next older sibling may demonstrate the same high achievement profile of first-borns.

2. This is a tricky topic and one on which data are fluid and interpretations vary wildly. My own data on 300 entrepreneurs, based primarily in the Northeast and on the West Coast, indicate that the vast majority are married, but since most men in their 30s are married, this alone isn't a significant finding. However, I found that successful entrepreneurs tend to have exceptionally supportive spouses who provide love and stability to balance the insecurity and stress of the work. Marriages without such support tend to end in divorce, and divorce among entrepreneurs is more frequent than among the

> Decisiveness blossoms from self-confidence.
>
> —Jeff Berner in *The Joy of Working From Home*

employed. Unsuccessful entrepreneurs have the highest divorce rates of all.

A supportive spouse significantly increases the entrepreneur's chance of success. Next most likely to succeed are divorced entrepreneurs. Least likely to do well are those in strained marriages.

3. Almost everyone gets this question right. Entrepreneurship is a male stronghold. Women have made much more progress as senior managers in corporations than in starting their own businesses. However, this may be changing. Recent data show a notable increase in the tiny percentage of women entrepreneurs.

4. This is a moving target. Entrepreneurs are getting younger. Studies in the 1950s showed first-time entrepreneurs were most often between 38 and 42 years old; in the 1960s, the average moved down to 35–40; in the 1970s, 30–35; now I'm noticing more people in their 20s launching their first businesses.

5. Entrepreneurial traits show up very early in life. Many youngsters begin little businesses before their teens. And by their late teens, more than 75 percent of today's entrepreneurs were engaged in coin and stamp collecting, dance and concert promotion, clothing and appliance sales, lawn-mowing, snow services, paper routes or other early enterprises.

6. This one is controversial and few other observers agree with my conclusion: a master's degree is the most common educational level attained by entrepreneurs. Research in the 1950s found that most entrepreneurs failed to complete high school, never mind college. Their willingness to challenge authority is among one reason cited. But a generation later, college is the norm for future businesspeople and most earn a bachelor's degree. Even higher achieving entrepreneurs tend to follow through to a master's. However, few feel a doctorate is worth that much more extra time in school.

7. There's good agreement on this one: Entrepreneurs are independent free spirits who tend to have difficulty working for others. They seldom leave a secure environment and a steady job simply to make money. Instead, they view the attainment of wealth as a by-product of a more important quest to be independent. To be famous is almost never the reason for entrepreneurship; there are much better ways for that. Starting a business as an energy outlet isn't it either. Entrepreneurs are more concerned with using time productively; they don't need things to do.

8. Clearly, relationships with fathers are key, at least for men (there is very little data on women). Mothers and fathers are predominant in a person's personality development; spouses and children arrive too late in life to affect basic personality traits. Sons tend to compete with their fathers, and many entrepreneurs are the sons of entrepreneurs. Their fathers' approval remains a lifelong motivating force.

9. The answer is a chair, and most people guess this correctly. Entrepreneurs fall in love with a good chair and prefer it to any other piece of office furniture, so much so that they tend to carry it from business to business. (By the way, although this isn't a statistically significant finding, most entrepreneurs start more than one business; few start one and stick with it permanently.)

10. You probably got this one wrong. The answer, believe it or not, is luck. We know that money alone isn't enough. Hard work and good ideas are certainly helpful. However, mere hard work seldom turns a troublesome situation into a success, and many good ideas are never acted upon. Luck is different and is seen compensating significantly for other weaknesses. Over an

---

Cleverness, as usual, takes all the credit it possibly can. But it's not the Clever Mind that's responsible when things work out. It's the mind that sees what's in front of it, and follows the nature of things.

—Benjamin Hoff in *The Tao of Pooh*

eight-year period, every successful entrepreneur agreed that luck was a key factor. A few key breaks, early, were what made the difference, they said.

11. The answer to this question always causes great difficulty, especially for money men. Universally, venture capitalists believe they are best friends with entrepreneurs and it's sometimes true, but only sometimes. Much more often there is great stress on the relationship. Most small businesses fail, and the vast majority need second and third rounds of financing, which moves the tone of the relationship from cordial to tense. Often there is a permanent split.

12. The overwhelming answer to this question is external management professionals. In my research, virtually every successful company has used a consultant at one time or another—and many unsuccessful enterprises have not. This is a fascinating finding but, unfortunately, other researchers haven't been able to corroborate it.

Entrepreneurs seldom rely on internal staff for policy decisions because employees tend to have their own interests at heart. Internal management, meanwhile, tends to agree with the boss. Outside financial advisers are even less likely to be asked; they are seen as too conservative and lacking a feeling for running a business. Optimistic, fun-loving entrepreneurs prefer outside professionals, including other entrepreneurs, consultants, college professors or successful businesspeople.

13. Entrepreneurs are doers. They do everything faster and better than anyone else, hence they're reluctant to delegate responsibility. Being both better and faster is a handicap for most managers and planners. They also seldom are effective as venture capitalists, even after they've accumulated

---

I don't like work—no man does—but I like what is in work: the chance to find yourself. Your own reality—for yourself, not for others—what no other man can ever know.

—Joseph Conrad in *Heart of Darkness*

wealth. Entrepreneurs are more at home with products, markets and technologies. The skills of a successful venture capitalist are at a much higher level of abstraction; entrepreneurs would rather find a market niche or exploit a new technology than manage money and make financial bets.

14. Contrary to popular belief, entrepreneurs aren't high risk-takers. Instead, they're moderate risk-takers. Entrepreneurs like to set realistic, achievable goals. They're very aware of the consequences of failure. This characteristic is especially true of successful entrepreneurs, but is also true for unsuccessful ones. Competitive events based on their own skills naturally increase their propensity to take risks, but those risks are never extreme. They bet on sports when they're players, but not as spectators.

15. A business starts with an order. An order comes only from a customer. All business revolves around customers, and it all begins when someone offers to buy something. Don't be deluded into believing that you have a business when you have a prototype ready to go. It's not a business until someone buys your product. Everything leading up to that is just a prelude; that's why nine out of 10 business efforts fail.

When you have a good idea, you're on the right track. But there are other trains there, too. Move a little faster and see if you can sell something. That's what gets the train rolling, and it can get up quite a head of steam when it gets loaded with customers.

Eugene Raudsepp, the late president of Princeton Creative Research in Princeton, New Jersey, found the following 12 traits to be key to successful entrepreneurhood. Many of them agree with Mancuso's, but there are some interesting additional ones:

1. An achievement motivation (though not necessarily to get rich).
2. An action orientation. Ready to make progress immediately.
3. A strong sense of reality. Few illusions. Can confront mistakes.

4. Internal control. Takes responsibility for what will be.

5. Self-confidence. A strong ego, but not self-important.

6. Opportunism. Can spot needs and imagine ways to fill them.

7. Moderate risk-taking. Not gambling on long shots.

8. Motivation and energy. Loves to work hard. Passion for success.

9. Long-term perspective. Can handle delays and frustration.

10. Persistence and tenacity. Determined to complete the job.

11. Ability to accept failure. Ready to learn from mistakes.

12. Effective problem-solving. Can combine analysis with intuition.

Maybe It All Boils Down to Three

Bill Radin, in *Breakaway Careers* (Hawthorne, NJ: Career Press, 1994), says it really comes down to just three things: idealism, the ability to execute and the desire to compete. Community involvement and volunteer work are good indicators of idealism. Basic business sensibilities are a must: ability to manage finances, organize record-keeping and communicate effectively. Then all you need is the desire to compete—the love of making a good deal.

Selling Yourself Over and Over

While you may be batting 1.000 on Bill Radin's Big 3, can I presume you possess all 12 qualities cited by Gene Raudsepp above? Hardly. In fact, I imagine someone could do rather well having serious amounts of even a handful of the 12 great traits. But identification with a clear majority of these characteristics is a very good start.

Well, why not? What, really, are you getting from your company job, aside from a steady paycheck, regular raises, job security, extensive medical benefits and comfortable pension? Hey, if that's all they think you're worth, well, in the words of the popular country-and-western song, "Take This Job and Let Me Hold onto It while I Start My Own Little Business on the Side.

—Dave Barry in *Claw Your Way to the Top*

If I had to pick two you can't do without, I'd say #5 (self-confidence) and #8 (passion for your work). Competence is the price of admission to entrepreneurism, but those who compete successfully must also be comfortable selling themselves and promoting their products and services. Ideally, your enthusiasm is obvious and abundant at all times.

"Often, people have wonderful ideas but little idea how to market or promote," says Silvana Clark, author of *Taming the Marketing Jungle* (Bellingham, WA: Memory Makers, 1994). She cites a couple of examples of low-cost creativity: an owner of a boarding home for senior citizens leaves a brochure when she leaves a tip in a restaurant (it generates calls), and a dentist who organizes a children's poster contest during National Health Week.

This kind of extra effort in letting people know about your business is essential, but can't happen if you aren't comfortable making it part of your persona. If you're not sure how it'll feel to be pitching yourself, try role-playing with a friend. Make your friend the potential customer and explain how your product or service will meet certain needs. Your comfort level will be obvious, and can be improved with practice.

But Be Ever so Humble

As Gene Raudsepp said, self-confidence is not self-importance. In fact, I happen to believe the world is a little short on humility right now, at least in well-developed nations and, especially, America. Almost everybody's quite caught up in what will glorify them, directly or indirectly. That makes people with even a touch of humility unusual. There may even be a market for it!

That's what Michael Baer found. Michael was laid off as an ad sales executive for General Media in New York City, a humbling experience that left him sufficiently desperate for work that he began driving a cab. He later picked up some front desk work at a budget hotel that catered to international tourists.

There, guests often asked him how to get to the airport, and he'd say, "I'll be back in the morning with my cab." "That's when it struck me to begin some sort of an airport shuttle business," he says. So he opened Baer's Shuttle Bus Plus, with two 15-passenger vans. That business led him to create custom tours for visitors to New York. "I like being of service. It makes me feel good," says Michael.

Aha! That kind of attitude is what made it possible for him to drive a cab and answer questions long enough to notice a real business opportunity. A little humility goes a long way, and can take you there. And it's not painful. Listen to Michael: "It makes me feel good!"

Be a Great Communicator

There are countless kinds of self-directed work, but they have at least one thing in common: a need to present yourself properly to customers, often in writing. So when asking yourself the big question (Is an alternative career for me?), consider this one of the big answers: if you thoroughly enjoy writing and speaking, you'll be a lot happier along the road to independent success.

We're not talking about penmanship here. The Hall of Business Fame is filled with illegible handwriters. I mean writing as in ripping off business memos and letters that impress and persuade, marketing copy that's at least crisp, if not sizzling, and personal notes that will remind your correspondents that there are brains behind this enterprise.

Similarly, speaking effectively, both one-on-one and in conference-room settings, is key to your image and, therefore, your business success. Most entrepreneurs got to the brink of entrepreneurship partly because of personal presence and an ability to get their points across verbally.

But many are ill-at-ease with the written word—more than you might imagine. I recently had the opportunity to assist a highly successful professional-development consultant (I'll call her Amy) well-known for her informative and entertaining workshops, but paralyzed by paragraphs. Amy had agreed to contribute a few hundred words to a trade journal, describing her work. Her deadline was near and she was in a panic. As comfortable as she was in person and in public, she had, so far, avoided all opportunities to show her stuff on paper. She couldn't believe she'd said yes to this one.

Her first instinct was to hire someone else to do it. A freelance writer acquaintance agreed to give it a try, but stumbled badly. The first draft was awful. There was no time and little hope in asking for a rewrite. What could she do?

"Forget, even for a few minutes, how impossible this appears to be and try it yourself," I said. "Pretend you're explaining to a friend what your work is all about. Don't worry about whether it's the definitive, perfect description. Get something down on paper that resembles your own conversation."

The block seemed to be that her work was so vital to her that she feared casting it in print awkwardly, and so she couldn't confront the idea at all. In this, as in so many other things, just getting started was key. Once she had a few words down, the next ones came a bit more easily and by the next day, she was faxing me a pretty solid stab at her article. We fine-tuned it together in a couple of hours. Now she has her magazine article, and a lot more: confidence and the satisfaction of having cleared a big hurdle in her self-directed career.

If anything, writing is rising in significance as communication technology advances. E-mail is a craft in itself that in many ways brings back the long lost art of the letter. Thoughtful faxed notes are another effective way to convey your efficiency and responsiveness.

How Do You Feel about Money?

Being honest with yourself about the importance of money in your work is a must in self-directed career planning. If it's that important, make room for it. In doing so, however, look for opportunities to let enjoyment of your work take precedence. Will Richardson is building a house in Dummerston, Vermont—a big, 5000-square-foot house filled with architectural detail. He's "living the project," as he says. "I really love what I'm doing. It doesn't feel like a job." Yet although he earns a good living in this business, Will feels "the craft doesn't seem to be driving the occupation any longer. Money does." Check out money's influence on your career planning and make sure it's in perspective.

Speaking of Money: How Can You Afford Not To?

That pretty much sums up the conclusion you should reach about finances as you enter entrepreneurship. While the specifics of your decision will clearly be guided by a business plan of some detail, at the conceptual level, you should be driven by forces that go beyond the bottom line.

If, for example, you're independently wealthy, have put a great deal of thought into engaging in an activity that will be thoroughly fulfilling and have a hands-down great opportunity to increase your holdings—you probably don't need this book!

But if you're wondering how you could possibly afford to go on your own, listen up for some unconventional wisdom: No business plan is sufficient. None can foresee all the consequences of your enterprise. Risk is inherent. In fact, the odds are likely to be against you. You simply have to be willing to battle an uncertain number of unknowns.

Please, do enough research on your intended line of work to provide plenty of appeal, on paper, for your opportunity. (Lots more on this in future chapters.) But for now, while we're determining whether a self-directed career is right for you, the only basic question we have to answer about finances goes something like this: If you could start tomorrow, independently, doing the kind of work you absolutely love, but running the risk that you will fail financially, would you? Or, would you prefer to wait five years while you save a year's worth of income, which would more or less guarantee your financial safety, and then begin your dream work? Which would you choose?

If your answer is the former, you can certainly wait until Chapter 4 to discuss finances, because you've already put finances in the proper perspective for a successful self-directed career! If your answer is the latter, go back three spaces and take Joe Mancuso's entrepreneur test again.

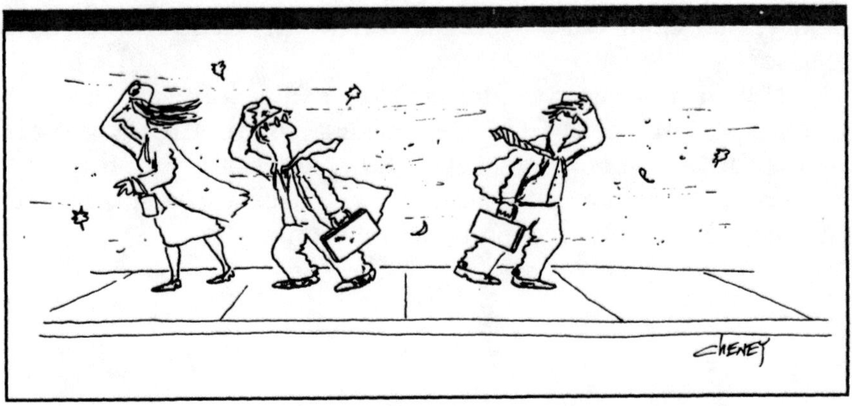
CHENEY

3

Choosing a Path

At some point in your journey toward self-employment, you'll cross a line between embracing the attitude and initiating action. We've reached that point in our discussion here. The path still isn't exactly clear, but it may be much better shaped than you realize.

"You'll be in business long before you open the door," says small-business maven Paul Hawken, author of the ahead-of-its-time landmark book, *Growing a Business* (New York: Simon & Shuster, 1986).

One of the key attributes of entrepreneurship is being able to observe the landscape in which your work is being carried out; to look at your own work from a distance, so you can see its intrinsic value and how else it might be applied profitably. There's nothing mystical about this. It's a discipline easily learned if you're willing to commit concentrated thought to it.

Here's how: Put aside the details of your specific work duties and begin to identify the general activities that are key to success in the way you work. It could be crafting or creating products or services, managing others to do so, knowing how everything works in your organization, engaging customers in the opportunity to do business with you . . . whatever.

These are the places to look for identification of your true strengths, as well as those that can be transported to another industry or another content area, if you will. These are your functional or "soft" skills (even though they may be highly technical).

General categories include finance, managing, marketing, training, sales, operations and systems. Now, define your strengths further: perhaps it's motivating professionals in a small sales office. List every strength you can think of. Just make sure you're listing functional tasks you excel at, not limited to your kind of business. Next, put a star beside any functional skill you've put to use at more than one job or enterprise. Pick one or two at which you feel you absolutely excel and love doing.

Now you can begin the imagining process: Where else would these skills be valuable? What would my business look like if I based it on these abilities and services? Who would my customers be?

This is really the key to a self-directed career: to pinpoint the greatest value that you bring to projects and identify the key customers for that value, whether it's within an organization where you're currently working, in your own enterprise or in some combination of the two. As soon as you begin applying that outlook, you're self-directed. And the self-directed attitude soon lights the path we're looking for. This is what Paul Hawken meant when he said, "You will be in business long before you open the door."

Alec Thorne, a Hartford, Connecticut-based management consultant, recalls that, before going on his own, he spent about a year at his previous employer weighing options for the kinds of work he'd seek if he began his own business. In his role as an accountant in a practice of 10 professionals, Alec had been exposed to dozens of local businesses and had often given his clients advice that went beyond basic accounting.

Several of the firm's clients were law firms, and he noticed that three law-firm clients in particular seemed to have extraordinary challenges in structure and operational issues. In his spare time at home, Alec began to study principles of management

Think and act incrementally, that is, with the smallest possible change that will get you where you want to go.

—Walter Kiechel in *Office Hours*

consulting. Then one day, a law firm client called to ask Alec a question about compensation plans for law firms. Alec seized the moment and three days later submitted a proposal for an organizational assessment project. He was in business before he even opened the door, and Alec's story illustrates several points that are key to the process of choosing a path:

☆ His new enterprise was based on first-hand experience with a similar service.

☆ He possessed enough curiosity and passion for his subject to study it before he knew he'd soon be earning his living at it.

☆ He recognized a new opportunity to add value to an existing relationship.

Building directly on your experience may be the best route to a self-directed career, but it's certainly not the only one. Often, the question is, "How much of a leap should I make between what I'm doing now and what I'd like to do on my own?"

What would you like to do? How can you afford to do anything else? You may always find a difference between what you like to do and what you're good at. But chances are, if you're pursuing the thing you really love, your ability will grow. It may also be true that love grows along with doing what you're good at. But why take any chances? Make loving what you're doing the top priority.

The Path with Heart

"You must always keep in mind that a path is only a path; if you feel you should not follow it, you must not stay with it under any conditions."

This is the beginning of one of the great lessons Carlos Castaneda learns in his 1968 classic anthropological allegory, *The Teachings of Don Juan: A Yaqui Way of Knowledge* (New York: Ballantine Books, 1968). Castaneda is about 18 months into his experiences with the enigmatic Mexican sorcerer when he asks the great master about choosing a path. Don Juan continues with these powerful, carefully chosen words:

To have such clarity you must lead a disciplined life. Only then will you know that any path is only a path, and there is no affront, to oneself or others, in dropping it if that is what your heart tells you to do.

But your decision to keep on the path or to leave it must be free of fear or ambition. I warn you. Look at every path closely and deliberately. Try it as many times as you think necessary. Then ask yourself, and yourself alone, one question. This question is one that only a very old man asks. My benefactor told me about it once when I was young, and my blood was too vigorous for me to understand it. Now I do understand it. I will tell you what it is: Does this path have a heart?

All paths are the same: They lead nowhere. They are paths going through the bush, or into the bush. In my own life I could say I have traveled long, long paths, but I am not anywhere. My benefactor's question has meaning now. Does this path have a heart? If it does, the path is good; if it doesn't, it is of no use. Both paths lead nowhere; but one has a heart, the other doesn't. One makes for a joyful journey; as long as you follow it, you are one with it. The other will make you curse your life. One makes you strong; the other weakens you.

There are many lessons in these words, but let's consider the most basic one: Learn to listen to your heart. If you can begin to notice your feelings more carefully and regularly, following them will come naturally.

Another wise person once said about life and marriage, "A person has to ask, 'Where am I going? And who will go with me?' If you ask them in the wrong order, you will be in big trouble." The same goes for choosing a career path. In this case, it's the "What would I love to do" question and another: How can I make the best living? If you answer the second one first, expect a disastrous result.

Let Skills Adapt to Love

Assuming you're working on doing something you really love, you should focus on the transferability of your functional skills. Ron Evans was long-time publisher of *Byte* magazine, the influential computer publication. Now he runs a consulting and business development practice focused on Asia and the Pacific Rim. Where's the connection? He'd spent his last five years at Byte developing the Asian markets in both circulation and advertising. He could imagine striking the same kinds of deals in a variety of businesses. Further, he has a life-long interest in Eastern cultures. Suddenly his move seemed not such a stretch after all. He loves it.

Sometimes it's the function you love, and the content isn't crucial: "You don't really have to know anything about ice cream to open a Baskin-Robbins," says Miami careers writer Gary Grappo. "But you do have to have the right soft skills: How to train, manage and motivate staff, for example."

Okay, What Are My Options?

You've chosen an area to work in that you really love, have taken an inventory of your transferable skills and identified a couple of strengths to pursue. Where shall we find the market for these skills?

One immediate possibility is to consider applying them in a different way for your current or recent employer. Tracy Steyer relocated to Rogers, Arkansas, from Minneapolis when her husband landed a job at Wal-Mart's corporate headquarters. But she didn't want to give up her job at an executive search firm, so she proposed taking her work with her: opening an office at home in Rogers and doing most of her work by phone from there, traveling occasionally to meet with clients and candidates. Her boss agreed and they established a working agreement; a year later, everybody's still happy. You can call Terry at her Minneapolis number and segue to Arkansas without a hitch.

Gary Grappo had another kind of deal: Until recently, he worked two weeks a month for Scanticon, a hotel and conference property development group based in Princeton, NJ. The other two weeks he wrote books at his home in Florida. It wasn't a rigid schedule—he could swap days—but it provided a framework in which he could turn on and turn off his full-time commitment and live guilt-free half-time, which is more than most of us get to do!

If, however, you're making a complete break with your previous job, you have even more interesting opportunities to consider! Ronnie Lessam, in the book, *Getting Into Self-Employment* (Toronto, Management Education and Development, 1984), defines seven approaches to self-employment:

1. *Turning a hobby into a business.* For this, you need longstanding passion for your product or service. The springboard is usually personal connections.

2. *Becoming a consultant.* This requires specialized knowledge and gets rolling through professional contacts. The ability and willingness to sell are essential here.

3. *Acquiring an existing business.* Managerial and marketing skills are critical. Financial resources are the trigger.

4. *Buying a franchise.* This one depends most on organizational ability. Again, financial resources put the plans in motion.

5. *Creating a business of your own.* Now we're talking a highly enterprising spirit. The key to action is a clearly identified marketplace.

6. *Matching personal and market potential.* This depends entirely on your personal knowledge and individual potential.

7. *Developing your vision.* For the highly creative and charismatic individual, this approach to self-employment is usually aimed at an economic or social need or potential.

Step Up to Your Level

Notice the progression in these seven approaches. They begin with passion and personal connections then add, step by step, specialized knowledge, professional contacts, management skills, financial resources and—at the top of the market—your individual "star" quality. (Keep this in mind as we discuss each of these kinds of self-employment in subsequent chapters.)

Regardless of which of these categories you end up in, it's unlikely you'll start at the top. Instead, you may very well spend time in several areas on your way to settling in—and it doesn't have to be the top to be satisfying.

Consider that virtually every career expert and entrepreneur says you must have passion for your work in order to be self-directed. This means your dream work probably started as a hobby at some point, or might have been something you studied

> If you want to change the world, start small.
>
> —Peace Corps ad

in school. Whatever this activity is, it stimulated you to engage in it with little or no regard for immediate return on your investment. This is what builds passion for your work and, not incidentally, notifies those close to you that you're making a significant personal investment in your subject.

Through this process, you acquire specialized knowledge that may prompt others in your field to seek your advice, thus the consulting route.

Additional skills in management, plus access to resources, might take you another step ahead toward buying a business. An option along the same lines, also requiring management and organizational skills, is to purchase a franchise.

Yet another notch up in creativity, plus management abilities, is starting your own business. And at the top of the heap is creating a business in which your personal creativity and charisma are the driving forces.

Discipline, but Freedom

There are two great lessons in understanding this progression:

1. A fantastic career and business idea is expansive in nature; the more you think about it, the grander it gets. Yet it can best be realized one step at a time. We must muster the discipline to reduce the idea to its essential elements of activity, in order. That's when the action starts: when we can see the first step.

"Every business I've ever started (there have been several) has started out of my house," says Gary Grappo. "And I've never put more than about $200 into a new venture." Here's an example: When Gary was closing down his job-fair business in Miami during the 1991 recession, he was scrambling for income. Discussing this one night with a friend visiting his house (again) for supper, the friend said, "You know, Gary, you're really a great cook, and I love eating here instead of cooking for myself! You could make money doing this for somebody."

Gary's pilot light went on; in fact, the burners were lit. He printed up a flyer billing himself as a private chef, took it to the swankiest apartment buildings in Miami and presented it to doormen, offering a $50 commission for every dinner party he could do as a result of the doormen's referrals. Gary grossed $3000 the first month and kept it up for six months until his next, more substantial opportunity arose.

2. You don't have to figure it out all at once. This sounds contradictory to the first lesson, but it's actually a happy byproduct of it. Because you're taking only one step, you don't have to figure out exactly where all the other steps are. You might have a few ideas about them, but it won't be too late for a mid-step correction.

This second lesson also is often expressed as, "Getting in motion is the main thing. It's much easier to alter the course of a moving object than to get one off dead center."

Jim Callihan, a self-employed marketing consultant in Peterborough, New Hampshire, puts it this way, "I don't care what you do, just do something. Don't sit back and worry about it. Just put out energy and when you put out energy, something comes back."

In my own experience, realizing that I didn't have to figure it out all at once was a revelation—and a huge relief. I'd spent some time trying to decide what things I would try if I went on my own. There were lots of ideas; someone suggested I develop a mini-business plan for each one to help select the best opportunities. But before I got too far in that process, a couple of the opportunities came looking for me, and I thought, "Well, it won't cost me anything to try these and see how I like them. Then I'll revise my long-range plan accordingly." I didn't have to figure it out all at once! This was the responsible thing to do: not figure it all out.

It carried over into my start-up phase: I didn't need every piece of state-of-the-art computer equipment immediately, just the basics. I could wait for a good deal on the right chair for my office. I decided to delay shopping for health insurance right away, taking advantage of my previous employer's obligation to continue me at its group rate. Just because I'm in business for myself doesn't mean I have to sign in blood a detailed plan of activities for years to come. In fact, the more I limit the outlay, the greater the flexibility. Paul Hawken says, "The self-owned, self-operated business is the free-est life in the world."

How Much Planning Is Enough?

The grand scheme must be broken down into manageable pieces with which to begin, but it's not necessary to know everything in advance about where a self-directed career will take us. What do these two things tell us about developing a business plan?

The answer, essentially, is that there should be a plan, but the extent of its detail can vary wildly. The greatest flexibility, as noted above, is with organizations that include only you. As soon as you start involving other people—as partners or employees—the demands on careful planning multiply greatly. If you're seeking financing, then your business plan becomes the central focus of your efforts.

We'll discuss the nuts and bolts of specific kinds of business plans in forthcoming chapters. For now, as we consider "choosing a path," business plans can serve another role: providing a framework for evaluating various directions.

In my own career-planning process, I looked at several ways of establishing myself independently and evaluated several types of projects I could pursue. I did this through a very rudimentary and informal business planning process:

☆ What, specifically, would be the scope of my service?

☆ What would be my market?

☆ What could I project for revenues?

☆ What resources would be required? Therefore, what expenses?

☆ What other impact on my career might I expect from this project?

Just answering those questions for each project, on one or two pages each with rough figures, gave me a playing field on which to compare possibilities. It helped me choose which ones to pursue. And, by the way, it wasn't all hard numbers. In the answers to the last question, there was loads of room for feelings, hunches and subjective reasoning.

> If one advances confidently in the direction of his dreams, and endeavors to live the life which he has imagined, he will meet with a success unexpected in common hours.
>
> —Henry David Thoreau

Later, when one or more of these business plans is put into use, the goal will be twofold: to make it complete and accurate, but also to make it flexible. Hawken calls this idea "plan to learn." He tells a story about a biology lab test that puts one frog in hot water (the frog immediately jumps out) and one in tepid water that's being heated. The second frog lolls around in the warming water and, by the time it notices the water's getting awfully hot, has become too weak to do anything about it. The lesson: "Enterprises fail more often because of the sum total of seemingly inconsequential events acting upon them than because of a sudden disaster."

Instead, Hawken says, as soon as a business learns to plan, it must plan to learn. "If a business sets itself up as a 'knowing' organization, confident of its models and sure of its needs and goals, its perception may be right. But will it be able to learn and change? Only an organization that does not presume to know will be able to detect and use fresh information from its environment. Planning must be firmly based on inquiry. Questions keep a business alive."

Product versus Service Considerations

Into which category does your selected enterprise fall? Service organizations dominate the small-business scene, and many of them are professional services. But as a professional, consider this: Your firm's ability to generate revenues is absolutely limited by how many hours you can work and how much you can charge for your time.

This concept also holds, albeit to a lesser extent, in any kind of service business. That is, the steady presence and involvement of the owner is virtually essential to the success of any service business. If, on the other hand, you're creating products, your market can grow exponentially—far beyond the physical limits on your own time—and deliver proportionally greater returns.

Many a professional services provider eventually asks, "How can I leverage my time in order to earn more?" It's a question worth anticipating.

Road Signs for Your Path

At this point you may feel you know your path and can't wait to get going, or you may still feel fuzzy about it. Either way, it can help to put a clearer, more specific label on these alternatives. Paul Hawken offers a helpful list of suggestions for a new enterprise; test your ideas against it and see where they fit in:

1. Recreate Something That's Been Lost

The consolidation of any industry into a few giant organizations—the current massing of health-care services comes to mind—tends to leave gaps that customized delivery of similar services or products can often fill. Look around your community for signs of things people really miss about the way certain services or products were provided before the chain came to town.

2. Enhance the Commonplace

Find a very ordinary product and give it new life. Hawken's examples include a charcoal fuel dealer whose sales caught fire when it began to market its mesquite charcoal as a gourmet barbecue item; New York City's corner groceries that have undergone a renaissance since a few Korean immigrants demonstrated that previous vendors had become lazy about displaying their products attractively; and his own Smith & Hawken garden tools, which took a truly dull-as-dishwater product and made it compelling through informative marketing.

3. Raise the Ante

Instead of simply trying to meet the competition, go one better and never look back. PC Connection in tiny Marlow, New

Hampshire, has grown from zero to $250 million-plus in annual sales in 14 years by pushing the service envelope. Customers can call as late as 3 A.M. and receive their computer accessories the same day, anywhere in the United States.

4. Reveal a Business within a Business

Hawkins' example: Chuck Williams of Williams-Sonoma, who took cookware out of hardware and department stores and put it on its own stage.

5. Restore a Business

Catch an outmoded enterprise that can be recast in a new light. Look at the recent emergence of family billiard parlors.

6. Be the Most Complete

Go deeper into a particular product or service line than anyone else. Sell 999 flavors of jelly beans or ice cream.

7. Be the Low-Cost Provider

Connect makers and buyers directly, cut your own costs to the bone and make room for spectacular volume at a paper-thin margin.

Be Creative

In applying these ideas to a selecting a specific enterprise, it's tough to underestimate the creativity component. You may have an idea that fits directly into one of the areas above, or it may blend two or more of the qualities. Either way, it should reflect creativity. Here are a couple of examples:

> Peggy Reed Bennett of Wichita, Kansas, was at loose ends, unemployed and looking for a clever way to make her own way, when she hit on the idea of becoming a mystery shopper. Peggy actually hated shopping so much she figured she ought to get paid for it, so here's what she did: She wrote to a number of corporations, telling them she'd be willing to visit stores as a typical (and inquisitive) customer and report back to the company on the honesty, knowledgability and helpfulness of clerks, cleanliness of the store, and other impressions—intended or otherwise—that customers might receive from their company. The idea clicked.

Soon after, Peggy was doing work for Montgomery Ward, Sears, Burger King, Pizza Hut and Arby's, plus several local banks, car dealerships, furniture stores and garden centers. A typical workday might include going to the bank to get money from an account without a withdrawal slip or check; going for breakfast at Burger King, where she'd take food temperatures, time the speed of service and check the restroom for supplies; stop by the garden center to find out how much the new clerk had learned about flowering shrubs; and call several apartment complexes to see how their rental policies were being administered.

The variety was endless. Peggy's main challenge was coming up with enough disguises to keep clerks and sales people from figuring out who she was. She has since moved on to other kinds of work, but the business was sufficiently successful that she was able to sell it to someone who continues to do well at it.

Or, how about Christopher Leo and Kay Keane of Lagrangeville, NY. As they pondered one of the battles working parents fight day after day—how to get the kids everywhere they need to go without leaving work—they came up with Kids on the Go. It's "a taxi service parents can trust," and it's doing so well locally they're considering expanding it to other communities.

In fact, "being creative" is often carried out simply by being observant—checking out each scene around you for clues to success—and open to opportunities. Sometimes this means being willing to do things whose immediate payoff isn't clear but which could, with good fortune, be worthwhile.

"If I can possibly fit it in my calendar, I try to do anything and everything that might advance a career or business opportunity," says Gary Grappo. "I have had some of the most serendipitous experiences." An example: Gary agreed to do a book signing at an out-of-the-way bookstore where he'd be lucky to attract a handful of readers. Sure enough, about five people came, but among them was the bookstore chain's national sales manager, who set Gary up on a book tour of South America for which he was paid $2000 a day, plus expenses!

Want to make even bigger bucks? Paul and Sarah Edwards, authors of *The Best Home Businesses for the Nineties* (Los Angeles: Jeremy Tarcher, 1991) list these home-based businesses in which a significant number of entrepreneurs earn six-figure annual incomes:

☆ Bill auditing.

☆ Business brokering.

☆ Business plan writing.

☆ Advertising/marketing copywriter.

☆ Desktop video production.

☆ Executive search.

☆ Export agency.

☆ Home inspection.

☆ Management consulting.

☆ Professional-practice consulting.

Research, Research, Research

Regardless of what kind of business you establish, don't fail to conduct thorough research, which has the dual effect of informing you as well as leading you to sources who may know of specific opportunities. Business libraries, trade associations and trade publications are obvious place to begin.

When Charles "Tony" Anthony of Dublin, NH, was thinking about entering the executive search field in 1986, he contacted Jim Kennedy, publisher of the leading trade publications in the industry. Jim loaned Tony several books on executive recruiting. Tony subsequently bought all the back issues of *Executive Recruiter News* and read them—twice!

"When I finished this, I had a very good understanding of the industry and the people in it. I could talk a good game, which helped me substantially in my interviews with people in the industry," Tony recalls.

When Can I Start?

Many would-be entrepreneurs who aren't being pressed by external factors into finding their next opportunity, ask "When should I quit my job and get started on my own enterprise?"

Several factors play into this, including:

☆ How much of an investment is required?

☆ How much of a financial cushion do you have?

☆ What are your on-going financial responsibilities (mortgage, other loans, car payments, school tuitions, etc.)?

☆ Will it be a home-based business? If not, can you establish your enterprise in another location while still holding down your regular job?

☆ Can you conduct your new business outside regular work hours?

☆ Is your family willing to make the necessary sacrifices for you to give up other responsibilities at home so you can engage in getting a new business started in your spare time?

☆ In sum, can you feasibly begin part-time at home?

This can require quite a bit of soul-searching. I'll offer my own very pertinent example: I agreed to write this book while I was still fully engaged in a relatively demanding regular job. I thought I could do it in my spare time at home. Everything seemed to indicate that this was feasible. I had a computer and space to work in; my family was fully behind me; there was no financial outlay—in fact, I was being offered an advance for agreeing to do it.

But I miscalculated. Though I was able to get started on the book while still holding my regular job, I found it was very difficult to do it off-hours. I couldn't reach sources during their business hours. And despite my desire, I found it difficult after a full day's work to muster the energy and creativity to tackle such a large project. Though my family was as forgiving as I could ever imagine, I had a tough time removing myself from all the activities I enjoy and responsibilities I feel in my home life.

So, for me, significant progress on my book didn't take place until I was on my own, could set my own schedule and work priorities, and have big chunks of prime-time daytime business hours in which to become immersed in my subject. Even then, it was a challenge. Starting your own business has its own demands (remember how I was doing at the beginning of Chapter 2?).

Follow your bliss.

—Joseph Campbell

My conclusion: Know yourself. Be honest about what you can and cannot accomplish in your "spare" time. Be clear about your priorities. And realize that the more significant your new enterprise is, the tougher it will be to get it going with small amounts of effort. Unless you're Superperson, be realistic about how much work this will be and make room in your life for it.

How Much Financing Do I Need?

A key point in the above tale of getting this book off the ground is that I was investing time and not money. Time is a very safe investment to make, especially in something you really love. But money will get you into trouble when it's lost.

How can you tell what a wise amount of borrowing might be? Economist Kathryn Stafford, in an interview with *The Wall Street Journal,* reminds us that undercapitalization is one of the three biggest mistakes an entrepreneur can make (the other two are underestimating the amount of work it takes to get a business going and failing to run the business like a business, through solid record-keeping and a combination of communications and marketing techniques). You must be realistic about what the financial needs will be to get the business going, having enough to not only develop the product or service, but also to sell it.

However, many see comfortable financing as the enemy. "I believe that, for the new and growing business, too much money is a greater problem than too little," says Paul Hawken. Gary Grappo agrees: "Too many get a grandiose idea, plop down $5,000 or $10,000 from Mom and Dad and fail to build a real foundation for their business because they have enough cash at the beginning to not worry. But those whose ship is in more

Speak the affirmative; emphasize your choice by utterly ignoring all that you reject.

—Ralph Waldo Emerson

danger of sinking at the outset learn more about how to stay afloat."

I'm with them: Following the same line of thinking as reducing grand ideas to first achievable steps, don't spend or even budget money for stuff you don't really need. Don't borrow money you can possibly live without and keep your overhead low. Everything you make will go to the bottom line.

Should I Work at Home?

This is one of the great debates of entrepreneurship for people who've never been in business for themselves. The answer is an unequivocal yes. But let me explain.

I feel strongly that in order to be successful in any self-directed career, you can't separate it entirely from your home life. If you seek to start a business of any kind and think you can "leave it at the office," you're either fooling yourself badly or lack the passion that will be necessary to succeed. It's natural, expected and—in my view—a requirement that at least some of your "space" at home be devoted to business planning and the myriad chores and activities that come with being self-directed. Put whatever limits on it you feel are necessary in order to recharge yourself for your work. Establish priorities for time with your family. But don't expect total separation of work and home.

Guess what? Knowing how to work at home is a blessing and may be a critical factor in helping you get off the ground effectively and inexpensively. Open a home office today, whether you intend to carry out all of your work there or not. If you can make that investment in time and money while you're otherwise employed, you will have already cleared a basic getting-started hurdle.

Gary Grappo says he's been able to launch several ventures for only a few hundred dollars each partly because he's well-set-up at home with computer and communication equipment, and doesn't have to make such an outlay part of every business plan he considers.

Also, remember our talk about transferability of skills at the beginning of this chapter? Consider these rather mundane but critical skills that are part of almost any business platform: thorough knowledge of the features and effective use of telephones, voice mail and fax machines, and basic computer capabilities, including word processing and spreadsheet programs and, soon-to-be de rigueur, electronic mail. These are just the foundation skills for functioning smoothly in business today before you even introduce the content of your work and basics of financial management, marketing and customer satisfaction!

You Mean Really Work at Home?

Whether you work there most of the time—whether this is corporate headquarters—is another question entirely.

The first consideration is, do you have to work at home? Are you restricted by finances or other concerns from even considering an office or place of business at another location? If so, consider yourself lucky. You're going to have a home office!

Second: Do you want to? Do you have the room? Would you enjoy the opportunity to set your own hours? See your family more? Or would you be uncomfortable with the interruptions? Feel cramped and begin to resent your housemates? These are very personal questions, and ones you might not know the answer to if you haven't tried working at home.

When I launched my self-directed career, I struggled a bit with the idea of working at home. I'd spent 18 years in office settings—10 in a daily newspaper newsroom with a big crowd of verbal literates, and 8 more in another open office in a small publishing company. I'd always benefited from the stimulation of others. What would it be like home alone? Or, at the other extreme, would I have enough privacy? Would I be comfortable and feel professional? Would my business appear professional? Would it be convenient out here on a dirt road in New Hampshire, miles from Kinko's, the bank and the post office?

I couldn't answer all those questions. But two thoughts took precedence: First, I had the beginnings of a home office anyway and certainly didn't intend to give that up. Second, if I formalized that office and then found I couldn't work there all the time, I wouldn't have gone too far wrong. I'd just have a nicer office at home than I'd planned.

So far, I'm in my glory at home. I have a comfortable upstairs room devoted entirely to my work (reasonably quiet even when my 10-year-old son is practicing his drums in the family room!), fully equipped with computers and telecommunications gear. All the overnight delivery services now know where I live. And, having given up my half-hour commute, I don't mind a bit going out to the post office—plus I get to pick up my kids at the school bus, something I was never lucky or near enough to do before.

I get all the professional stimulation I need through the phone, fax and mail (e-or snail-), and on my once-a-month visits to New York, the occasional day in Boston and speaking engagements and conferences farther afield.

Best of all, I'm not paying rent on office space. It's as if someone came along and said, "David, since you're going into business for yourself, we've decided to pay off your mortgage for you"—that's how much I'm saving!

But that's just me. Your circumstances are bound to be different, and the basic nature of your business may require you to use commercial property. In subsequent chapters, we'll discuss how to proceed smartly in that direction. But before moving on here, let's weigh the question: Could this business be conducted at or from home?

If you're thinking of opening a computer services store and imagine it on Main Street or in the mall, have you also thought of serving customers by appointment at their offices and homes, maintaining only a minimum inventory at your home office? As you develop a business plan for your idea, keep it flexible long enough to address the opportunity of working at home. You might be surprised.

It's Almost Like Job-Hunting after All

Now, as we take our first steps down self-directed paths, let's pause for a moment to take one look back at the old world of jobs. Consider the following five all-star items to consider in job-seeking compiled by New York recruiter and career adviser/author John Lucht. Notice how well they apply to starting your own business:

1. *Your highest and best use.* What do you do especially well that employers (clients, customers) need most and

pay most for, which your accomplishments (not self-assessment) prove you can do?

2. *Your most impressive achievements.* What have you actually done that demonstrates you'll perform the job (deliver the service or make the product) you want to be hired for (you're selling)? What achievements show you were outstanding in earlier and lesser positions (businesses)?

3. *Your most enthusiastic and prominent supporters.* Who are the outstanding people in your field who know from first-hand experience that you're outstanding, and are willing to put their credibility behind you?

4. *The likeliest and strongest reasons not to hire (buy from) you.* Why are you most likely to be turned down? What's likely to be held against you, correctly or incorrectly, fairly or unfairly? Only by identifying your vulnerability can you defend and launch a counteroffensive.

5. *What do you really want to do?* If you want work you'll enjoy (your career will flourish when you find it), you'd better carefully consider what positions (enterprises), industries and companies (customers) would be best for you . . . and target your search toward them.

How are you doing? Does your new enterprise fit both your highest best use and your life's true desire? If so, consider yourself lucky. But success is clearly possible without meeting all five of these criteria perfectly. On the other hand, this is a good place to note big gaps in your ability to answer these questions confidently.

Note also the importance of the final question: What do *you* really want to do? Find a path with heart.

Perfect freedom is reserved for the man who lives by his own work and in that work does what he wants to do.

—R.G. Collingwood

"Little" Things That Make a Difference

Somewhere in the high drama of sweeping employment trends and life-changing career decisions are sometimes lost the details, or truly helpful "small" ideas that can have a big impact on your worklife success. I'll conclude the discussion of choosing a path with this thought: Get a board.

When I decided to test my mettle independently, a good friend, executive search consultant Nick Gardiner, suggested that I try something he did early in his career: form a board of directors. Ask a handful of your best business friends and contacts—insightful people who care about you—to be part of a group that reviews your options and makes recommendations about how to proceed. It could be convened once at a critical career-decision point, become a quarterly lunch or a biweekly on-line bulletin. You make up the rules. The point is, you can learn a lot, and you've established a mechanism to thwart the isolation that is sometimes overwhelming when you go out on your own.

Nick did this in 1978. He had been working for a Rockefeller family company called International Basic Economy Corp. that was being dissolved, and was one of those responsible for executing the divestiture. The last of the business units was sold in June and Nick spent the next several months investigating his options. "I was completely open to change and looked at all sorts of things."

He was also going through a divorce and was sharing a sublet with friends. "I was down to one suit, and it had a cigarette hole in the left knee, so when I went on interviews I had to cross my right leg over my left knee," Nick recalls. "And I remember standing one day on the subway platform at Columbus Circle with 200 resumes under my arm, sweating like a pig in this winter suit, and asking myself, 'What's happening to Mrs. Gardiner's little boy?'"

He decided to set a deadline: By noon on Dec. 22, he would choose among whatever options were available and be done with it. Then, while he explored and surfaced a few choices, he asked a half-dozen people "exceptional in their good judgment and who'd shown concern for my personal welfare" to be his directors. "I treated my decision as a corporate one."

> The return from your work must be the satisfaction which
> that work brings you and the world's need of that work. With
> that, life is heaven, or as near heaven as you can get. Without
> this—with work you despise, which bores you, and which the
> world does not need—this life is hell.
>
> —W.E.B. DuBois

The group convened for lunch on Dec. 22 and began to quiz
Nick on four opportunities for which he'd provided written
briefings: a job in banking, one in investment banking, and two
opportunities to enter executive search. The board's unanimous
recommendation was for Nick to take a crack at executive
search, with one of the great search firms at the time.

"Many years later, I can say it was a very good choice," says
Nick. And though circumstances have altered the group's membership, Nick has used his board several times since then at
major decision points in his career.

At about the time I went on my own and was planning to
pursue Nick's suggestion, something came to me, in a nifty bit
of good fortune, that meets the same need in another way. A
group of people a lot like me—independent consultants, at various stages of their careers, of different but complementary disciplines—invited me to join their once-a-month meetings in
New York to brainstorm on business ideas and share concerns
about how to do this thing we call being in business. Our inven-
tive facilitator's name is Sam, so we're Friends of Sam (not yet
incorporated).

There may be a group like this lurking informally in your
network, or there may be a professional or trade group that offers the right people and setting. But if you can't find one, form
one. Again, you make up the rules, but we've noticed a few
things that make it work: keep it very confidential, so you can
be as open as possible; keep it sufficiently intimate to truly address the concerns and suggestions of all members; keep *obligations* between meetings minimal, but offer a receptive hearing
to efforts people make because they *want to;* and, significantly,
make regular attendance a matter of high honor.

The benefits of these meetings have been extraordinary. Friends of Sam helps alleviate the occasional fear that creeps up when I wonder whether the next engagement will be there for me after I complete this one. Even though I can trace only one billable, small project to Friends of Sam to date, I know that if and when I do run out of work, there are eight people I can call for ideas.

The monthly meetings in New York (I live a commuter plane-hop away in New Hampshire) tie me to a time when I'll be there. Appointments with current and prospective clients seem to magically fit around my schedule when I'm able to say, "I'll be in the city on the 17th," rather than not knowing when I'll be there or picking a date that's of convenience to only one client or friend. And if the 17th isn't a good day, I'll catch you on my visit the following month.

I've gained confidence in setting my fees because I have a peer group that shares experiences on this and related issues (trade groups can't help here). Friends of Sam gives me a running start on being able to respond to an opportunity that's beyond my resources. Perhaps it's something I can do with just one other member of the group rather than with everybody, which isn't a problem: we can meet separately before or after Friends of Sam.

Finally, at a minimum, I get a sense of professional support and camaraderie connected to my new career. It juices me up. I recommend it wholeheartedly.

"I beg your pardon! That just so happens to be the buck that *I'm* chasing!"

4

Starting a Business

As we explore the relative merits of several kinds of self-directed careers, let's start with an in-depth look at starting your own business—the new American dream.

Starting a business is first among self-directed career options because it's actually a foundation for all the others: buying a business, starting a consulting practice, buying a franchise and becoming a freelancer or project manager. Don't skip this chapter, even if you've already focused on one of the other alternatives. You would be missing a few important building blocks.

Let Your Personality Shine

Establishing an enterprise, particularly one in your own name, is the ultimate opportunity to make your mark in the business world. However humble at the outset, and however small you might stay, this business will bear the unique mark of your personality and will reflect your values as clearly as the mirror you look into each morning.

> Being in business is a lot like riding a bicycle: You keep moving or else you fall down and get hurt.
>
> —small-business adviser Gary Cloutier

Some people are intimidated by that burden. Even those who aren't will occasionally become uncertain of their ability to create or decide on a necessary next step. In this chapter, we'll learn how to deal with those problems, among others. For now, it's enough to know that you've cast your fate with the self-directed, have a rough path in mind and are ready to pursue your business dream. We'll begin with a few truisms about starting a business and see how well they hold up. These are based on conclusions reached in a terrific *Wall Street Journal* article entitled, "Nine Myths About Starting a Business," written and reported by Dave Kansas.

1. A Business Plan Is Essential

You have to have a solid plan for any kind of business. This is an accepted fact of business life, and no responsible adviser will tell you differently.

"Without a plan, and a good assessment of a new business's needs, it's unlikely that someone can succeed at starting a new business," says Peter George, director of the Small Business Development Center at the State University of New York at Albany.

Risking heresy, my view on this sacred cow is at odds with conventional wisdom. I believe that a business plan is simply the best available means for demonstrating that a venture is likely to succeed. It must be formal and complete in order to obtain financing. And it should be at least semi-formal for enterprises that immediately involve employees and other significant obligations, such as a lease. But plenty of successful sole-proprietorships are born without a 50-page supporting document that projects monthly cash flows for the next five years.

Granted, more businesses without plans fail than do those with them. But it's definitely possible to start casually. I believe success results from the merit of the enterprise itself, along with a healthy dose of good fortune. A business plan simply gives us the best possible opportunity to evaluate the merit of the enterprise and choose not to participate in it (this includes yourself if its conclusions indicate a strong possibility of failure).

My business plan is a Manila file folder called David A. Lord, filled with notes to myself—in pencil, on lined yellow pads—that I made before leaving my job at a small business-information publishing company, and during the first few of months on my own. There's a working list of envisioned services and products that's been whittled down, added to and refined again as I've gone along, appearing more formally in letters of introduction and promotional materials I've published during my start-up. There's a list of potential clients—people I've helped in the past who know me to be a reliable writer, market analyst and adviser. There are pages of budget notes: the capital costs of opening an office at home and operating expenses (where the writing practically goes off the page with little things I hadn't thought of earlier).

Then there's my $100,000-a-year plan—a humble attempt at income forecasting. As I weighed the question of what to project for revenues in my new business, I asked myself what my personal income goal should be. Though our family lives modestly in rural New Hampshire, I have three children soon to be in college and am motivated to work hard for that to become possible. I also hope to be prepared for years further down the road after my prime. (Right now, I can't imagine retiring, and I am not sure retirement as we currently know it will even be possible for baby boomers and beyond.)

I felt that net (after tax) income of $65,000 would meet our minimum needs and even provide some discretionary spending with which to celebrate the long hours I'd be devoting to my business. Then I plugged in the estimates of operating expenses I'd made:

☆ Taxes.

☆ Insurance.

☆ Repayment of a $5000 home equity loan I'd taken to cover part of my start-up costs.

☆ Travel for business development.

☆ Telephones.

☆ Stationery and postage for an initial announcement/ marketing letter, plus routine correspondence.

☆ Other office supplies, including computer advice and maintenance.

All of this added up to about $40,000.

The business would require gross revenues of $105,000. It seemed to be an achievable number, given indications from prospective clients of their intentions to use me. If I could earn more, wonderful, but despite the current spate of news stories about executive families suffering with incomes of $150,000, I felt we could survive at $105,000 (net $65,000). My wife, who freelances on arts and special-events projects, would be kicking in an occasional paycheck as well.

Next question: How many full days of consulting and writing work could I expect to bill for in my first year? My answer: Income from writing is so unpredictable—and often low—I should assume I'll have none and see if I can construct something based on consulting fees alone. Any writing revenues will be a bonus; mad money. I'll write for show and consult for dough. The latter will feed the former.

I budgeted 270 workdays for the year: Monday through Friday plus Saturday mornings, with two weeks of vacation and five essential holidays. Of the 270, I made an educated guess that I might be able to bill for one-third of them. For every day of billable consulting work, I'd be spending two days developing the business, going the extra mile to ensure my work's full value, conducting the on-going affairs of being in business, and filling in with writing projects.

I'd learned from other consultants over the years that this was a reasonable ratio (though there are really no widely applicable formulas for the wildly varied world of consulting). At 90 billable days per year, what would I have to charge per day to attain $105,000 in gross income? $1200 a day would generate $108,000—a worthy goal.

Next, I asked a few consultants doing similar work what their rates were. My magic number—$1200—came up immediately from the consultant whose practice most closely matched my own projected work. All the other answers were higher—all the way up to one fellow at the top of our field who charges $9000 a day. I decided I was safe starting at $1200.

To profit in these network-building times, entrepreneurs don't need to be bigger than anybody else or richer than anybody else. They just have to know how to do their part of the job better than anybody else.

—John Case in *Inc. Magazine*

It became my pricing plan and the basis for my final income and expense projections. I made additional informal calculations of what our personal assets and liabilities might look like at the end of such a year, and decided to go for it.

That was—and is—my business plan. It's worked because I was able to get the kind of work I thought I could, execute it and get paid for it—not because I did or didn't have a formally prepared document. I recommend business planning appropriate to the nature of the enterprise.

2. Lack of Sufficient Capital Is the Greatest Single Reason for Small Business Failure

This is true for many enterprises, but it won't be true for mine. I may fail for other reasons, but I picked a field—consulting and writing—in which start-up costs are minimal. I spent about $5000 renovating and furnishing an upstairs room in my home, bought about $5000 worth of office equipment, ordered a few phone lines, had some stationery printed and was in business.

In fact, one of the great discoveries about the whole process has been that, as long as I keep financial obligations at a minimum, I don't have to figure everything out all at once. A note to myself in my David A. Lord folder even says so. My objective is to keep the enterprise as simple as possible: to have no employees, but to joint-venture with other individuals and/or organizations on projects too big for me alone; to take on no debt; to track expenses carefully for which I can be reimbursed by my clients; and to keep other on-going expenses at a minimum.

Before you commit to an operation that will require a big capital investment, and therefore a big obligation, consider whether your goal of doing a particular kind of work can be carried out in a simpler format that will actually give you more time to do the work you're dreaming about doing.

In fact, while most small businesses fail due to a lack of working capital, "that's like saying the cause of most divorces is conflict," says small-business guru Paul Hawken. "The question is, what causes the lack of working capital? In a business, money doesn't create anything at all, much less ideas and initiative. Money goes where those qualities already are. Money follows, it doesn't lead. As a businessperson, you foster money with thought, strategy, demeanor and deed."

The bottom line, says Hawken, "You should start a business with just as much capital as makes you feel comfortable, and you should obtain it from sources you're most comfortable with. Embarking on your first business venture, you should start slowly and steadily, preferably using your own money. And if you borrow from yourself, you'll have the right attitude about money right away, which is that it's hard to come by and hard to keep. It's easy to remember this with your own money, but you can lose perspective when spending borrowed money or invested capital," he says.

3. "I Had No Other Choice, so I Started My Own Business," Is a Classic Prescription for Failure

People who prefer the security of an established organization usually fail, while those who can't stand working for someone else and have to do it their own way rack up lots of points on the "am-I-an-entrepreneur" test. Carol Hyatt, author of several forward-thinking career books, agrees that there's a big difference between "forced entrepreneurs" and "ones with mission."

Perhaps, but I've had a different experience. I thoroughly enjoyed working within companies owned by others. I especially loved the camaraderie of being part of a team of professionals until, that is, I found myself being asked to make a long-term commitment to a situation in which too many doors were closed. There'd be no chance for me to advance to full leadership of my business, or even my business unit. The value of my ownership share would depend on decisions in which I had no formal vote. I offered to buy out my business unit but was rejected. In that context, I became a "forced entrepreneur." I felt I had to start my own business.

Does this mean I'll fail? On the contrary, I believe that most of the qualities that made me a valuable and effective employee will also help me become a successful entrepreneur. It's a question of motivation. But just because you didn't open a lemonade stand when you were three, sell the most *Boy's Life* subscriptions or Girl Scout cookies, and make trouble at every job you've held since because you just had to be in charge, doesn't mean you can't start your own business today.

In fact, a successful New York City entrepreneurial program called Workshop in Business Opportunities (WIBO) is based on the inspiring premise that "most people are capable of starting and running their own businesses as long as they're taught necessary skills and are committed," says Rafael J. Gerena, co-owner of a small advertising agency, who completed the course.

4. Starting a Business Will Strain Your Marriage

If your marriage isn't rock-solid, don't throw a new business into the fray. "A weaker marriage or partnership can be, and often is, torn apart when someone is working hard at starting something new," says Thomas Dandridge, business professor at the State University of New York at Albany. "It's not really some fun adventure. Starting a business usually creates real stress."

To me, however, it's simply a shifting of stress, from meeting the expectations of others to meeting our own. Yes, I have a great bond with my wife, but even if I didn't, I feel I have more opportunity to control stress levels than I did working for someone else. And, by the way, working at home is an especially intense form of self-employment. I've invaded the space my wife has enjoyed as virtually "hers" while I've been at work all these years. But let's be up-front about the pluses. We're at home together a whole lot more than ever before, and we can make choices about how to spend our time with much more flexibility than ever. I'd say being self-employed can be a big positive in a marriage. If it's not a good marriage, on the other hand, then self-employment will make that issue all the more obvious.

5. Start Young

"Most people see the window of opportunity coming sometime right after college," says Wendell E. Dunn, academic director of the Sol C. Snider Entrepreneurial Center at the University of Pennsylvania's Wharton School. "At that time, it's less likely that you'll have a family, a mortgage, car payments or other expensive responsibilities."

True. So what happens if you're 44? Or even 64? Too many financial obligations? This can be the case at almost any age and is a separate issue. Johnny Come Lately? Over the hill?

Forget it! We're talking about what people can do today to advance their careers in a stimulating, meaningful way. I can't think of a business in which age should preclude involvement at some level. Don't reject a self-directed career because you think you're too old to do so.

On the other hand, if you truly believe that you're not up for the challenge, no matter your age, then don't take it on just because others say it's a good idea. No one knows your limitations better than you do.

You Make the Rules

There are a great many good rules about being in business. One of them is that you can make up a lot of your own rules. The trick is to know which of the others you really need to pay attention to!

Among those rules that must be followed in some form is solid, thorough business planning. While I've already noted that it's quite possible for a journeyman professional like myself to enter self-employment without a full-blown market analysis and detailed cash-flow chart, your enterprise is probably more elaborate than mine. You may be entering a field in which you'll be making significant capital investments and employing people simply to be in the game. Great! This is where business planning gets serious.

So let's walk through the process. (And, by the way, even if you're like me and don't need to crunch big numbers to persuade others that your enterprise is worth their money, it's instructive to do this.)

Will your business have legs? That's what we want to know. Business planning isn't something other business people thought up just to slow you down on your exciting journey (or keep you out of their markets). It turns out that business planning has lots of benefits beyond the obvious: obtaining financing. It's actually a low-cost test run that will help you avoid years of professional and financial misery—if that can be determined ahead of time—and give you a great big green light and a way to direct traffic to your door if the test proves successful.

At best, your idea is so straightforward and so well-developed that writing the business plan will be a breeze. But it may not be a breeze, which is okay, too. Many great businesses have come from plans that were agonizingly difficult to pull together. That's why, and how, some entrepreneurs succeed where others have failed. One was a better business planner.

The plan isn't just a plan. It's a way of thinking. It forces you to confront, in what can be a conveniently brief format, the basic questions about your business. If it's not already your style to:

☆ Step back from situations.

☆ Ask the basic question about what's going on.

☆ Answer it.

☆ Then take the obvious next step.

Writing a business plan will be a great experience in showing you how. It will help you recognize issues that are, in fact, irrelevant to your central purpose. It also will stimulate you to build on your dream by making you think about it from several points of view.

Again, business planning isn't about throwing cold water on your raging enthusiasm or simply wanting to be successful and being inspired to do so in a particular field. It's an opportunity to see the future. If your idea is truly exciting, writing the business plan is a chance to go for a ride in your new career without having to buy it—until you decide it's a good investment. What could be more fun, as well as responsible?

If, after taking this to heart, you still dread the thought of putting fingers to keyboard and documenting your dream in writing, stop here and reread Chapter 2, "Be a great communicator."

Business planning has even more benefits beyond helping you see the future, sharpen your business thinking skills and enhance your idea by considering several points of view:

It Helps You Gather Wisdom from Others

Regardless of how unusual your enterprise may be, in the big picture, there will be remarkable similarities to other businesses, plus relatively accessible people with vast, and telling, experience in those remarkable similarities. Get their advice! You can do this both casually and formally. It should be part of your modus operandi to be alert to the opinions of others, especially potential and existing customers.

Get comfortable describing your plan in a few words and getting off-the-cuff responses from a variety of friends and business contacts. But for people whose reactions are key to your success—perhaps essential to your next step—you can't ignore the formal approach.

This means putting your thoughts into a basic business plan format so that the power-brokers of your idea—including, and especially, yourself—can give it full and proper consideration. Anything less is an insult to your enterprise. And the more effort you put into the plan, the more valuable the advice you gather from it will be. You can't lose.

It Will Help Develop Customers and Become the Basis for Establishing Your Image in the Marketplace

It turns out that the things you say about your business in a basic statement of purpose, and in explaining how your business will meet customers' needs as no others can, are the best kind of advertising copy possible. Your words here can become the essence of your message in a variety of media you'll use to promote the business once it's up and running.

It Will Help You Measure Your Progress after You Get Started

The early days of entrepreneurism are likely to be a bit confusing. Even if your business is a runaway hit and you're giddy with apparent success, there will be questions about whether this suggests new strategies. Running forecasts of your new initiatives through the business planning process will help you make these next-step decisions.

At the other extreme, if things turn out to be much tougher than expected, you'll be able to get quickly to the cause by looking at the business plan as you would the gauges on your car's

---

An institution is the lengthened shadow of one man.

—Ralph Waldo Emerson

dashboard. It'll tell you whether your receivables are overheating, your invoices undercharged, your expenses speeding or your income at a dead stop.

Key Elements to Consider

Let's now consider the elements of a basic business plan. And, in case you're still resisting the written word, remember: You don't have to write the whole thing at once, and it doesn't have to be a book. What we're looking for are simplified answers to basic questions. Be brief, using charts and graphs wherever possible to convey quantifiable information.

To make it even easier, let's try this: Suppose I'm writing a book about starting your own business and have just called you to hear about your new enterprise. I'm going to ask you a few questions, and offer a bit of advice about how to answer them. Simply jot down your replies, and you've got a business plan.

What's Your Mission?

This is the central summarizing statement of what you seek to create. It can, and generally should, be as short as a sentence, "To be the leading supplier of gourmet baked goods to local stores and restaurants." It can be more detailed than that, including descriptions of specific products and services. But the briefer the better. It's the answer you give to someone who doesn't want to hear the whole story but wants to know the gist of what you're doing—the big-picture part.

How Will Your Business Achieve This Mission?

Again, briefly—in less than one page—summarize the activities your company will undertake in order to achieve your mission. Cite two or three key short-term objectives you'll establish in pursuit of your mission, and explain how they'll be achieved.

How Did You Get Here?

Understanding that the plan you're writing will be used not only to guide further efforts, but also to sell your enterprise to prospective participants, you may want to include some background about your expertise and involvement, what your resources are and will be, and your current status as an organization. Are you legally structured yet and, if so, in what category: sole proprietorship, partnership or corporation? Who else is involved and what roles will they perform?

We'll discuss the relative merits of various corporate structures in Chapter 9 (Getting Started), but I'll include one comment here on partnerships: Many entrepreneurs reach out for partners for security in starting new businesses and, in their desire to do so, are blind to differences in long-term goals that come back to haunt them.

"People say, 'I need to have a partner so I can have confirmation every day that I'm doing the right thing,' " says Marge Lovero, president of The Entrepreneurial Center in Purchase, NY. Many of these people would be much better off alone.

Lydia Soifer, a speech and language pathologist based in White Plains, NY, went into business with an older expert in the field, but later found she wanted to grow the practice more vigorously than her partner did. The split was difficult and bitter, but Soifer eventually found she could succeed on her own.

"There were days when I was scared out of my socks and didn't think I could do it at all," she says. But she hired appropriate advisers and began to grow the business the way she believed was possible, and now is happier than ever.

Who Will Be Your Customers?

A business is born when a customer demonstrates a need and you're there to meet it. Just having the goods isn't sufficient.

At the beginning, there's a customer with a desire. "The purpose of a business is to create and keep a customer," says Harvard University marketing expert Theodore Leavitt.

Indeed, "a business opportunity occurs when there's a problem to be solved or a need to be met," says David McNally, author of *Even Eagles Need a Push* (Eden Prairie, MN: Transform Press, 1990). "The entrepreneur seizes the opportunity and produces a product or service that will solve the problem or meet the need. The key ingredient to the success of the business, however, is the ability to attract and retain customers. Without customers, absolutely nothing else is possible, nothing else matters."

You may have a picture in your mind of who your first customer will be. Better yet, you may have already identified your second and third customers. It could be someone you're already working with, or have another relationship with—even in a context unrelated to the service or product you intend to provide. It could be the company you currently work for, and to whom your new company will become a supplier. Or, it could be a mass of unknown individuals, in a market you know for another reason, or in a market you know almost nothing about.

You may think you know who your customers will be, but later find out they're someone else. This can rattle your board of directors, but can also be a happy discovery of an additional or expanded market you hadn't expected to reach. Stephen Campbell, owner-editor of the Home Business Review in Austin, Texas, left a career of writing at major corporations to publish what he thought would be a local publication about home employment. In just its fourth year, Home Business Review has gone national with 19,000 far-flung subscribers, and is accessed more than 3000 times a day from around the world on its World Wide Web site.

You may have no idea who your potential customers are, or will be. You may have a great product that you're considering distributing, either on a wholesale or retail basis, but haven't yet decided which to pursue. In that case especially, and in general for all of the above circumstances, it's time for market research. Ask questions like:

☆ How much do I know about the customers I'm targeting?

☆ What do they want?

☆ I've identified a need not being met, but why is that so?

☆ What can I learn about previous efforts to provide this product or service to this particular market?

☆ How large is the market and why have I chosen it?

The very act of pursuing a venture is a continuous reward. Each day will present its own challenges and problems that you will meet and solve. Each small battle won will bring a jolt of satisfaction, charging you up to continue the quest.

—Jim Lang in *Make Your Own Breaks*

Your answer to the last question will help you decide whether you've investigated your potential customers sufficiently, and whether more research is needed. The size and nature of the audience will determine your technique.

"You'd be surprised how many business plans I review where people have never gone out and talked to their prospective customers," says Wendell Dunn at Wharton. "They made a lot of assumptions about why people should buy the product, but they've never bothered to go out and talk with, say, 15, 20, 25 people who would be exactly the kind of person they would want to have as customers." Why will they buy from you? Find out.

Have you analyzed your likely competitors in this market? List them and note their strengths and weaknesses. Provide any information or insight available about how they're doing. But be careful when criticizing competitors in your business plan; it may not reflect well on you.

"When you first write your plan, you'll probably take a dig or two at your competition," observes Paul Hawken. "Be relentless in editing it out. It's the degree to which you know and understand the competition that speaks well for your plan, not your distaste or feeling of superiority. Ironically, the reader will learn more from this section about your character than about the character of the competition."

Key to describing the competitive setting for your enterprise is explaining how you'll distinguish yourself from thé competition (or, if there is no competition, move your customers from the status quo). As the old saying goes, you can provide customers with two of the following qualities: good, fast and cheap" (inexpensive). Customers can't have 'em all. My advice is to make "good" your top priority, "fast" second and "cheap" the one you can't get to.

How will you reach them? Marketing 101. What's your action plan for getting your product or service in front of buyers, and how will you turn prospects into paying customers?

"Selling strategy is a serious weakness in many business plans," says William J. Stolze, author of *Start-Up, An Entrepreneur's Guide to Launching and Managing a New Business* (Hawthorne, NJ: Career Press, 1994). Be specific about how you'll sell your services, and describe your distribution channels and how you plan to use them.

What will affect demand? Before leaving the essential focus on customers and their needs, provide any other information here about their buying patterns that may be relevant. Are there seasons or cycles of demand? What influences purchasing decisions? How important is price?

Have you identified secondary markets that may be pursued if you have success in your initial market? If so, how will you enter those markets?

Do you know your business? How well? This is your opportunity to go into greater detail about your abilities and the unique resources your organization will offer.

Specifically, how will you carry it out? Go all out here in describing how you'll produce and deliver your product or service and how you'll assure consistent quality. Describe your location, relationships with any suppliers, distribution system and pricing strategy.

What are your financial projections? This question will take more than five minutes to answer and be worth more than all the others combined. The basic elements to be provided here should include:

☆ A multi-year revenue projection.

This will be only as good as your market research, and it will never be perfect. "Financial projections are important because of the thought that goes into them, not because of their putative accuracy in forecasting," says Paul Hawken. "You cannot forecast five years into the future without a detailed examination of virtually every single aspect of the business and economy. Not only are plan and strategy revealed, but so are the myriad details that comprise a successful business. It's of vital importance that they be carefully and slowly crafted."

☆ Monthly cash flow projections.
☆ Profit and loss projections.
☆ Capital expenditure projections.

In general, "be careful not to use the hockey stick approach to forecasting," says Stolze. This is the plan that foresees little growth in sales and earning for the first few years, followed by a sudden rapid surge toward unrealistic returns.

"Many are the business plans I've read where after-tax margins of 40 percent and higher are projected in an industry where 10 percent to 15 percent is considered good performance," Stolze says.

An excellent resource for your work in this area will be *Industry Norms and Key Business Ratios,* published by Dun & Bradstreet. Here's where you'll find out what typical profit margins are for businesses like yours. Your local library should have a copy; if not, ask your local Small Business Administration office.

Is It a Wrap?

These, then, are the basic questions that should be covered in your business plan, and I'll leave it to you to decide how elaborate yours needs to be. Once completed, does this mean we're done with the business plan? Never! A business plan is a living thing, never truly complete when you start up and always evolving as your business develops. The value you get from it at the outset will be proportional to the effort you put into considering and responding to the guideline questions above. If you've addressed them all, and your business idea still sounds plausible, you've done very, very well. Success is likely.

But you still need to answer a few more pesky questions, the responses to which you needed to know to prepare your business plan, but which I want to mention as reminders—and for special attention.

Who's Putting Up the Money?

The first question is financing. Who's footing the bill for your dreams? As soon as you begin pursuing a plan that requires financing beyond your own means, you begin to confront in your business a different point of view. This new view of your enterprise, which you now must share, is focused entirely on the likelihood of predictable, near-term success, and has little to do with the overall merit of your business concept.

"Most entrepreneurs are looking for someone to invest in an idea, but the venture capitalist seeks to invest in an opportunity. There's a real difference," says Sandy Weinstein, a partner at KPMG Peat Marwick Thome in Toronto.

"Where the entrepreneur envisions the ultimate success of a valuable idea, the venture capitalist sees only an opportunity in its infancy," he says. "The entrepreneur's objectivity may be clouded by an emotional attachment that comes from spending countless hours and personal funds on the idea. Venture capital investors remain detached. They realize that a detailed feasibility study, product development and professional marketing are required before an investment will return even one dollar. These differing points of view can make it difficult for entrepreneurs to accept that venture capitalists expect a great deal in return for their investment. Annual returns of 25 percent to 35 percent may be requested, along with an equity position approaching 50 percent and a controlling position (at least until certain conditions are met)."

This clash of purposes comes as a surprise for too many would-be entrepreneurs. As you prepare to seek financing, prepare as well for its effect on your business philosophy.

Start Small

Any business that can imaginably be run from a home office should be, and this extends to financing. Despite all that's said about most failed businesses being undercapitalized, don't go into debt unless you have to. Seek outside financing only if you must in order to start the business you want, and even then, spend time investigating whether there's a way to get into your field without incurring a financial obligation that may wind up driving your business (instead of you).

As an experienced newsletter editor thinking about going out on my own, I evaluated the prospects of starting a new publication, and realized that even if I could get the financing, I'd be risking not only all my efforts, personal savings and probably our family's home, but would be making payments to my lender well beyond the foreseeable future.

On the other hand, in pursuit of a customized consulting practice based on my particular knowledge of my markets, I was able to get started by borrowing only about $5000 on a home equity loan (in addition to about $5000 in personal savings). I paid off the $5000 with a retainer I received the month I opened, and have stayed in the black with a pay-as-you-go approach ever since. The beauty of this is that I could still decide to launch a publication or participate in one. The fact that I haven't incurred debt frees me to pursue other projects if such opportunities present themselves down the road.

"Conventional financing for most home-based businesses is minimal," says Gene Fairbrother, a consultant with ShopTalk 800, a toll-free hotline service of the National Association for the Self-Employed, a group based in Hurst, Texas, with 300,000 members.

Unfortunately, the need for financing typically runs well beyond the $10,000 I invested in starting up. While any kind of financing may be hard to get, or require personal collateral, even fewer lenders are willing to be bothered with loans of less than $25,000. However, a Small Business Administration "microloan" program that began in 1992 makes loans like this available to very small businesses, and the SBA may advise you of other state and federal programs targeted to this need.

Most advisers agree that if you borrow money, borrow plenty. "If I had it to do over again, I'd have borrowed more . . . six months to a year's worth," says Janice Caldwell of Rockville, MD. Janice launched a law practice from her home in 1982 with two months' worth of capital. Since it takes a while to bring clients on board, she had to lean on relatives for financial help." I still haven't paid them back," she admits.

Similarly, Loretta Larimer says she wishes she'd had about $50,000 instead of the $3000 she started with when opening P&P Sewing in Janesville, CA. Loretta bought P&P, which sells and services sewing machines, for $3000 in 1990, but had nothing beyond that to invest in its growth. With an extra $47,000, what would she have done? Among other things, avoided borrowing small amounts at higher rates. "I'm in debt up to my ears," she says.

Where Money Comes From

About 75 percent of new businesses are funded by their owners; about 13 percent receive financing from outside investors and through strategic alliances; about 8 percent are backed by banks. In Chapter 9 (Getting Started), we'll go into detail about a variety of nontraditional sources of financing. But in general, and for the purposes of our discussion here, my advice is: Don't ignore nontraditional sources. More small businesses find money there than through banks.

But beware of borrowing from a friend or relative. About 10 percent of small-business owners do so, according to the U.S. Census Bureau, and the results of a failed agreement can ruin a relationship. For those who do, it's best to put it in writing and pay a fair interest rate. (There are tax implications on each side here: write-offs for the lender if the rate is below-market, and extra levees for you on any difference between what you're paying in interest and the going rate, since that amount is considered taxable income.)

Finally—and this applies to any kind of lender—be very cautious when offering shares of ownership to your lenders. You may be introducing a voice in managing the enterprise that you hadn't counted on. And, if you succeed, you'll wish you didn't have to share the reward.

According to George McDonald, commercial loan officer at Savings Bank of Walpole in southern New Hampshire, the picture will look something like this:

Whereas banks have traditionally cared most about collateral, today the name of the game is cash flow. Show cash flow in a new business and you can talk turkey. A bank will match whatever you're investing (but would invest up to 75 percent of what you need to buy an existing business; see Chapter 5).

To further qualify, George's advice is to:

☆ Choose your bank carefully.

Some favor bigger businesses. A 1995 Federal Reserve System study found multi-office banks often skimp on small-business loans. Try to find a local decision maker for your loan.

☆ Don't apply for an SBA loan at more than one bank.

It's a waste of time.

☆ Fifty-fifty partnerships don't work.

Just don't do it.

☆ Get enough money the first time.

"Put a little cushion in there," says George. (Why does this sound like my banker talking?)

☆ Make sure you need it.

"Every other person who seeks financing doesn't need it. Lack of working capital is just a symptom of an underlying problem," he says.

And Have You Considered . . . ?

Numerous other issues are apt to jump up and grab you in the course of starting a new business. We'll grapple with several in more detail in Chapter 9, but I'll mention these now in case you need something else to keep you awake at night:

☆ Are your personal finances sufficiently stable that they won't present an unreasonable burden on your new business? (How's that for a loaded question? Put down that new car ad!) Seriously, are you and your family prepared for the kinds of sacrifices that may be necessary to get your business airborne? Many of us can point to a time in our lives when we got by on next to nothing. Are you ready, if need be, to revisit those good old days?

☆ Are most businesses in your area prospering? Or, if not in your area, in your market? Since "location is everything," is yours ideal, both in terms of a proper setting for your work that reflects the image you seek to create, as well as in cost?

☆ Is there equipment you could lease rather than buy, in order to minimize outlay?

☆ Do you have adequate health, disability and liability insurance?

☆ Is your record-keeping shipshape (and appropriate to the size of the enterprise)?

☆ What happens if you're successful beyond your wildest dreams? It could happen.

Luckily, there's a limit. Even if you can't answer all of these questions, take heart. There really are only five things that can go wrong:

1. You don't truly know what your objectives are.
2. You failed to insure yourself against known risk.
3. There's a great big hole in your financial plan.
4. You don't really know this field.
5. You procrastinate (I saved this one for last).

Sweet business dreams. Next up is buying a business, which has its distinct advantages.

"Like I was saying . . . the small businessman really has it rough these days."

5

Buying a Business

Seeking a quicker way to the top? Daunted by the demands of starting a business from scratch? Want to benefit from lessons learned by successful business founders? Perhaps you should consider buying a business. In most cases, it's a safer bet than starting a company your own.

New businesses started from scratch have a failure rate of more than 90 percent during their first five years. But half or more of all businesses that are sold survive at least the first five years of new ownership, according to Kent Foutz, a professor at West Chester University in West Chester, PA.

In fact, buying a business, turning it around, then selling or operating it for a profit is one of the fastest routes to entrepreneurial success. However, "Don't look only for companies that are in trouble or losing money. Purchasing a successful, profitable enterprise often is the best way to go," says Gary Benson, director of the Entrepreneurship Program at the University of Wisconsin in Whitewater.

While logic tells you that successful, profitable enterprises are rarely for sale, there are several kinds of situations in which good businesses become available:

☆ The owner becomes sick or dies and there's no obvious successor in place.

☆ A parent company is trying to raise cash by selling a division.

☆ A business owner has decided to cash in sooner, rather than later, on his or her creation.

☆ A partnership is dissolving.

☆ An owner is selling a business as part of a divorce settlement.

Good businesses may be more available than you realize. Just because the enterprise is surviving, or even profiting nicely, doesn't mean its founder wants to stay with it forever. Many entrepreneurs say they simply need to move on to the next challenge.

My own experience consulting to companies that are seeking to make acquisitions indicates that—at least in the industries in which I specialize—owners of many of the top businesses in the field are willing to at least listen to an offer. Very few reject a buyout approach out of hand, and many will entertain a serious discussion almost anytime. Under the right circumstances, a very high percentage are consistently available, even if the price is high.

Cash Flow Is King

If, in fact, you develop an opportunity to purchase a solidly performing business, you'll have a much better chance of finding financing than you would if you were starting with nothing. The magic words in commercial lending today are "cash flow." If you've got it, banks will work with you. If you don't, it's much less likely.

> Synergy means behavior of whole systems unpredicted by the behavior of their parts.
>
> —R. Buckminster Fuller

New businesses don't have cash flow; ongoing ones do and, even if the business you're eyeing isn't generating a profit, lenders will often find merit in your idea based simply on revenues. This becomes all the more likely if you can demonstrate a few ways to cut costs. But it all begins with a known quantity— a market for your goods or services as evidenced by some kind of revenue stream.

"Known quantity" is a key phrase here. When you buy a business, you'll likely be borrowing more money than if you were starting one. So it's that much more important that you're aware of all current and potential problems. You may think a company has a good reputation until you discover too late that it has severely disappointed some key customers. And you're always taking a chance that, after you take over, several key employees, suppliers or customers will bail out because of the change at the top, or by coincidence at a time when you can least afford it.

Therefore, virtually all experts on business buying advise careful study of a target organization's finances, reputation and relationships.

How and Where to Go Shopping

But first, you've got to find an attractive business to buy. What's the best way to go about it?

Joseph Mancuso, founder of the Center for Entrepreneurial Management in New York, says the key is to put yourself in the flow of a steady stream of business opportunities. This has several benefits:

☆ It gives you more choices.

☆ You'll develop skill in evaluating opportunities.

☆ The experience in looking at potential deals will help you refine your own criteria.

There's one danger in putting yourself in the middle of a big stream of business opportunities: you'll get into the habit of turning down deals, which can begin to work against you.

Eventually, referrals will dry up. The way to avoid this trap is to be committed to pursuing an opportunity that meets your criteria; and to work hard on your criteria so that when you find a deal that meets it, you can move forward with confidence. (That includes broadening your criteria if you can't meet the dream specs, but don't want to abandon your overall goal.)

If you're committed, set solid criteria and evaluate lots of possible deals, you'll be more likely to feel good after choosing one. You'll know it was an informed choice, which goes a long way toward maintaining your enthusiasm down the road.

So where do you find that steady stream of opportunities? And how can you avoid the sea of ill-advised ones? The basic strategy for this is to emphasize what Mancuso calls "positive deal flow techniques." That is, if you sit back and wait for opportunities to appear, using only one or two sources, you're not likely to hear about the most attractive deals—the ones that never get advertised. But if you take the active position of considering nearly everyone you deal with as a potential lead to a great opportunity, you're building "positive deal flow."

Mancuso recommends 16 particular places to look for business opportunities:

☆ *Your own company.* What organization hasn't at least entertained thoughts of a restructuring that would involve outside participation? Many haven't only considered it, but carried it out, and the pace of this trend is quickening. For countless organizations, it's a way of life. Therefore, while the owners of your company may not have put your division on the block, they're quite likely to be willing to hear your proposal. (Your only risk is that, if your offer is rejected, your future with the company may be in doubt. If that's not an issue, you have nothing to lose here.) Mancuso says some of the best deals he's seen came from this category.

☆ *Business brokers.* This is an avenue not to be ignored, but which, at lower levels, will also be a source of stale leads and lackluster opportunities. The reason is that for deals under $1 million, sellers have likely tried other alternatives before turning it over to a broker. Therefore, heed Mancuso's advice on how to maximize

> Great deeds are usually wrought at great risks.
>
> —Herodotus

your exposure to deals that will be good for you: Meet with brokers early in your opportunity search, let them know your criteria and level of commitment to the process, then keep in touch so you'll be alert to good deals that emerge via this route. At higher levels, for deals of up to $20 million, you'll work with an intermediate group of brokers whom you'll likely meet through your banker, lawyer or accountant. Investment bankers enter the picture at about $20 million and up.

Mancuso says significant caution is necessary in dealing with business brokers, especially in deals under $1 million. "Beware of those that want to charge you an up-front fee to review your financials or to list you with their companies as a buyer," he warns. "Check them out thoroughly," through former buyers and sellers, real estate brokers, bankers and the Better Business Bureau. And make sure other professionals represent you in actual negotiations, since the broker is almost always working for the seller. Remember, though, that before you begin talking turkey, brokers can be of significant help in answering questions that would take you time and money to undertake yourself.

☆ *Printers.* Who's better informed about what's going on in the business community than the people who print stationery, business cards, marketing materials and such, for virtually every business in town? Printers know who's hot and who's not. Mancuso suggests getting to know them, since they can be a great source of leads.

☆ *Newspaper ads.* This can be a viable vehicle for the extremely specialized business, even though most listings will be for opportunities that have already been passed over by others. Read them for the rare chance of a fit within your niche.

☆ *Newspaper back issues.* Look for articles in recent months about your industry or target area. Divestitures often follow purchases, and "divestitures can be some of the sweetest deals around," says Mancuso. "Management is so glad to get rid of a headache that it's willing to take back some of the financing at favorable terms," he notes. "In addition, many localities are quick to grant loans, tax abatements, free land in industrial parks and other incentives to retain businesses."

☆ *Bankers.* Though their actual work takes place toward the end of the deal rather than at the beginning, bankers can often point you to opportunities based on their knowledge of what's going on and who might be thinking about selling. Mancuso cautions, however, that "bankers will tell you about profitable businesses for sale and ones facing foreclosure without saying which is which. You have to learn that yourself."

☆ *Lawyers.* Ask attorneys you know which lawyers in town do the most business and corporate law, then get in touch with them.

☆ *Accountants.* They are another excellent source that should be contacted early and often during your search.

☆ *Insurance agents.* Again, they may have an inside track on when businesses are for sale.

☆ *Trade associations.* Every industry has a trade group (usually several), with either paid staff or volunteer directors whose responsibilities include knowing what's happening among member firms. Consult the Encyclopedia of Associations (Gale Research) at your library for contact information on associations in your field. Then, attend their conferences or local/state chapter meetings, subscribe to their publications, and you'll soon be hearing about opportunities.

☆ *Buyer's brokers.* While most business brokers represent sellers, you might retain someone to act on your behalf. Pay them by the hour, by the number of qualified deals presented, or for discounts secured through the process—but don't pay a percentage of the deal, since the broker would then be motivated to recommend a higher price. Look under "business brokers" in the Yellow Pages.

☆ *Small Business Administration liquidation officers.* Many businesses on the SBA's bad loan list are for sale. Ask discreetly at your local SBA office ("Do you have any clients currently seeking buyers?"). Find out who your local liquidation officer is (call the SBA at 202-205-6600 or 800-827-5722). Then visit in person.

☆ *Bankruptcies.* Taking that route a step further, since there are plenty of opportunities among businesses that have failed, consider learning about businesses filing for Chapter 11 protection from creditors, or otherwise engaged in bankruptcy proceedings. A key resource here is *The National Bankruptcy Reporter* (Andrews Publications, Westtown, PA), which, because of its expense ($900 for six months), you might want to look for at a local law library or bankruptcy attorney's office. Also ask local bankruptcy judges and trustees—or even consider seeking a position as a bankruptcy trustee to help turn a company around or liquidate it.

"Several famous venture capitalists started this way," Mancuso notes, since assets of troubled companies can often be purchased at bargain prices, free of creditors, from owners trying to raise cash to get out of debt.

Look also for a local credit reporting agency, which will give you leads based on local bankruptcies or lawsuits. Your chamber of commerce or your attorney will know where to get these reports.

☆ *Corporate partners.* More and more, large companies are cutting overhead by outsourcing parts of their business, or licensing lines of business to entrepreneurs. Examine corporations in your industry or area for clues on what operations they might be willing to hand off. (And see Chapter 8, which includes more tips on outsourcing opportunities.)

☆ *Your own ads.* Cast an even wider net by advertising your willingness to invest in the right enterprise. With a tone of professionalism, describe the kind of opportunities you'd consider and run it in the classifieds under "capital to invest" or "business wanted."

☆ *Knocking on doors.* Let your interest in a particular kind of company teach you more about it. If it's a retail operation, become a customer to measure the service you receive at different operations. Notice everything about each one. Then, when it's time to approach the owners, consider Mancuso's straightforward, general advice about how to make a cold call in the world of business-buying:

"Be businesslike and courteous when talking to owners. Explain that you're looking to acquire a business and ask if he or she knows of any for sale. Owners probably won't mention their own businesses unless they're anxious to sell, but they'll talk about others to determine whether you know the field or are seeking inside information. Once they trust you, there'll be plenty of time to discover if their businesses are for sale."

How Much Should You Pay?

Gary Benson says most buyers of businesses pay too much, because they don't accurately determine how much a business is worth. In general, a company's value is determined by the value of its assets (preferably book value or lower), plus some multiple of earnings (usually not more than three) or net income. All kinds of individual considerations can enter the picture here, but this rule of thumb isn't normally exceeded. Get a professional, independent valuation of any business you become serious about before buying.

Next, give serious attention to the terms of the sale, which many buyers consider even more important than the price. If you're being pushed to pay a handsome sum for the business, try to win concessions in the size of the downpayment, the interest rate on any loans, the amortization schedule and the extent to which the seller is willing to assist in financing.

Mistakes Not to Make

Buying a business should be fun, but—even more so than when starting your own business—it's practically consumed with activities designed to protect yourself from the unfortunate and unforeseen. In *Breakaway Careers* (Hawthorne, NJ: Career Press, 1994), Bill Radin offers five places to look for "surprises" in a business you're considering:

1. *Physical damage or deterioration.* Check the building, equipment, furniture and fixtures of the business for hidden (or even obvious) signs of wear or obsolescence.

2. *Worthless inventory.* Make sure that what you're buying is worth what you're paying. The goods in the warehouse could be the ones that were on the shelves for years and never moved. Along the same line, customer lists may bring little value to new owners, depending on their quality—which may be very difficult to verify—and the nature of the business.

3. *Ailing customer or supplier relationships.* Before you buy a business, make sure a measure of good will already exists between the business and those who'll be critical to its success, ranging from bankers to vendors.

A major advantage to buying an existing business is having a track record to review. The business already has its financial and marketing plans put into action. It already has an established location, inventory, customer base and trained staff. At least, it should. And these features are what you're paying for—so be sure they are benefits.

—Vickie L. Montgomery in *The Smart Woman's Guide to Staring a Business*

4. *"Pending" sales or business growth.* Listen carefully for wishful thinking. You can't take "if only," "hopefully" or "any day now" to the bank. If possible, be sure to follow up by contacting several potential customers directly.

5. *Suspicious motives.* Exactly why is the owner trying to unload the business? Is he or she sick, retiring or sick and tired of beating a dead horse? If necessary, use your private eye skills to ferret out critical information.

Even Smart People Make Them

Wouldn't you think someone with enough megs of RAM to be a programmer at Microsoft Corp. could go into business for himself without crashing on business basics, such as those described above?

Robert Kjelgaard (pronounced KELL-gard) of Lynnwood, Washington—who'd burned out repairing software code for Windows NT—provides a wonderful example of all the dumb things an intelligent, if naive, person can do (even after spending several months reading about how to become an entrepreneur!).

Briefly, as Kjelgaard told *The Wall Street Journal,* he used the proceeds from the sale of his stock options at Microsoft to buy a laundry: 75 washers and dryers and a small dry-cleaning operation. It seemed like a simple business he could enter for under $100,000, hire someone to manage (his brother-in-law had just lost his job and could do this) and, according to the rather disorganized records, turn a nice profit. He put down $30,000 in cash and signed a note for $50,000.

Almost immediately, the laundry became a heavier load than Kjelgaard had imagined. The brother-in-law didn't work out, so Kjelgaard began spending quite a bit of time there. As a result, he was spending much less time with his wife Penny and their 3-year-old daughter. Everyone was tense and Kjelgaard was exhausted. Then, abruptly and impulsively, Kjelgaard quit Microsoft (foregoing significant additional stock options) to take over the laundry full-time.

Only then did he begin to see the laundry's real problems: cash flow wasn't what the previous owner had indicated; there were far too many small machines and not enough big ones; and a careful reading of the six-year lease that came with the laundry revealed that Kjelgaard's building-maintenance responsibilities—beyond the $3300-a-month rent—made his space much too expensive for what the business could bear. In a rash move to make ends meet, he raised dry-cleaning prices dramatically . . . and virtually killed that part of the business.

The bottom line: Less than a year after buying the laundry, Kjelgaard was losing $4000 a month. He put it up for sale, returned to Microsoft in a much lower paying position, hired a manager for the laundry and directed some of his paycheck toward keeping the laundry afloat. Losses were narrowed to $2000 a month, but no one's snapped up the chance to buy the laundry, and the lease will last several more years.

Kjelgaard's experiences are like a Harvard Business School case study on what not to do when buying a business. Let's examine his story for lessons:

☆ *Transferring your skills.* Kjelgaard's steady history of success at Microsoft lulled him into thinking he could succeed at something as apparently straightforward as owning a laundry. The lack of connection is almost laughable, yet it's frighteningly possible to imagine someone making such an assumption. In fact, beneath the obvious differences there is a certain similarity: Kjelgaard enjoys tinkering, whether it's with computers or coin-changing machines. But the lesson here is: A single transferable skill isn't enough. What makes you a winner in one environment doesn't guarantee success in another.

☆ *Know the business.* You may not need experience in every part of your prospective company's activities, but you should at least have an appreciation for what's required. Owning a laundry looked like a no-brainer to Kjelgaard. Very few things are. More knowledge of what's important in owning a laundry could have helped Kjelgaard at the outset if, after learning this, he still wanted to get into it at all.

☆ *Researching the market.* Kjelgaard bought the very first laundry he looked at. If only he'd looked around for comparable opportunities! This is so basic, not only for the purpose of buying the business, but forever after in keeping tabs on your competition. When else do you have this kind of opportunity to ask your competitors about their activities? Preparing to buy a business is one of life's greatest moments for leveraging your position into valuable market knowledge. Don't squander it! Learn everything you can under the umbrella of looking for an opportunity to make an investment. Be Peter Falk as Columbo: "Oh . . . I was just wondering . . . what kind of net profit does someone make in this business?" You'll be surprised.

Remember that market research can include the following: What are the pros and cons of buying this business versus starting my own? Why, really, is the seller selling? How useful will that equipment really be? What do this business's customers and suppliers think of it? Do not overlook this last point: Interview, in depth, every employee and supplier possible.

☆ *Getting the facts.* Kjelgaard let the previous owner get away with vague or downright misleading information about the laundry's performance up until the time of purchase. The owner also described weaknesses in a way that made Kjelgaard feel he could easily overcome them. You simply must have reliable financial information about the business you're buying. If you're not skilled in this area—and in most cases, even if you already are—get professional help here. It's well worth the investment.

Similarly, he overlooked the inappropriateness of the equipment he was buying. Only an experienced laundry owner, or an especially inquisitive buyer, would have known before the purchase that the laundry lacked enough big machines and had too many small ones. These facts—beyond the financials themselves—escaped him.

Gary Benson suggests looking for three potential red flags in the financials: evidence that the seller has inflated sales (perhaps by selling off assets) or reduced costs (perhaps by layoffs) to improve apparent profit just before the sale; unlikely financial ratios (i.e., income as a percentage of sales; check industry averages); and trends that don't make sense (inconsistencies during the past three to five years).

Many former corporate executives make the mistake of buying failing businesses with the assumption that they can turn them around by virtue of their considerable managerial skills. However, the experience gained by climbing the corporate ladder and the experience needed to run a small business are like apples and oranges.

—Bill Radin in *Breakaway Careers*

☆ *Reading the fine print.* Get the little facts as well as the big ones. Kjelgaard simply failed to read his lease carefully, discovering too late that it was a significant burden on the business.

☆ *Hiring the right people.* Kjelgaard chose his brother-in-law to run the laundry initially, because the fellow was in a pinch and needed the job. This is never a good reason to hire anyone, especially a relative. Hire someone because they'll do a good job, not because you want to help them out. A new business simply can't afford that kind of charity.

☆ *Resisting wild impulses.* Kjelgaard developed a pattern of rash behavior that only heaped more trouble onto his pile of woes. He bought the laundry almost on a whim. Then he quit his regular job in frustration at a most inappropriate time—just before he would have earned significant new stock options. He raised dry cleaning prices dramatically, without realizing it would stifle business entirely. Key moves affecting your basic business plan should be made slowly and carefully, with full consideration to possible negative outcomes. In buying and running a business, patience is as important as ambition.

☆ *Keeping your balance.* Kjelgaard bought the laundry toward the end of a massive project at Microsoft—development of Windows NT—during which he worked long days and weekends at his regular job before he could even think about the laundry. Kjelgaard's family came last, which caused a terrific strain at home on top of the business challenges that soon developed. By taking on a much-too-ambitious role, he began to fail everywhere, which nearly cost him his marriage as well as his business. It's paramount to budget time for your family when you engage in business activities that extend beyond normal work hours.

Final Question: Must You Buy?

Buying a business has at least one major, built-in problem that other forms of self-employment do not: Incurring significant debt. Unless you're extraordinarily cash-rich, you'll likely be taking on the biggest financial burden of your life. If the business is really worth it, and you're truly committed to seeing the whole thing through, then go for it. But if you have even a single serious doubt about whether this is a good deal and whether you'll want to stay with it until that debt is paid off, wait. Consider whether there's any other way you could get into this kind of a business without buying one.

Just before I resigned to go into business for myself, I proposed buying the newsletter division of the publishing company where I worked. The newsletters were nicely profitable; I was entirely capable of publishing them; I was motivated to do so; and I was well-known to our customers. All indications were that this was a solid opportunity for me.

However—and perhaps to my everlasting benefit—the owners refused to sell the newsletters to me (they didn't want to divide the business in that way). Only then did I realize that my reputation and abilities were sufficient for starting my own business without incurring any significant debt. What a revelation this was!

Suddenly, I understood that since I wasn't taking on an obligation to pay off hundreds of thousands of dollars to a previous owner, I had all the freedom in the world to pursue my own work. All I had to do was cover my family's income needs. There would be no sweating over the books to see if we'd be making enough this month to meet all our obligations—no five or 10 years of waiting until I was truly the owner of my own business.

On my own, I remain free to borrow and buy if I see the right opportunity, but I'm not tied to it. It's a great feeling.

Before you burden yourself with a big long-term payout to a previous owner, consider whether there's a way to make your dream work without buying a business. You may be pleasantly surprised.

6

Operating a
Franchise

Once you've decided to launch a self-directed career, you still have many options to consider when setting a course of action. At one extreme, you could be wildly independent, with full responsibility for creating and operating every aspect of your own business. Conversely, you could sign a contract with one employer that would create a working life only slightly different from being a full-time employee.

Somewhere in between is franchising—a unique form of self-employment within a structure established by others. You're in charge, yet you're also subject to a corporate image and operational methods that dictate many of your business activities (and strongly influence others). Despite the vast array of opportunities that fall under the general category of franchising, this form of business ownership isn't for everyone.

Yet more and more managers, executives and professionals are choosing this route. The Small Business Administration says there currently are more than 500,000 franchised units in the United States with total sales of more than $700 billion, or about 34 percent of this country's total retail sales. By 2000, franchised sales are expected to claim 38 percent of the retail market, the SBA reports.

Most of the growth is occurring in what's called business-format franchising, in which you create the product or service within an established format, such as a fast-food outlet. This kind of franchising accounts for about three-fourths of the field. The remaining 25 percent is in product-trade name franchising, in which you simply obtain the right to distribute and sell a brand-name product within a particular market. Gas stations and car dealerships are good examples of that.

The giants of business-format franchising—those with more than 500 outlets—dominate the franchising market, garnering significantly more than half of all franchise sales. But the greatest growth area in franchising is with small companies—those with fewer than 10 units.

What'll It Be?

You can spend from less than $5000 to more than $1 million in an initial investment in a franchise. Then, you can expect to pay somewhere between 4 percent and 8 percent of your revenues as an ongoing royalty. In addition, there are likely to be cooperative advertising costs of perhaps 2 percent to 3 percent of sales. In return, you'll receive:

☆ Name brand recognition and good will,

☆ Advice and training,

☆ A tried-and-true operational methodology that reflects lessons learned by previous franchisees,

☆ Bulk-rate discounts on supplies,

☆ The benefits of cooperative advertising, and

☆ Moral support, if not invaluable assistance, as you move forward.

In many ways, franchising offers the best of two worlds. It has the simplicity of buying an on-going business. (You don't have to invent every move; somebody's done all the ground work.) Franchising has the clean-slate atmosphere of a new enterprise. It's like buying a new car that includes a road map to all the places you need to go in order to afford the payments.

Is Franchising for You?

Joseph Mancuso, founder of the Center for Entrepreneurial Management in New York, has a few questions for you to answer to help assess whether you're the franchising type. Circle the single answer that best fits your personality:

1. I have generally been regarded as:
   a. one who loves to plan vacations
   b. always willing to work hard
   c. one who seeks benefits and rewards for my work

2. Financially, I:
   a. am very conservative
   b. am very liberal
   c. have always been able to put money aside
   d. have never been well off

3. Taking directions from others is:
   a. one of my strong talents
   b. something I don't like
   c. often a must
   d. acceptable if not constantly required

4. Work-related pressure:
   a. can cause physical illness
   b. is something I try to avoid
   c. is a definite problem in business today
   d. seldom causes me any discomfort

5. I have generally been regarded as having:
   a. the ability to sell things
   b. a good grasp of what makes people tick
   c. physical strength
   d. emotional warmth

6. To reach your optimum level of success, you must:
   a. have luck on your side
   b. be happy in your work
   c. be willing to take risks
   d. know the right people

7. Personally, I:
   a. am dissatisfied with my present position
   b. have had a variety of life experiences

    c. have strong business and sales skills

    d. have not had much business experience

8. A major factor in business success is:

    a. an appetite to learn more about what you do

    b. a happy and stable personality

    c. physical stamina

    d. extensive business experience

9. I am best described as:

    a. an intelligent person

    b. a highly verbal person

    c. a hard-driving person

    d. a person who can relate to other people

10. A strong desire to learn is:

    a. a valuable asset, both personally and professionally

    b. often necessary to advance in business

    c. not very important once you complete school

    d. uncommon in the business world

11. When a superior tells me what to do, I:

    a. wish I had his job so I could give orders

    b. often try to present a new, more efficient way of doing the task

    c. secretly resent being ordered around

    d. learn from the instructions and complete the task

12. With the statement, "To succeed in business, it's often more important to be hard-working than to be a creative, talented person," I:

    a. strongly agree

    b. agree

    c. disagree

    d. strongly disagree

13. I've been best known for:

    a. getting involved in my community

    b. having good general business knowledge and skills

    c. being a good parent

14. As a business owner, it would be most important to me to:

    a. provide jobs for my family

    b. be well-thought-of by my staff

    c. be able to set my own schedule

    d. be closely aware of and prudent with my finances

15. Work hours should be:
   a. as long as needed
   b. paid for, especially for the boss
   c. flexible—long only when needed for special projects
   d. equally divided among all employees

16. A description of someone with a good chance to succeed in business is someone who:
   a. likes to get away regularly to avoid stress
   b. is always curious to learn more about doing his job
   c. works best by himself
   d. has a business degree from a top university

For questions 17–30, pick the statement that best describes you:

17. a. I have a strong affinity for sales.
   b. I'm highly energetic.
18. a. I have moderate experience in the type of business I would like to get into.
   b. I take directions well.
19. a. I'm a creative person.
   b. I'm a good listener.
20. a. I'm a previous business owner.
   b. I'm able to fully commit my finances to my business.
21. a. I don't mind working long hours.
   b. I have strong corporate skills.
22. a. I'm a very careful, organized person.
   b. I'm a people-oriented person.
23. a. I'm a charitable person.
   b. I'm a diplomatic person.
24. a. I'm highly spontaneous.
   b. I'm highly goal-directed.
25. a. I'm able to take charge with people.
   b. I'm a quick decision maker.
26. a. I have some basic financial knowledge.
   b. I have previous management experience.

27. a. I need to be in control.
    b. I can take directions from others.
28. a. I have extensive business skills.
    b. I'm always willing to do what it takes to get things done.
29. a. I often use weekends to unwind.
    b. I'm very resistant to stress.
30. a. I have money in the bank.
    b. I'm willing to do without if necessary.
31. For this question, circle the five statements that are least like you:

    a. I'm a slow starter.
    b. I can sell anything.
    c. I prefer to work by myself.
    d. I'm interested in learning new skills.
    e. I would rather live spontaneously than set long-term goals.
    f. I thrive on stressful, busy, deadline situations.
    g. I work best by taking charge and issuing orders.
    h. I'm rich in people skills.
    i. I prefer large, corporate environments.
    j. I have a history of working long hours at favored activities.

Scoring

For each answer you choose, give yourself the corresponding amount of points listed below:

1. a = 0, b = 4, c = 0, d = 2
2. a = 2, b = 0, c = 4, d = 0
3. a = 4, b = 0, c = 2, d = 1
4. a = 0, b = 0, c = 1, d = 4
5. a = 4, b = 2, c = 0, d = 0
6. a = 0, b = 2, c = 4, d = 0
7. a = 0, b = 2, c = 4, d = 0
8. a = 4, b = 1, c = 0, d = 3
9. a = 1, b = 0, c = 2, d = 4
10. a = 4, b = 2, c = 0, d = 0

11. a = 0, b = 2, c = 0, d = 4
12. a = 4, b = 3, c = 0, d = 0
13. a = 0, b = 4, c = 2, d = 1
14. a = 1, b = 0, c = 0, d = 4
15. a = 4, b = 0, c = 2, d = 0
16. a = 0, b = 4, c = 1, d = 1
17. a = 2, b = 1
18. a = 1, b = 2
19. a = 1, b = 2
20. a = 1, b = 2
21. a = 2, b = 1
22. a = 1, b = 2
23. a = 1, b = 2
24. a = 1, b = 2
25. a = 2, b = 1
26. a = 2, b = 1
27. a = 1, b = 2
28. a = 1, b = 2
29. a = 1, b = 2
30. a = 2, b = 1
31. a = 1, b = 0, c = 1, d = 0, e = 1, f = 0, g = 1, h = 0,
    i = 1, j = 0

Total points possible: 97

What Your Score Means

Less than 50 points: You're a questionable candidate. A low score on this test might indicate that you'd be more comfortable and successful as an independent business owner or salaried employee. You may be more independent and have a stronger business background than most franchisees. Rather than trying to squeeze your talents into a field for which you may not be suited, you should probably seek other opportunities.

If you still feel strongly committed to becoming a franchisee, examine how your test responses differ from the suggested answers. This can uncover areas in your personality or background that you need to reassess to improve your chances of becoming a successful franchise owner.

50–79 points: You're a potential candidate. Many of your traits are close to those found in top franchise candidates. However, you may not be completely committed to the concept of running a franchised outlet of someone else's business. Although you may be interested in becoming a franchisee, your quiz answers differ from those of more "traditional" candidates. Perhaps you have a strong streak of independence or are more comfortable giving directions than taking them. If you can determine where you differ from the model franchisee, you may be able to conclude if these are fundamental differences or slight discrepancies. If the latter is true, you might be a good candidate.

80–97 points: If you've answered the quiz questions frankly and received a score in this range, your personality traits, attitude, experience and temperament are good matches with the attributes many franchisers say are found in their most successful franchisees. You likely have a well-defined desire to learn and a willingness to follow directions in the quest for your own success. If you are financially able to do so, you should investigate becoming a franchisee.

Personality Tests Are Key

Because franchising is such a structured activity, it's possible for personality tests such as this one to play a fairly important role in determining whether you're a good fit for a franchise.

In fact, one testing outfit—TIMS Time Management Systems in Tucson, AZ—is officially endorsed by the International Franchise Association to test franchisers to determine personality characteristics ideal for each organization, and to test prospective franchisees for suitability.

In their book, *The Franchise Kit* (New York: McGraw-Hill, 1993), Kirk Shivell and Kent Banning discuss four aspects of personality often studied in matching people with franchise organizations: dominance, influence, steadiness and compliance.

A highly dominant person is more likely to succeed as a pure entrepreneur than as a franchisee, but a moderate amount of dominance is considered ideal for franchiseeism. People high in dominance tend to be difficult to please, easily frustrated and always ready for a new challenge. They're great completely on their own. Someone with moderate dominance will be more like the team-player franchisee type.

"Franchisers want people who may be strong-willed, but are also disposed to sacrifice some of their ego and play within the rules of the game," say Shivell and Banning.

Highly influential people—star salespeople, for example—would seem to natural franchise owners. Yet, franchisers aren't looking for pure salespeople and much prefer those who register only moderately in influence. The reason is that high-influence people are often so focused on being charming that they overlook the hard realities of being in business.

"Often, they become trapped by their own trust and acceptance of people," say Shivell and Banning. "High-influence people often need close supervision to meet their objectives" and, therefore, aren't always successful in the semi-independent world of franchising.

You may think, then, that the ideal franchisee is a steady worker: a calm, easy going, dependable team player, right? Nope. Rather, successful franchisees tend to measure low in steadiness. Why would Steady Eddie be a drag as a franchisee? Because steadiness also breeds sensitivity, resistance to risk and change and an inability to make quick decisions. Thus, the preferred franchisee is someone who's not overly sensitive, but instead can take heat on the front line, is ready to respond rapidly to changing market conditions and opportunities and can solve problems quickly.

"Franchisers should be able to project the probable outcome of a certain course of action and have the will to follow a new course quickly," say Shivell and Banning. "High-steadiness personalities are neither decision-makers, planners nor moderate risk-takers, yet all of these attributes are crucial to the success of a franchisee."

Finally, determine how you rate on the compliance scale—your relative desire to avoid conflict (often through diplomacy and caution) and accommodate the wishes of others. Depending on the type of business, this is an important characteristic. In general, organizations that are highly structured, and especially those requiring franchisees to have strong technical skills, seek more accommodating franchisees.

"Sophisticated technical-service franchises (quick-print shops, computer and medical-service businesses) tend to prefer higher compliance scores than those involved in retailing," say Shivell and Banning. High-compliance types are valued for their attention to detail and problem-solving skills, and they're also diplomatic. However, they can be slow decision makers. Some franchisers want people like this, who aren't likely to buck the system, while others want franchisees who are more creative and assertive.

Hey, I'm the Type!

Suppose, after taking one or more of these personality tests, you fit the mold for at least one category or style of franchising (or, you've decided to disregard such frivolous distractions and plow ahead). What next? Well, there are financial, attitude and experience questions to address.

How's your financial health? Much like lenders, most reputable franchisers want to know your credit history, current obligations and resources. Then they'll decide whether you're a reasonable risk, comparing your current standing and history with the size of the investment required. If it's $5000, this should be no big deal, but the difficulty of qualifying will rise proportionally for buy-in fees in the tens (or hundreds) of thousands.

Don't give up simply because you lack financial resources, however. Real strength in other areas can make this the least important factor in qualifying.

Attitude will be reflected through applications and interviews. Franchisers will also draw conclusions about your attitude toward business responsibilities through your personal credit history. Your level of commitment should be obvious to all involved.

Perhaps trickiest is a judgment about your business skills, or potential for developing them. Having experience in some customer-service capacity is virtually required. But beyond that, it's open to opportunities for you to draw a connection between your experience and what the franchise is all about. In this regard, don't make too many assumptions.

"While you may have considerable experience in management, it may be of a type that isn't applicable to franchising," say Shivell and Banning. "Experience gained as a large-company executive may be considered irrelevant, or even detrimental." At the same time, it may be worth bringing into the conversation your childhood memory of the day that was so hot you opened multiple lemonade stands near entrances to the city park.

Any life experience that bears on what you're about to do next is worth looking at for clues on what your enterprise will look like, and whether or not it'll succeed. Make enough positive connections and you've made a case for the opportunity to run a successful franchise.

Still in the running? If so, then you're ready to consider the four-step process of selecting a franchise company, as outlined by Sandra L. Oluwek, a Hoboken, NJ, consultant who helps entrepreneurs start businesses through network marketing and franchising.

First Step: Identify Your Interests

Think about a product or service that connects with an area of special interest and ability for you. As with any enterprise, financial success is much more likely if you truly identify with the value you bring to your customers. The connection may not be as obvious as "I've always loved cars, so I opened a Jiffy Lube" (although that's not a bad example). It could be that you've been a stamp collector and decide to open a travel agency because you've learned so much about the world through stamps. Follow your bliss, even if you're also keeping an eye out for high profit potential.

At the same time, it's usually a good idea not to stray too far from your current career. For example, refugees from managerial jobs are likely to have the best luck on familiar turf, such as in business services, says Mary Tomzack, author of *Tips and Traps When Buying a Franchise* (New York: McGraw-Hill, 1994). "The typical corporate person who gets into fast-food franchising doesn't know what he's getting into," she says.

First Step, Part Two: Figure Out How Much Money You Have to Invest

This is a perfectly straightforward process. And while you're going through it, look for signals about your level of commitment to the idea and how it plays into your overall outlook on investing and borrowing (and meeting obligations they create).

Second Step: Research

Look for specific franchises that meet your interest and financial criteria. Information abounds on what's available, and there are several organizations that perform a "watchdog" or recommending role, including the Federal Trade Commission in Washington, the American Franchisee Association in Chicago, and the American Association of Franchisees and Dealers in San Diego.

In addition to your interests and financing outlook, begin considering the relative risks and rewards for well-established franchises vs. ground-floor opportunities with great-idea-based appeal.

Third Step: Give Them the Once-Over

Once you've cut the pack to a select few, evaluate the qualification process. For the one or two companies that really seem to meet your dreams, visit company headquarters and see what's in the Uniform Franchise Offering Circular (UFOC)—a disclosure form required of all franchisers by the Federal Trade Commission. It gives you 10 working days to study the agreement carefully without contact by the (sales motivated) franchiser. Have your lawyer and accountant check it out, too.

Fourth Step: Give Them the Twice-Over

Investigate the franchise company, and develop a business plan for your first three years. Get advice from fellow franchisers named in the UFOC about whether your projections are on-target. Then ask them how much fun they're having and whether they're making any money. Verify all information in the UFOC, and make sure you understand how to get out of the deal if things don't go as planned.

What Makes a Good Franchise?

In its annual report on "The Nation's Best Franchise Buys," the *National Business Employment Weekly* cites a handful of qualities to look for in a franchise you seek to buy. Here are six consistently cited basics:

1. *Name recognition.* This can be one of the chief values of franchise ownership. A good reputation is even better.

2. *Exceptional product/service quality.* Naturally, you'll be looking for products and services that delight customers. Anything less should be a red flag.

3. *Proven profitability or outstanding potential.* If the franchise is well-developed, you'll be looking for a solid track record of profits among franchisees. If it's a young operation, you'll have to look more carefully at whether the company has truly succeeded in matching a great idea with a real market in a unique way.

4. *Superior franchisee relationships.* It's difficult to imagine success in this field without solid communication. Though some franchisees are remarkably independent, most thrive on a healthy give-and-take of information, advice and requests.

5. *Attentiveness to trends.* This is a happy by-product of good communication, combined with other corporate activities, that keeps the organization alert to changes in the market and new opportunities for success.

6. *Willingness to change.* Even the best concepts—both in the marketplace and in managing the company—are continually fine-tuned and updated. That's how companies remain market leaders. Being attentive to trends isn't enough. The company must address the trends quickly and effectively. Ask for examples of grassroots-driven change in every franchise you evaluate.

Anybody Seen One Lately?

What's the likelihood of running across an organization with all of these qualities. They're out there but, like many of life's attractions, franchising may not be as smooth as it seems on the surface.

"Theoretically, there's a symbiotic relationship between the franchise company and the franchise operator. But in reality, they're often at each other's throats," warns *New York*

The franchise prototype provides the means through which the small business owner can finally feed his three personalities—the entrepreneur, the manager and the technician—in a balanced way while creating a business that works.

—Michael E. Gerber in *The E Myth*

Times business writer Earl C. Gottschalk, Jr. "The franchise company wants royalties, and the franchise operator hates paying them. The franchise company wants as many outlets as possible, but the franchise operator doesn't want new competition."

More often than the franchise industry is willing to admit, things don't work out, says Gottschalk. While the industry claims franchises have a 95 percent success rate, he cites a study by Wayne State University economics professor Tim Bates that draws a much different conclusion. Bates looked at 7300 small businesses started during the 1980s, including 400 franchises, and found that 35 percent of the franchises had gone out of business by late 1991, vs. 28 percent of the other small businesses surveyed.

Danger Zones

If you've made it this far and feel confident that you've identified a franchise that has a strong likelihood of success, run it past this final group of danger-zone questions to make sure you're not missing something that would cause you to think twice. Several of these are noted by Meg Whittemore, Andrew Sherman and Ripley Hotch in their book, *Financing Your Franchise* (New York: McGraw-Hill, 1993):

☆ Does the franchise have a high "churning" rate? Churning is the buying out of less-than-successful franchises by the franchiser, who then resells the franchise in order to collect a new franchise fee.

☆ Is the franchiser telling you it isn't necessary to read all the fine print in the disclosure document? Amazingly, the Federal Trade Commission finds 40 percent of new franchisees sign on without reading it.

☆ Is the franchiser making projections about what your earnings will be, but refusing to put the claims in writing? This is actually a violation of federal law. Projections based on what franchisees have earned must be conveyed to you in writing.

☆ Is the franchiser really interested in you? Good franchisers don't want unqualified people to buy their franchises. The more selective they are in approving you as a buyer, the better.

☆ Is the training program unusually long or short? If too long, the program may be too difficult teach effectively. If too short, the program may indicate a shallow operation.

☆ Must you buy supplies from the parent company? If so, watch out. This may be another profit center for the franchiser rather than a service to franchisees.

☆ Can you get out easily? Make sure there are no rules preventing your exit should things fail to work out.

The Nation's Best Franchises

There are many lists that rank franchises by category, sales, locations or other variables. Yet all should be viewed with a grain of salt, since there really isn't any completely objective way to measure which franchisers best serve the interests of their franchisees.

In an attempt to offer some sort of an objective round-up of franchises to consider, the *National Business Employment Weekly* asks a panel of distinguished franchising specialists each year to select their choices of best franchises. Their picks are separated into two categories: franchises costing less than $100,000 each, and those costing more.

The panelists represent a wide range of backgrounds and interests. For the list of best franchises that follows, the panel was composed of: Ann Dugan, director of the Small Business Development Center at the University of Pittsburgh; Kathryn Taylor, a franchising attorney with Crowe & Dunlevey in Tulsa,

---

The main advantage of buying a franchise rather than starting a business from scratch is that the failure rate among franchised businesses is lower. You are buying a proven business idea, and you get a lot of help running it.

—William J. Stolze in *Start Up*

OK; Dr. Gary Benson, a professor in the college of business and economics at the University of Wisconsin-Whitewater; Robert Purvin, Jr., chairman of the American Association of Franchisees & Dealers in San Diego, and author of *The Franchise Fraud* (New York: John Wiley & Sons, 1994); Michael Seid, a franchising consultant and managing director of the Strategic Advisory Group Inc. in West Hartford, CN, Susan Kezios, president of Women in Franchising, and the American Franchisee Association, both in Chicago; Lois Marshall, a franchise industry recruiter and president of The Marshall Group in Salinas, CA; and William Slater Vincent, an assistant professor in the department of management and entrepreneurship at Kennesaw State College in Kennesaw, GA.

The franchises cited by the NBEW's panel as the best being offered for *less* than $100,000 each, in alphabetical order, include:

Advantage Payroll Services
126 Merrow Rd.
P.O. Box 1330
Auburn, ME 04211
(800) 876-0178
Payroll and payroll tax services
Year Business Started: 1967
Year Started Franchise: 1983

American Leak Detection
888 Research Dr., #100
Palm Springs, CA 92262
(800) 755-6697
Water/gas leak detection
    services
Year Business Started: 1974
Year Started Franchise: 1984

**Better Homes & Gardens
Real Estate Service**
2000 Grand Ave.
Des Moines, IA 50312-4996
(800) 274-7653
Real estate services
Year Business Started: 1977
Year Started Franchise: 1978

Blimpie Int'l Inc.
1775 The Exchange #600
Atlanta, GA 30339
(800) 447-6256
Submarine sandwiches
Year Business Started: 1964
Year Started Franchise: 1970

**Chem-Dry Carpet Drapery &
Upholstery Cleaning**
1530 N. 1000 West
Logan, UT 84321
(800) 841-6583
Fabric care
Year Business Started: 1977
Year Started Franchise: 1978

Computertots
10132 Colvin Run Rd.
Great Falls, VA 22066
(703) 759-2556
Children's computer education
Year Business Started: 1983
Year Started Franchise: 1988

Cost Cutters Family Hair Care
300 Industrial Blvd. N.E.
Minneapolis, MN 55413
(800) 858-2266
Hair care
Year Business Started: 1982
Year Started Franchise: 1982

Coverall North America Inc.
3111 Camino Del Rio N. #950
San Diego, CA 92108
(800) 537-3371
Commercial office cleaning
Year Business Started: 1985
Year Started Franchise: 1985

Creative Colors Int'l Inc.
5550 W. 175th St.
Tinley Park, IL 60477
(708) 614-7786
Vinyl repair
Year Business Started: 1980
Year Started Franchise: 1991

E.K. Williams & Co.
1020 N. University Parks Dr.
Waco, TX 76707
(800) 992-0706
Accounting, tax and counseling
  services
Year Business Started: 1935
Year Started Franchise: 1947

Furniture Medic
277 Southfield Pkwy., #130
Forest Park, GA 30050
(800) 877-9933
Furniture repair
Year Business Started: 1992
Year Started Franchise: 1992

Futurekids Inc.
5777 W. Century Blvd., #1555
Los Angeles, CA 90045
(310) 337-7006

Computer learning centers for
  children
Year Business Started: 1983
Year Started Franchise: 1989

General Business Services Inc.
1020 N. University Parks Dr.
Waco, TX 76707
(800) 583-6181
Business counseling, financial
  mgmt. and tax services
Year Business Started: 1962
Year Started Franchise: 1962

GNC Franchising Inc. (General Nutrition Centers)
921 Penn Ave.
Pittsburgh, PA 15222
(800) 766-7099
Vitamin and nutrition stores
Year Business Started: 1935
Year Started Franchise: 1988

Great Harvest Franchising
28 S. Montana St.
Dillon, MT 59725
(800) 442-0424
Specialty whole-wheat bakery
Year Business Started: 1970
Year Started Franchise: 1978

H & R Block Inc.
4410 Main St.
Kansas City, MO 64111
(816) 753-6900
Tax preparation
Year Business Started: 1955
Year Started Franchise: 1956

Heel Quik! Inc.
6425 Powers Ferry Rd., #250
Atlanta, GA 30339
(800) 255-8145
Shoe repair, clothing alterations
Year Business Started: 1984
Year Started Franchise: 1985

Hot Stuff Food Systems Inc.
2930 W. Maple
Sioux Falls, SD 57101
(605) 336-6961
Pizza kiosks
Year Business Started: 1986
Year Started Franchise: 1994

Jackson Hewitt Tax Service
4575 Bonney Rd.
Virginia Beach, VA 23462
(800) 277-3278
Computerized tax
  preparation/filing services
Year Business Started: 1960
Year Started Franchise: 1986

Jani-King
4950 Keller Springs Rd., #190
Dallas, TX 75248
(800) 552-5264
Commercial cleaning services
Year Business Started: 1969
Year Started Franchise: 1974

Jazzercise Inc.
2808 Roosevelt
Carlsbad, CA 92008
(619) 434-2101
Dance/exercise classes
Year Business Started: 1977
Year Started Franchise: 1983

Kinderdance Int'l Inc.
Box 510881
Melbourne Beach, FL 32951
(800) 666-1595
Movement/education programs
  for young children
Year Business Started: 1979
Year Started Franchise: 1985

Kitchen Solvers Inc.
401 Jay St.
LaCrosse, WI 54601
(800) 845-6779

Kitchen-cabinet refacing and
  remodeling
Year Business Started: 1982
Year Started Franchise: 1984

Mail Boxes Etc.
6060 Cornerstone Ct. W.
San Diego, CA 92121
(800) 456-0414
Postal/business services
Year Business Started: 1980
Year Started Franchise: 1980

**Management
Recruiters/Sales
Consultants**
1127 Euclid Ave., #1400
Cleveland, OH 44115-1638
(800) 875-4000
Personnel placement and
  recruiting services
Year Business Started: 1957
Year Started Franchise: 1965

Merry Maids
11117 Mill Valley Rd.
Omaha, NE 68154
(800) 798-8000
Residential cleaning
Year Business Started: 1980
Year Started Franchise: 1981

Mini Maid
1341 Canton Rd., #C-1
Marietta, GA 30066
(800) 627-6464
Residential cleaning
Year Business Started: 1973
Year Started Franchise: 1976

Molly Maid
540 Avis Dr.
Ann Arbor, MI 48108
(800) 289-4600
Residential cleaning
Year Business Started: 1978
Year Started Franchise: 1978

Newcomer's of America
210 Wisconsin Ave.
Waukesha, WI 53186
(800) 282-2414
Home inspection service
Year Business Started: 1989
Year Started Franchise: 1994

Nutri/System Weight Loss Centers
410 Horsham Rd.
Horsham, PA 19044-2014
(215) 442-5300
Weight-loss programs
Year Business Started: 1971
Year Started Franchise: 1994

Once Upon a Child
4200 Dahlberg Dr.
Minneapolis, MN 55422
(800) 445-1006
Children's clothing and
  equipment
Year Business Started: 1984
Year Started Franchise: 1992

Padgett Business Services USA Inc.
160 Hawthorne Park
Athens, GA 30606
(800) 323-7292
Accounting, consulting and tax
  services
Year Business Started: 1965
Year Started Franchise: 1975

Pressed4Time Inc.
124 Boston Post Rd.
Sudbury, MA 01776
(800) 423-8711
Dry cleaning pick-up/delivery
Year Business Started: 1987
Year Started Franchise: 1990

Re/Max Int'l Inc.
P.O.Box 3907
Englewood, CO 80155-3907
(800) 525-7452
Real estate
Year Business Started: 1973
Year Started Franchise: 1975

ServiceMaster
855 Ridge Lake Blvd.
Memphis, TN 38120
(800) 752-6688
Commercial contract cleaning
Year Business Started: 1947
Year Started Franchise: 1952

Snap-On Inc.
P.O. Box 1410
Kenosha, WI 53141-1410
(800) 775-7630
Professional tools and equipment
Year Business Started: 1920
Year Started Franchise: 1991

Supercuts
550 California St.
San Francisco, CA 94104-1006
(415) 693-4700
Haircare
Year Business Started: 1975
Year Started Franchise: 1979

Sylvan Learning Systems
9135 Guilford Rd.
Columbia, MD 21046
(800) 284-8214
Supplemental education
Year Business Started: 1979
Year Started Franchise: 1980

The Coffee Beanery
G-3429 Pierson Pl.
Flushing, MI 48433
(800) 728-2326
Gourmet coffees, desserts, etc.
Year Business Started: 1976
Year Started Franchise: 1985

The Historical Research Center Int'l
632 S. Military Trail
Deerfield Beach, FL 33442
(305) 421-8713
Heraldic and heritage kiosks
Year Business Started: 1988
Year Started Franchise: 1992

The Lemon Tree
3301 Hempstead Tpke.
Levittown, NY 11756
(800) 345-9156
Hair care
Year Business Started: 1974
Year Started Franchise: 1976

The Medicine Shoppe
1100 N. Lindbergh Blvd.
St. Louis, MO 63132
(800) 325-1397
Pharmacy
Year Business Started: 1970
Year Started Franchise: 1970

The Packaging Store Inc.
5675 DTC Blvd., #280
Englewood, CO 80111
(800) 525-6309
Packaging and shipping
Year Business Started: 1980
Year Started Franchise: 1984

TravelPlex Int'l
655 Metro Pl. S., #250
Dublin, OH 43017
(614) 766-6315
Travel agency
Year Business Started: 1984
Year Started Franchise: 1989

Two Men & a Truck/USA Inc.
1915 E. Michigan Ave.
Lansing, MI 48912
(800) 345-1070
Local moving service
Year Business Started: 1984
Year Started Franchise: 1989

Wild Birds Unlimited
3003 E. 96th St., #201
Indianapolis, IN 46240
(800) 326-4928
Bird-feeding supplies and nature
    gifts
Year Business Started: 1981
Year Started Franchise: 1983

Ziebart-Tidy Car
1290 E. Maple Rd.
Troy, MI, 48007-1290
(800) 877-1312
Auto appearance
    services/accessories
Year Business Started: 1954
Year Started Franchise: 1963

The franchises cited by the NBEW's panel as the best being offered for *more* than $100,000 each, in alphabetical order, include:

Aaron's Rental-Purchase
3001 N. Fulton Dr., N.E.
Atlanta, GA 30305-2377
(800) 551-6015
Household goods
    rentals/purchase
Year Business Started: 1955
Year Started Franchise: 1992

AlphaGraphics Printshops of the Future
3760 N. Commerce Dr.
Tucson, AZ 85705
(800) 955-6246
Printing/related business services
Year Business Started: 1970
Year Started Franchise: 1980

Applebee's Neighborhood Grill & Bar
4551 107th St., #100
Overland Park, KS 66207
(913) 967-4000
Restaurant
Year Business Started: 1983
Year Started Franchise: 1987

Auntie Anne's Inc.
160-A Rte. 41
Gap, PA 17527
(717) 442-4766
Soft pretzels
Year Business Started: 1988
Year Started Franchise: 1989

Ben & Jerry's Homemade Inc.
Route 100, Box 240
Waterbury, VT 05676
(802) 244-6957
Ice cream
Year Business Started: 1978
Year Started Franchise: 1981

Betsy Ann Chocolates
322 Perry Highway
Pittsburgh, PA 15229
(800) 426-8027
High-quality chocolates
Year Business Started: 1938
Year Started Franchise: 1994

Bonjour Bagel Cafe
225 S. Lake Ave., #M-153
Pasadena, CA 91101
(818) 304-9023
Bagel/bakery cafe
Year Business Started: 1992
Year Started Franchise: 1993

Bruegger's Bagel Bakery
159 Bank St., P.O. Box 374
Burlington, VT 05402
(802) 862-4700
Bagels and sandwiches
Year Business Started: 1983
Year Started Franchise: 1993

Churchs Chicken
6 Concourse Pkwy., #1700
Atlanta, GA 30328
(800) 848-8248
Fried chicken and biscuits
Year Business Started: 1952
Year Started Franchise: 1972

Computer Renaissance
4200 Dahlberg Dr.
Minneapolis, MN 55422
(800) 868-8975
New/used computer equipment
Year Business Started: 1988
Year Started Franchise: 1993

Discovery Zone
205 N. Michigan Ave., Ste. 3400
Chicago, IL 60601-5914
(312) 616-3800
Indoor children's playground
Year Business Started: 1990
Year Started Franchise: 1990

Dunkin' Donuts
14 Pacella Park Dr.
Randolph, MA 02368
(800) 543-5400
Donuts and bakery products
Year Business Started: 1950
Year Started Franchise: 1955

Ecomat
147 Palmer Ave.
Mamaroneck, NY 10543
(800) 299-2309
Environmental garment care
Year Business Started: 1993
Year Started Franchise: 1994

Fastframe
1200 Lawrence Dr., #300
Newbury Park, CA 91320
(800) 521-3726
Custom framing and art gallery
Year Business Started: 1986
Year Started Franchise: 1987

Fastsigns
2550 Midway Rd., #150
Carrollton, TX 75006
(800) 827-7446
Computer-generated vinyl signs
Year Business Started: 1985
Year Started Franchise: 1986

Great American Cookie Co. Inc.
4685 Frederick Dr., SW
Atlanta, GA 30336
(800) 336-2447
Retail cookie stores
Year Business Started: 1977
Year Started Franchise: 1978

Hilton Inns
P.O. Box 5567
Beverly Hills, CA 90210
(310) 205-4407
Hotels and resorts
Year Business Started: 1946
Year Started Franchise: 1965

Holiday Inn Worldwide
3 Ravinia Dr., #2000
Atlanta, GA 30346
(404) 604-2100
Hotels
Year Business Started: 1952
Year Started Franchise: 1954

Hooters Restaurant
4501 Circle 75 Pkwy., #E-5110
Atlanta, GA 30339
(404) 951-2040
Casual full-service restaurant
Year Business Started: 1983
Year Started Franchise: 1988

I Can't Believe It's Yogurt!
P.O. Box 809112
Dallas, TX 75380-9112
(214) 788-4788
Frozen yogurt
Year Business Started: 1977
Year Started Franchise: 1983

ITT Sheraton Corp.
60 State St.
Boston, MA 02109
(617) 367-3600
Hotels, resorts, etc.
Year Business Started: 1937
Year Started Franchise: 1962

Jiffy Lube Int'l Inc.
P.O. Box 2967
Houston, TX 77252-2967
(800) 327-9532
Auto fluid specialists/
    maintenance
Year Business Started: 1979
Year Started Franchise: 1979

Kampgrounds of America Inc.
550 N. 31st St., 4th Fl.
Billings, MT 59101
(406) 248-7444
Campgrounds
Year Business Started: 1961
Year Started Franchise: 1962

Krystal Restaurants
One Union Sq.
Chattanooga, TN 37402
(800) 458-5912
Hamburger restaurants
Year Business Started: 1932
Year Started Franchise: 1989

Kwik-Kopy Corp.
One Kwik-Copy Ln.
Cypress, TX 77429-0777
(800) 231-1304
Printing and copying services
Year Business Started: 1967
Year Started Franchise: 1967

Maaco Auto Painting & Bodyworks
381 Brooks Rd.
King of Prussia, PA 19406
(800) 296-2226
Auto painting and body repair
Year Business Started: 1972
Year Started Franchise: 1972

Manpower Temporary Services
5301 N. Ironwood Rd.
P.O. Box 2053
Milwaukee, WI 53201
(414) 961-1000
Temporary help service
Year Business Started: 1948
Year Started Franchise: 1954

McDonald's
McDonald's Plaza
Oak Brook, IL 60521
(708) 575-6196
Hamburgers, etc.
Year Business Started: 1955
Year Started Franchise: 1955

Miami Subs
6300 N.W. 31st Ave.
Ft. Lauderdale, FL 33309
(305) 973-0000
Submarine sandwiches
Year Business Started: 1983
Year Started Franchise: 1986

Midas Int'l Corp.
225 N. Michigan Ave.
Chicago, IL 60601
(800) 621-0144
Car exhaust systems, etc.
Year Business Started: 1956
Year Started Franchise: 1956

Moto Photo Inc.
4444 Lake Center Dr.
Dayton, OH 45426
(800) 733-6686
Film processing, etc.
Year Business Started: 1981
Year Started Franchise: 1982

Mountain Mike's Pizza
1014 Second St., 3rd Fl.
Old Sacramento, CA 94818
(800) 982-6453
Pizza/oven-baked sandwiches
Year Business Started: 1978
Year Started Franchise: 1978

My Favorite Muffin
1006 E. Park Blvd.
Cranbury, NJ 08512
(609) 395-9292
Muffins, bagels, cappuccino
Year Business Started: 1987
Year Started Franchise: 1987

Play It Again Sports
4200 Dahlberg Dr.
Minneapolis, MN 55422
(800) 433-2540
New and used sporting goods
Year Business Started: 1983
Year Started Franchise: 1988

Popeyes Chicken & Biscuits
6 Concourse Pkwy., #1700
Atlanta, GA 30328
(800) 848-8248
Fried chicken and biscuits
Year Business Started: 1972
Year Started Franchise: 1976

Precision Tune
748 Miller Dr., S.E.
Leesburg, VA 22075
(800) 231-0588
Engine diagnostics,
    maintenance, etc.
Year Business Started: 1975
Year Started Franchise: 1978

Rent-a-Wreck of America Inc.
11460 Cronridge Dr., Ste. 118
Owings Mills, MD 21117
(800) 421-7253
Auto/truck/trailer rental
Year Business Started: 1973
Year Started Franchise: 1978

Rocky Mountain Chocolate Factory
265 Turner Dr.
Durango, CO 81301
(800) 438-7623
Chocolate and confections
Year Business Started: 1981
Year Started Franchise: 1982

Seattle's Best Coffee
1333 Stewart St.
Seattle, WA 98109
(800) 243-5206
Coffee cafes and kiosks
Year Business Started: 1969
Year Started Franchise: 1994

Sonic Drive In Restaurants
101 Park Ave.
Oklahoma City, OK 73102
(800) 517-6642
Fast-food drive-in restaurants
Year Business Started: 1954
Year Started Franchise: 1959

Staff Builders Inc.
1981 Marcus Ave.
Lake Success, NY 11042
(800) 444-4633
Home health-care staffing
   services
Year Business Started: 1961
Year Started Franchise: 1987

Straw Hat Pizza
6400 Village Pkwy.
Dublin, CA 94568
(510) 829-1500
Pizza, salads, sandwiches
Year Business Started: 1969
Year Started Franchise: 1969

Taco John's Int'l Inc.
808 W. 20th
Cheyenne, WY 82001
(307) 635-0101
Mexican food
Year Business Started: 1968
Year Started Franchise: 1969

The Athlete's Foot
1950 Vaughn Rd.
Kennesaw, GA 30144
(404) 514-4719
Athletic footwear/sports apparel
Year Business Started: 1972
Year Started Franchise: 1973

The Body Shop
45 Horsehill Rd.
Cedar Knolls, NJ 07927
(201) 984-9200
Skin/hair care products
Year Business Started: 1988
Year Started Franchise: 1990

The Italian Oven
11 Lloyd Ave.
Latrobe, PA 15650
(412) 537-5380
Italian family restaurant
Year Business Started: 1989
Year Started Franchise: 1990

The Pro Image
563 W. 500 South, #330
Bountiful, UT 84010
(801) 292-8777
Sports-fan gift store
Year Business Started: 1985
Year Started Franchise: 1985

Uniglobe Travel
1199 W. Pender St., 9th Fl.
Vancouver, B.C., Canada V6E 2R1
(604) 662-3800
Travel agency
Year Business Started: 1980
Year Started Franchise: 1981

**United Consumers Club
Franchising Corp.**
8450 Broadway
Merrillville, IN 46411-3006
(800) 827-6400
Consumer buying club
Year Business Started: 1971
Year Started Franchise: 1972

Wallpapers to Go
P.O. Box 4586
Houston, TX 77210-4586
(800) 843-7094
Wall coverings
Year Business Started: 1977
Year Started Franchise: 1986

Wendy's Int'l Inc.
4288 W. Dublin Granville Rd.
Dublin, OH 43017
(614) 764-3100
Quick-service restaurants
Year Business Started: 1969
Year Started Franchise: 1971

Western Auto/Auto America Stores
2107 Grand Ave.
Kansas City, MO 64108
(614) 764-3100
Auto aftermarket sales and
   services
Year Business Started: 1909
Year Started Franchise: 1935

Wicks 'N' Sticks
P.O. Box 4586
Houston, TX 77210-4586
(800) 231-6337
Candles, home fragrance, etc.
Year Business Started: 1968
Year Started Franchise: 1968

ZuZu Handmade Mexican Food
2651 N. Harwood, #200
Dallas, TX 75201
(800) 824-8830
Handmade Mexican food
Year Business Started: 1989
Year Started Franchise: 1992

"I'm sure that Mr. Pangfield will be seeing you shortly, but in the meantime, can I get you another cup of pencils to chew on?"

7

Consulting

Consulting has become the great umbrella for those drenched by downsizings. These days, everybody's a consultant—at least until they find their next salaried position.

In a recent survey of 670 executives and professionals in the $50,000 to $125,000 income range and actively seeking new jobs, executive recruiter William Mangum found 32 percent were working as consultants during their searches. Of those, 65 percent were consulting part-time; 35 percent were full-time.

Consulting is much more than a temporary haven for job-seekers. It's a $20-plus billion industry booming at all levels, from such giants as EDS and Andersen Consulting, all the way down to (and of special interest here) solos practitioners like you and me. Consulting is among the most common forms of home-based employment.

If you can get the work, consulting can be golden: the initial investment is minimal, you're likely to be able to work from home, set your own hours, have few or even no employees (according to your wishes and business opportunities), and make very good money (though it's generally limited by the availability of your personal time).

All in all, consulting is ideally suited to the New Economy. You assist organizations with your special knowledge and skills exactly when they need them. There's lots of variety, and it's a kick to be selected for an engagement.

133

But if you can't find the work, or are suffering through the inevitable dry spells that even the best consultants encounter, it can be tough—more of a roller-coaster than many other occupations.

It can also be lonely. One day a consulting project will look like a smooth series of steps along familiar paths and—perhaps even the same day—you can fall into a funk of dead ends and begin to think you took a wrong turn a long time ago. Only your very best friends will listen to (or do anything about) your travails, so it becomes your challenge to learn to enjoy the ride and to stay in shape for the hills and valleys.

Consultants are always selling, and they are always outsiders. As a consultant, you'll often lack the resources you'd like to have and you'll occasionally deal with clients who seem to be thwarting your every opportunity for success, either by nature or because of organizational issues beyond everyone's control.

Then there's the travel—usually too much of it to make it attractive. There are the incredible hours (sometimes someone else's hours, sometimes yours, depending on your practice—but always a lot). There's the uncertainty of consulting: Unless you pull your weight every day by delivering results and developing the next piece of work, there's nothing to put in the bank.

For all of these reasons, consulting as a career choice clearly involves the same kind of commitment that's needed in starting or buying a business. Just because it requires minimal start-up costs, doesn't mean you can enter this field lightly and be successful.

"You must really commit to starting the business," says Alex Schibanoff, executive director of The Consultants Bureau in New Brunswick, NJ. "It's impossible to promote a consultancy and look for a new job at the same time."

In fact, consulting's easy entry—and perennial low standing as a career that people are committed to—make it even tougher for those starting out to establish themselves as serious enterprises. In my own experience, aside from whatever merit there may be in the work I'm doing and future demand for it, there's been lots of skepticism and confusion among people I encounter. It's not the same as taking a new job that's too good to resist. It's not like starting a business in which you're being backed by lenders convinced of your likelihood of success. It's not like buying a business of known value. Instead, it's vague and kind of slippery. There's an undercurrent of "we'll see" in each conversation.

> It is better to know some of the questions than all of the answers.
>
> —James Thurber

Such are the challenges of those who choose this tricky path. It takes an extra bit of chutzpah.

But for me, and for many, the pros of consulting are way ahead of the cons. Instead of looking at the number of hours I work and wishing I could be home more, I'm home most of the time, couldn't care less how many hours I work and instead count only the number of *billable* hours I can put in—always trying to make it bigger!

Are You the Type?

In his helpful book, *From Executive to Entrepreneur: Making the Transition* (New York: Amacom, 1991), Gilbert G. Zoghlin, a partner in an employee benefits and financial planning consulting firm in Wilmette, IL, lists 10 questions executives should ask themselves before jumping into consulting. They are:

1. Are you between 35 and 55 with at least 10 years of business experience?
2. Is your area of consultancy directly in line with your area of expertise?
3. Do you have a significant amount of marketing and sales experience?
4. Were you a middle manager or higher level?
5. Have you developed, with relative ease, a network of contacts within and outside your organization?
6. Have you enjoyed corporate assignments that have been challenging and diverse (vs. those that required little homework and few new approaches)?
7. Are you going into consulting with the idea that you'll do it until you retire?

8. Do you dislike delegating tasks and relying on others?

9. Are you curious about how well ideas that work in your organization would work in others?

10. Have you enjoyed the brainstorming as well as the details of your corporate job?

The desired answer to each question is an obvious "yes," and if you find yourself responding that way to most or all of them, great. Even though your consulting practice could become derailed for all kinds of other reasons, you're at least beginning with much of the right experience and attitude.

But there's more to the personality of the successful consultant. Writing in *Consultants News,* Donald Baiocchi of D.P. Baiocchi Associates in Chicago, a career management consultant to senior executives and their organizations, describes these areas in which to look for at least adequate, if not superior, abilities:

☆ *Intellect.* You should be highly analytical, expert in critical thinking and curious. You should enjoy tackling complex issues and be objective yet able to identify with clients' problems. You must be comfortable with ambiguity, uncertainty and unstructured situations and able to handle constant scrutiny by clients and partners.

☆ *Leadership.* You need vision and initiative, the willingness to challenge yet also inspire confidence, respect and trust. You must be able to work with clients as well as for them.

☆ *Managerial abilities.* You must be well-organized and able to balance selling and doing. You need experience in planning the work of others, developing and teaching staff members, controlling the project, coordinating feedback to the client, projecting a sense of urgency and meeting deadlines.

☆ *Communication skills.* There can be no doubt about your ability to express yourself clearly in writing and present yourself convincingly in person. You must be a good listener who can promote dialogue, identify problems and persuade others to help solve them.

☆ *Personal qualities.* You need good health, high energy and a personal life that supports the significant commitment you make to your clients and colleagues. You must be resilient, highly ethical, discreet and always ready to learn.

☆ *Interpersonal skills.* Tact, diplomacy and sensitivity are essential. You need poise, a professional appearance and manners, and the ability to project an accurate self-image. You'll have to intervene successfully in tough situations, and be willing to disagree without being disagreeable. Most of all, you must be comfortable with yourself and your role as a consultant.

Says Geoffrey Bellman, an organizational development consultant in Seattle and author of *The Consultant's Calling* (San Francisco: Jossey-Bass, 1990), "I must have the opportunity to be myself while I work. Work that continually requires me to hide who I am is too burdensome to pursue. One of the reasons I do this work is that it provides me with the possibility of being myself while I'm in service to others."

A Great Consultant: James O. McKinsey

For a bit more insight into what makes a good consultant, look no further than James O. McKinsey, founder of the world's most successful and influential management consulting firm.

McKinsey was raised in poverty in the Ozark farming town of Mexico, Missouri, in the early 1900s. He showed early abilities not only to learn, but also to teach. While in high school, he was asked to instruct a class in algebra. Later, after earning a law degree, he studied bookkeeping and accounting and, in addition to becoming a CPA, taught accounting at the University of Chicago.

At the same time, he began an extensive series of writing projects: books that advanced the approach to accounting from one based in record-keeping to one in which the information being gathered could be used to address and solve business problems. He pursued analytical thinking and focused on *why* managers do things rather than *how* they do them, and on how better use of information could affect the why.

In 1925, after working for several years at a Chicago accounting firm, McKinsey left to establish his own consulting firm while continuing to teach. By following McKinsey's analytical approach, combined with learnable skills in developing clients, the firm's consultants became the pre-eminent business problem solvers of our time.

> Can you make it as a consultant? Only one in three are left after five years, only one in 10 after 10 years.
>
> —James H. Kennedy in *Consultants News*

In his career, and in his life in general, McKinsey exhibited several qualities that made his outstanding success possible (as noted by Cornell University professor William B. Wolf in *Management and Consulting: An Introduction to James O. McKinsey,* Ithaca, NY: Cornell University, 1978):

☆ He had a great deal of humility, combined with a need for status and recognition, which led to a powerful motivation to achieve.

☆ He made his work his life's top priority.

☆ He had an amazing memory, which appeared to be pure mental ability, but in fact was based equally on systematic recording and the remembering of facts and lessons learned. He also used anecdotes to illustrate those ideas so others could remember them.

☆ He could tell it like it is. McKinsey had no sentimentality or tenderness. He wanted to be respected, not loved. And his devotion to logic and analytical thinking drove him to tell others bluntly what had to be done.

Marvin Bower, who continued McKinsey's work as the firm's leader for many years, recalls that McKinsey "believed in personal coaching, and that meant really telling a person about his mistakes and opportunities to improve. He was rigorous but fair."

Wolf reports that McKinsey believed consultants need three things for success: unquestioned respectability, a reputation of expertise and professional exposure.

In his own career, McKinsey achieved the first through his academic achievements and connections, especially at the University of Chicago. He developed true expertise through his writings. He then put his expertise into action through relentless business and social contacts with those in positions to make use of his advice.

McKinsey was a pioneer of the power meal and was said to eat all his lunches, half his breakfasts and one-third of his dinners with clients or prospects. In addition, through involvement in community activities, he methodically and persistently pursued opportunities to meet influential people. This approach to business development remains at the heart of the McKinsey & Co. approach even today.

Nevertheless, simple exposure to the right people is no guarantee that they'll pay for your advice. In addition to respectability, expertise and exposure, is the crucial skill of being able to discern a specific need, then propose, in a persuasive manner, how it should be addressed.

McKinsey's style in this area has also become a hallmark of his firm, and of successful consulting in general. It includes these elements:

☆ *Establishing comfort.* In addition to his obvious drive and enthusiasm, McKinsey became a compelling counselor to business leaders by making them feel comfortable. He focused on mealtime appointments—times at which, away from their offices, chief executives could view their work with some perspective and a sense of relaxation. He became a master storyteller, mostly by diligently recording and remembering anecdotes that would both entertain and make a point. He took no written notes—to avoid intimidating clients—but made a careful mental list of what was being covered. In general, he tried to make the client as comfortable as possible in discussing often-thorny business challenges.

☆ *Asking good questions.* "McKinsey didn't pontificate," recalls William Newman, a McKinsey protege. "He was much more conversational. One of the standard techniques he outlined to us in staff meetings was that you ask questions, you don't start giving answers. He often used an illustration about selling textbooks, emphasizing that you first learn what the teacher is concerned with, and then explain how your book can help serve that purpose. You can appear a lot smarter if you ask questions than if you simply give answers."

☆ *Being a good listener.* If you really want to help someone, says Newman, "you'd better not begin to guess how to go about it until you understand the nature of his problem." Think carefully about what the other person is telling you before jumping in with a solution.

☆ *Responding constructively.* McKinsey followed through on opportunities to formally propose being of assistance.

The overall effect of this apparently informal, four-part approach can be magical. Here's how Newman describes it:

> Usually after pleasantries or the lightness of a joke, he would try to find out what was on the man's mind. Having done that, he would try to see if he couldn't suggest something that would be helpful to him. Sometimes he would bring problems back to the office and have a few of us dig up information, and then he would write the fellow a letter. He just felt that he would like to be constructive and helpful. In doing this, the man would then begin to look to McKinsey as a person to whom he could bring a problem and get some help. This was something I think Mac thoroughly enjoyed, but it was also something that was good for the firm.

Nothing has occurred since McKinsey's day that diminishes the effectiveness of this basic approach to successful consulting, and the continuing success of the firm bears this out.

Today's "Typical" Consultant

While McKinsey's principles of effective consulting haven't changed, today's entrants in the consulting world are more likely to be those whose fates have been recast by restructurings and downsizings. Gilbert Zoghlin presents a good example in the story of John Seastone.

During 25 years at the Walgreen Company, John had risen to vice president in charge of the Wags food-service division. But when Marriott bought Walgreen's in 1988, it appeared John would have to relocate. Faced with moving his family out of his native Chicago at age 55, he resigned and accepted a substantial benefits package. But opportunities to land another job like he'd had were slim. Reluctantly, he began exploring alternatives.

John wasn't thrilled with the idea of consulting. Yet people were calling him after reading of his departure from Wags to seek his help. Still, he resisted, fearing failure and unwilling to accept that he'd no longer have all the resources at his disposal that he'd enjoyed at Wags. "I felt a consulting career would be like starting over," he says.

Nevertheless, he decided to try a couple of projects, which went well. Clients were pleased and paid him accordingly. He became comfortable networking for more work and, gradually, began to enjoy his new role. "I went from holding the corporate security blanket to realizing I didn't need it," John recalls.

John noticed several things he liked about consulting: variety in his work, no pressure to meet corporate objectives (only the ones he established for himself) and opportunities to be quite flexible with his work schedule. On the down side, he found himself lonely at times and had trouble getting comfortable with his fees—at first feeling they were too high, then cutting them perhaps too much, and still not sure where the middle ground was.

John also learned a few lessons:

☆ That he needs to be flexible and can no longer dictate action. "I learned there was no sense in making a recommendation when you know the person isn't interested in making that type of change," John says. "You have to take it slow, find out what makes your client tick, including his concerns and values. Once you learn the direction he's coming from, you can ease into your recommendation and make it acceptable."

☆ That he shouldn't come on too strong or too slick. John has shifted his appearance from strictly buttoned-down to more relaxed—sport coats instead of suits for smaller clients—and his manner, from aggressively stating his strong opinions to being a better listener.

☆ That he has to make the phone ring. A few months after leaving Wags, John was no longer getting calls based on relationships he'd built there. So he learned to initiate calls well beyond his old network.

☆ Humility. He's gotten used to being kept waiting, and to chilly receptions to cold calls. Fortunately, he's having enough success that he can suffer the realities of being a seller, rather than a buyer, of services.

A Theme Emerges

Notice the emphasis on selling in these case histories? Many skilled executives enter the consulting field with much too little appreciation for the amount of time and effort that must be devoted to developing business. Says New Jersey-based career management consultant Neal Rist of Manchester Inc., "While consultants need specialized expertise in a particular field, their success is directly related to how well they can sell. It's not what you know, but how well you sell that will make or break your career."

Scary! Doesn't anybody care about expertise? Of course. It's a given, and you can certainly fail if you don't have it. But what Rist is saying is that an inability to bring in business is more often the cause of failure than a lack of expertise. So think about it. Are you excited about the value you can bring to others? Do you enjoy being of service? Can you communicate that to potential clients? Can you picture yourself spending more than half of your time getting the business and less than half doing it?

You may not know until you have your first client. Then, once you have a client on board, you'll find there's something else more important than expertise and sales ability. It's results. Since that's the only thing clients will pay for the second and third time they use you, you've got to deliver the goods. When you do, sales get the biggest lift there is: repeat business.

Consulting observers Ted Nicholas and the late Howard Shenson, authors of *The Complete Guide to Consulting Success* (Chicago: Dearborn Financial Publishing, 1993), agree vigorously on this point, "Few consultants are the world's leading authorities in their specialty. Instead, they're active, practical, energetic people who put the theory to work and make it pay." It's not what you know but what you can do that counts.

But even results must be supported by sales activities as a significant on-going part of life as a consultant. And lest you be tempted to hide under the excuse that promoting your practice is somehow undignified or unprofessional, consider this advice from consultant Gil Gordon of Gordon Associates in Monmouth Junction, NJ, "Lose your inhibitions, study sales methods and internalize the idea that selling is merely need satisfaction.

Being right is easy. Effecting change is hard.

—Robert O. Metzger in *Profitable Consulting*

Uncover needs, figure out if you have the solutions and try to match the two."

Square One

Let's look at the process of launching and operating a consulting process step-by-step. First, you've got to define your service and the market for it. Because these two elements are interdependent, there must be a match. An idea for a consulting business that's too heavily weighted in what you can do—but with little or no sign that there's a market—will fail, as will the one for which there's an obvious market but a question about whether you can deliver. Therefore, testing should begin immediately.

While evaluating your own expertise, identify potential customers and ask them what they think. One especially useful vehicle for this process is the development of your initial marketing materials, whether they be as simple as a letter announcing your new enterprise, or as ambitious as a full-scale brochure. Get feedback on what you're planning to say about your practice from people who'd be in a position to use you, or at least direct business your way.

After doing so, you may well be advised to narrow your niche. Says Gil Gordon, "A jack of all-trades stance will confuse clients, dilute your energy and force you to compete with more consultants. Focus on what you love to do, what you do better than anyone else, what you can describe clearly in very few words and what people will pay cash for."

That last part—what people will pay cash for—is a killer! How do you find out? Asking helps, of course. If you have in mind a particular group of people and organizations you think are likely clients, look for other signals. What do their actions say about what's really important to them?

Next, when you've gotten a micro pulse on your market from a few key prospects, look at the bigger picture. Does the type of service you're considering have a favorable outlook?

Hot Fields in Consulting

Consultant Ron Tepper has attempted to put his finger on that one in "The 10 Hottest Consulting Practices" (New York: John Wiley, 1994). They are, according to Ron:

1. Business strategy and strategic alliances.
2. Communications and public relations.
3. Executive search.
4. Site services and meeting planning.
5. Sales training.
6. Sales and marketing effectiveness.
7. Management consulting.
8. Outplacement.
9. Compensation.
10. Organization and reorganization.

Process or Content?

As you zero in on exactly what it is that you'll offer, consider the difference between process-oriented consultants and those that are content-driven. For content-driven consultants, knowledge of a particular industry or market is key. What they know is at least as important, if not more so, than how they deliver their services. Process consultants, on the other hand, are focused on the process of consulting: activities that can be carried out in a variety of situations in order to generate results.

In *The Complete Guide to Consulting Success* (Chicago: Dearborn Financial Publishing, 1993) Messrs. Shenson and Nicholas cite the example of a hospital planner specializing in critical-care units who decides to become a consultant. If she chooses a content-oriented approach, she'll likely pursue as clients other hospitals seeking help in planning critical-care units. But if she decides her skills at organizing and carrying out the planning process are even more valuable than her knowledge of hospital critical-care units, then she could seek clients in a variety of industries as a planning process consultant.

"Obviously, your market is broader and your prospects brighter if you take a process-oriented approach," Shenson and Nicholas say. But look before you leap into that broader market, because it may be more difficult to distinguish yourself as extraordinarily skilled in the consulting process. It requires experience as well as outstanding "people skills."

For me, success in my initial months as a consultant stems directly from content—my special knowledge of the markets I follow. That's why clients call. They know I'm not an experienced consultant yet, but they know I know their business. And for now, I'm ignoring Shenson and Nicholas' suggestion that there's a bigger market for me if I focus on process. In my view, process will come with experience as a consultant, but since I've recently made the jump from journalist to consultant, I've decided to keep as a constant my industry specialization. Compare your own abilities and experience and you'll have a good idea of where to position yourself on the content-process continuum.

Start Acting the Part

Though every business truly begins with its first customer, work must start even earlier backstage in preparing the product—you—for your market research and initial sales calls.

First, make sure you've mastered the basics of business etiquette that will get you in the door and keep you inside long enough to get comfortable. Jan Yager, a Connecticut consultant on business behavior and communication, and author of *Business Protocol: How to Survive and Succeed in Business* (New York: John Wiley, 1991), offers these reminders to stick on your bathroom mirror:

☆ *Stress confidentiality.* A consultant should practice and convey the same level of discretion that we expect of lawyers, accountants, doctors and the clergy.

☆ *Be honest about what you promise.* Overdoing it can not only put you behind the 8-ball in carrying out the engagement, it can even get you into legal trouble.

☆ *Be careful with criticism.* Weigh it carefully, deliver it gently and precede it with praise.

☆ *Never bad-mouth a client.* You never know how or when it might return to haunt you.

☆ *Perfect your presence.* Send a professional message by using high-quality materials and solid grammar in all your correspondence. Keep your communication gear (voice, fax, e-mail) running smoothly to acknowledge the time and effort spent by those contacting you. Return phone calls promptly. Dress appropriately. Be punctual, courteous, upbeat and positive. Always say "Thank You."

☆ *Consider everyone a customer.* You never know who will be in a position to influence the award of an engagement to you. Treating everyone with respect improves your likelihood of success from an unexpected direction.

What to Call Your Practice

Perhaps more than any other kind of organization, consulting firms suffer from an inability to describe themselves well through their name, and therefore settle for variations on two cliches:

1. Unbelievably broad and impossible-to-remember generic facades, such as Business Solutions, Management Resources or Strategic Decisions.
2. [Fill in Your Name] & Associates, Partners, Group, etc.

To this end, and with tongue firmly in cheek, *Wall Street Journal* contributor John Buskin offers the following advice (John, by the way, is President, CEO and El Exigente of International Buskin: Not a Corporation, a Way of Life):

Today, the phrase "I'm doing a little consulting" is ominous, leaving the distinct impression that the speaker is a "re-org" victim, logging heavy time in front of daytime reruns of "The Great Chefs of New Orleans" on the Discovery Channel. Hence, if you've actually chosen consulting as a business, you need a company name that implies what you do without actually spelling it out.

Since the essence of consulting is to first listen, then consider and finally respond, a most accurate name for a concern engaged in that process might be Hmm Communications. Muttered by a medical doctor, spin doctor or doctor of mixology, the sound "hmm" implies the nodding, serious consideration given weighty matters worthy of sage revelation. But you can't call your business Hmm—even though it would be a great way for a consulting group to answer its phone. "Communications," on the other hand, is the most wonderful word in the classic pantheon of vague small-business names. All it needs are introductory initials—a spouse's, the children's, a favorite ballplayer's—and your firm has a handle. And if your favorite ballplayer was Heinie Manush, so much the better.

In other words, don't be too cute, too generic or too grandiose. Ideally, you can capture the nature of your service in no more than three truly descriptive words: Family Business Strategies. Unfortunately, the next best thing is to use cliche number two: Your name in a dignified way. If you settle for this, add a subtitle: Travis and Co., executive search consultants.

How to Propose

While there's no guarantee every client will fall in love with you, there's plenty you can do at the proposal stage to make that more likely. Most of all, it has to do with putting yourself in your client's position and developing the kind of proposal you'd respond to if you were that person.

In *Writing Winning Business Proposals* (New York: McGraw-Hill, 1995), consultants Richard Freed, Shervin Freed and Joseph Romano describe in detail the sophisticated models of logic that are at work whenever a buyer and seller of professional services begin to talk. I encourage you to explore resources such as this, to make sure your pitch is hitting all the right notes.

But even more important than using logic to win engagements is to understand the feelings of clients as they embark on a relationship with you, the consultant. Freed, Freed and Romano note that clients often feel:

- ☆ Worried, because the changes you propose may not reflect well on them;
- ☆ Threatened that they'll lose control to you and become vulnerable;
- ☆ Impatient, because the problem at hand is a pain;
- ☆ Suspicious, because they've been burned before.

In response, therefore, you, the consultant must first make the client completely comfortable that there's nothing to fear in working with you. Only then can you achieve the second part of your goal: to persuade the client that you're able to do the work effectively.

What Else Does It Take?

Consultants were born with a magic marker in one hand and a flip chart in the other. Many can't even tell a joke without these props (Some can't tell a joke with them!). But consultants who can truly communicate at the conference table give added value to all the hours of work that lead up these client presentations. Marya Holcombe of Strategic Communications in New Haven, CT, has this advice to consultants:

1. *Tell a story.* Crisp and complete as your research may be, it will be hard to digest unless you can present it as illustrations along a journey that reaches a

meaningful conclusion. Draw analogies to give your facts impact.

2. *Present only what the client needs to make a decision.* Don't tell them everything you know. Tell them everything they need to know. Get your findings on the table concisely enough so that decisions about next steps are based on central issues unfettered with details.

3. *Be flexible.* No matter how carefully you've trimmed your message, be prepared to speed up if interest flags or the client is ready for closure. Adjusting in midstream proves you're responsive as well as confident.

4. *Never overestimate eyesight.* Slides aren't the full message; they're highlights that support the message. If they can't be read—or if they're so wordy your audience is spending more time reading than listening to you—you've defeated your purpose.

5. *Don't tell what it is; show what it means.* Graphs and charts show information visually. Don't get trapped explaining how the graph was built. Instead, use headings to tell what's being measured and reinforce the visual by explaining what it means.

6. *Deliver, don't read.* You may very well have a written version of your presentation to leave with your client, but don't waste their time reading it aloud. Become confident enough of the content of your presentation to deliver it without verbatim notes.

7. *Look and listen.* Most of the content of any communication is nonverbal. Body language, facial expressions and tone of voice may reveal far more than the client's actual words. When you sense hesitancy, probe until you know what's on the client's mind and have responded. Too often we are so busy talking we take the absence of outright hostility as acceptance.

8. *Act like a professional.* Watch your body language: up posture, open hands, solid eye contact, enthusiastic facial expressions.

9. *Be a person.* Get out of your robot gear and let your personality, including your sense of humor, shine through. Smile. Engage the group in conversation, even as you control it.

10. *Plan ahead.* Consider whether one additional day of analysis is worth the potentially devastating impact of sloppy slides and uncoordinated delivery. This can result from handling the transparencies warm from the copying machine on the way to the airport, then discussing who will play what role in the presentation while in the taxi on the way to the client's office. You'll do a lot better if you're relaxed, so meet production deadlines and give yourself time to be yourself at showtime.

"You may not like to dwell on it, but clients do talk to each other about your presentations, especially the disasters," says Holcombe. "It's worth your time to get it right."

Choose Your Clients Well

Another aspect of the famed McKinsey marketing mystique is the firm's "client selection" process. Rather than approaching your practice with the idea that you're hoping someone will want to buy what you do, this line of thinking says, "Fortunate are those with whom I choose to work." Now, you may not want to use that line during a sales call, but it can have an interesting effect on your confidence level if you say it to yourself in the elevator on your way to the call.

And it's more than just braggadocio. It's smart practice management. Why not work for the most attractive clients you can imagine? Wouldn't that add dramatically to the value of the experience you earn in your all-important initial engagements? Further, as a tool to help you avoid working for the wrong clients, it's helpful to apply this approach to any situation that looks like it will lead to an engagement with a new client.

Richard Jacques, a marketing and strategic planning consultant in Hartford, CT, asks himself 10 questions before accepting an engagement with a new client:

1. Is it a quality organization: performance-oriented, substantial, knowledgeable?

2. Does the opportunity have promise of a long-term working relationship with significant repeat services?

3. Does the client or market area served represent real growth potential?

4. Are the client and project adequately funded?

5. Does the project represent a good market fit for my firm?

6. Do I have the capability to serve the client and project well (i.e., talent, experience, manpower and interest)?

7. Will the project be challenging and demanding, yet enjoyable and rewarding?

8. Is the client a good fit for us in terms of values, philosophy and culture?

9. Before devoting more work to winning this engagement, do we have a strong likelihood of getting the assignment?

10. What's our gut feeling?

If you can't say yes to most of these, proceed at your own risk.

I've Got a Client! Now What?

Suppose someone buys your client selection process and says they want to use you? Wow. Time to think again on how this might go, because no matter how many fingers you've held up to check the prevailing winds, you're in the water now and have to start sailing. And what you know so far about the client is like an iceberg, says Bob Schaffer of Robert Schaffer & Associates in Stamford, CT, who consults to consulting firms. Most of the things that could sink your engagement are still lurking below the surface.

Many potential problems center around client readiness, Schaffer says. Illogical as it may be—and that's often life in consulting—the fact that the client has hired you for this engagement doesn't mean it's actually ready for change based on your work. It could even mean the opposite: that you're part of some kind of obfuscation in which the client is creating the appearance of addressing critical issues, but is instead simply buying time.

So, Schaffer says, look for clues to what the organization is truly willing and able to accomplish. What could you do to turn up more such clues? How well does the company convey performance expectations and how are they received? Do I know the names of all the key players: the single, accountable "client"; subordinates who will oversee implementation of our

> Relationships are built on trust, and trust is built on evidence of all kinds. You must demonstrate that you are unfailingly dependable in all things, big and small, and you must make a habit of delivering what you promised (or, preferably, more). Then you will be in a position to say with authority, 'Follow me.'
>
> —Stephan Schiffman in *The 25 Sales Habits of Highly Successful People*

recommendations; others whose cooperation we'll need; still others whose jobs will be affected?

Specifically, try to ask the client questions that offer an opportunity for both of you to discuss the organization's willingness to create change. Schaffer believes that, too often, consultants focus only on technical questions. For example, if they're discussing inventory levels, the consultant will want to know such details as how many items are being stored and how long they take to manufacture. Instead, Schaffer says, consultants should ask such questions as, "What will be different around here if we're successful?" and "What's your vision of what could be achieved?"

Perhaps the key item in revealing client readiness for change is this (which often doesn't appear until after you're engaged): How well is the organization communicating the mandate for change?

Since no engagement is ever perfectly free of resistance to change or other ill winds, Schaffer makes two suggestions about structuring the project:

- ☆ Share ownership of the project with client personnel and track their involvement every step of the way.
- ☆ Avoid projects in which there are long periods of time between opportunities to deliver results. "Even the most competently performed consulting project can fail to produce returns for the client if the work extends over many months," Schaffer says. "Client priorities may shift or the recommendations may go beyond the client's capacity to respond."

Instead, use incremental strategy on any significant assignment: that is, break the work up into limited, focused subprojects with clear beginnings and endings, then start with one that has a better-than-average likelihood of success.

Still Selling?

Now that you're fully engaged with a great client, guess what? Time to start marketing again. "Market consistently, in good times and bad," said the late Howard Shenson in *Shenson on Consulting* (New York: John Wiley, 1990).

Fortunately, some of the best on-going marketing is indistinguishable from your performance. For example, doing outstanding work and letting word of mouth do your talking is central to the growth of any practice. Beyond that:

☆ Are you projecting an image that will keep current clients proud to be using you and attract new clients?

☆ Do your offices have the appearance of professionalism and success?

☆ Does your brochure or marketing letter continue to reflect the best of what you can deliver?

☆ Are you active in professional associations and community groups that expose you to potential clients?

☆ Do you do any pro bono work to build goodwill?

☆ Are you having breakfast or lunch at least once a week with client prospects or others in a position to recommend you?

☆ Have you done a mailing lately that informs clients and prospects of your recent achievements?

☆ Do you advertise, and should you?

☆ Would you benefit from some well-placed PR? Could you generate it by writing an article, or doing some research that would merit news coverage?

☆ Do you make the occasional (or regular) cold call?

Eggs and Baskets

One of the big reasons for continuous marketing is to avoid the mistake Robin Sykes made. Soon after entering consulting as an independent air-conditioning contractor, Sykes hit paydirt with a $180,000 contract from a large company that manages apartment complexes. He figured he was set. Who needed to market beyond that?

Sykes found out four months later when his client changed gears and decided not to renew. The client gave Sykes a week's notice. As Sykes told *The Wall Street Journal,* "You can be rolling along with one major relationship, pulling in great money, and boom! You're history. You're just a bum out of work."

The secret, when you're highly dependent on one client, is to take advantage of the moment to explore other opportunities. Says Chicago financial consultant Townsend Albright, "Having the comfort level of one big client and the energy to explore opportunities to make the client less important to you is the best position to be in."

Some consultants say, on the other hand, that the best situation is never to have a client so important that you can allow yourself to get lazy. Scrambling for business, and having a variety of small-project experiences, may contribute more to your professional development than any single extended engagement with a key client. Being overly dependent on one client can also compromise your ability to challenge your client appropriately in order to achieve results.

Best of all, a nice mix of clients eventually turns the traditional insecurity of being a consultant into something that's actually more secure than having a job. After all, having a job is really like having only one client who, when fortunes turn, can make you "just a bum out of work." But having a generous, well-balanced handful of clients lessens greatly the chances that a single defection will have significant impact on your career.

I started my consulting practice with a key client that, at the time, had the power to make or break me. So, while agreeing to work on a per-diem basis, I asked that client to guarantee me at least 30 days of work, and to pay half that amount in advance. The client agreed.

With that much of a cushion to help me get rolling, I busied myself in accepting a variety of smaller projects to lessen the load of significance my initial client carried. (I was very lucky not to have to solicit beyond a simple announcement of my launch.) Sure enough, just over halfway through that first big engagement, client Number One shocked me one day by announcing that the engagement could end abruptly; management was balking at committing to our recommendations. At this writing, the project is continuing, but at a slower rate. I count 10 other active clients among my great blessings.

These clients are blessings not only for my financial security, but for the dignity of my practice. With pride, I can say to client Number One: "Look, I want to work for you only if we have a reasonable likelihood of achieving results. I'm not here because you're the only organization that wants me."

A Word on Fees

Consulting fees are literally all over the map—they vary according to where you're located and the kind of client base that's available there. In small towns, consulting to small businesses, you might find that fees of $50 to $100 per hour are all the market will bear. In major urban centers, Fortune 500 corporations are comfortable spending much more than that for highly skilled and experienced advisers.

In both kinds of work, many consultants make the mistake of charging too little. "A lot of people who become consultants somehow think less of themselves and are afraid to charge what they're really worth," says Marge Lovero, president of The Entrepreneurial Center Inc. in Purchase, NY.

She cites the example of a senior executive who'd been earning a high six-figure salary, lost his job, entered consulting at $1000 a day, then discounted it to a prospective Japanese client that wanted to enter the U.S. market. Yet his proposal was turned down.

Lovero suggested that the consultant raise his fee, reasoning that the client may have felt that at such a low rate, the consultant didn't have enough regard for himself, and therefore may not be the best person for the job. Soon after he quintupled his per diem to $5000 a day, he won an engagement from a German firm that wanted to enter the U.S. market.

You may not have to quintuple your fee to get your client's attention, but $1000 a day is on the low side of what a consultant with solid expertise should earn working for a large or highly sophisticated organization. Here's one way to figure it: A general rule of thumb is to earn one billable day of consulting for every three days worked. In other words, for every day in which you're actually executing client work, you'll likely spend two days developing that business and carrying out all the other duties of running a consulting practice.

I used this same rule of thumb (see Chapter 4) when I established a goal of billing for 90 days during my first year. If you were to establish a similar target number of days and charge $1000 per day, you'll gross $90,000, which may or may not be enough, depending on your overhead and personal needs.

Some experienced consultants push themselves to much higher utilization rates once they're well-established. Dr. C. David Weimer, an engineering consultant in Poway, CA, now in his 18th year of solo consulting, bills for about 220 consulting days per year, which generates a very nice living while keeping his rates quite reasonable. His secret: A high rate of repeat business (about 70%).

Most consultants end up considering rates comparable to what lawyers and accountants charge, but with a greater range. That's due to the variety of work and the possibility of extreme specialization, which gives rise to such exceptionally high rates as the $5000 per day I cited earlier.

If you plan to buck the trend, and are thinking that you will afford to sell your services for only a few bucks more than you earned on a corporate salary, forget it. The costs of being in business—and of bringing in business—require much higher rates than that. Never underestimate the value of what you'll contribute.

Still Need a Lift?

If the concept of pricing your services still scares you, consider the inspiring words of Alan Weiss, author of *How to Maximize Fees in Professional Service Firms* (E. Greenwich, RI: Summit Consulting Group, 1994), "There's nothing intrinsically unethical, illogical, impractical or illegal about trying to maximize the fees you charge clients. If you raise fees beyond the value that clients perceive in the relationship, market forces will drive them away. Conversely, if they perceive even more value for your services than you're charging, there will be no reciprocal pressure from the market to drive fees up. You must control this dynamic, or you will chronically suffer from the lack of control."

In addition, Weiss offers some creative ideas about whether to raise fees or maximize income, such as:

☆ *Never base fees on time units.* There are a limited number of hours in the day, but no limit to the potential value you bring to a client. Base fees on fulfilling value, not performing tasks. (I haven't broken out of the per-diem mode yet, but I sure like the reasoning here!)

☆ *Never negotiate fees, only value.* If you reduce a fee without a reduction in perceived value, you're indicating that your fees are inflated and not value-based.

☆ *Be visible.* Are you sitting by the phone or using it? Reading the paper or being quoted in it? Listening to dull speeches or delivering sparkling ones? In addition to putting you in front of clients, these activities substantiate your expertise and, therefore, boost your value.

☆ *Set fees within market ranges.* Identify where you want to be with each service. There's nothing wrong with deliberately seeking to be in the lower range of the market as a strategic decision. But if you want to be perceived as delivering higher competence and better service, your fees must reflect this pursuit. Buyers actually adjust evaluation of performance based on their association of higher quality with higher fees.

☆ *Differentiate fees based on the client.* Unless you provide increased value to existing clients, pressure on fees will always be downward. And unless you're willing to charge higher fees for new clients, there will be no relief on that end, either. Don't accept referral business on the same basis as the referent. Maximize value and fees in all new business.

☆ *Raise fees for difficult business.* Recognize that because some business is acceptable only at a premium fee, you must be mentally prepared to walk away from difficult assignments. This attitude will help you demand an appropriate fee structure; raise fees until your level of discomfort is alleviated.

☆ *Cull low-end business.* Abandon any business you've accepted in the past that's at fees more than 15 percent below your firm's average.

☆ *Control payment velocity.* Try simply stating that terms are full payment in advance. Or, use a mild incentive: usual terms are 50 percent payment on initiation, 50 percent within 45 days, but 10 percent off for full payment in advance.

☆ *Focus on innovation, not fixing.* Don't view yourself as merely a problem solver. Try to bring higher value through improvements, not just repairs, and charge accordingly.

How Can You Lose?

Ron Tepper, in addition to selecting the top 10 consulting fields, also cites 10 reasons why many consulting practices fail:

1. Improper research.
2. Overselling but underdelivering.
3. Poor listening habits.
4. Inadequate marketing.
5. Building business, not relationships.
6. Lack of business skills.
7. Undercapitalization.
8. Ill-conceived and poorly written proposals.
9. Communications gap.
10. Failure to properly explain fees and expenses.

Write these common mistakes down on an $8\frac{1}{2} \times 11$ piece of paper and stick it on the wall where you'll see it regularly.

What It's Like Long-Term

Will consulting be just an umbrella during your current employment storm? Will it be a medium-term bridge in your career, but still not a permanent way to work? Is it possible for you to remain happy and grow your income as a solo forever? Dr. David Weimer, the consultant mentioned earlier, offers valuable insight on these questions based on his 18 years in the field.

I interviewed David for *Consultants News* in 1989, 12 years into his solo consulting career, to find out what he liked best and least about consulting. Six years later, I asked him the same questions. The similarities and differences in his outlook tell a great deal about consulting as a long-term career.

Now 60, David spent 10 years in engineering program management, plus 8 years in federal defense contract research, before starting his own consulting practice in 1977. At the time, he charged $250 to $275 per day; by 1989, his rate was up to $975 a day and he was billing for an impressive 220 days per year at that rate. Today, he charges $1,250 a day (very much on the low side, given his experience) and is still ringing up about 180 consulting days a year (he's begun turning down some short-term engagements). He's still on his own, consulting to companies that do business with the government, assisting in market development and implementing growth strategies.

In 1989, what David liked best about consulting included the opportunity to help solve new problems, help companies compete successfully, make new friends, grow as a person and enjoy professional and financial independence.

When asked what he likes best now, without prompting him by repeating his earlier answers, David hit the first item squarely again, "I still enjoy the excitement of a new assignment with new problems. I've never been on an assignment that was exactly the same. Recently, in fact, I had a two-day assignment on a review team—something I've done a hundred times. I really thought I had seen and done everything in this area, but guess what? There was a new problem involved, and not an easy one. My energy level went up 400 percent!"

David's other favorite aspects of consulting have changed, however, at least in order of importance. While he still enjoys helping clients, making friends, growing as a person and being self-sufficient, today—with a few more years under his belt—he gets special pleasure helping young managers and feels he's a much better tutor than he was earlier in his consulting career. He also enjoys a general improvement in his own confidence level as a solo consultant, and takes special pride in engagements in which he's paired with a large consulting organization and is able to hold his own.

In many cases, he says, the other consulting firm starts out quite skeptical about what he might contribute, then finds that he offers a great deal. This is one of David's greatest rewards, he says.

With a bit more perspective, David finds pleasure in the fact that consulting can accommodate his less-than-aggressive personality. "My mode is about 80 percent corporate chameleon, in which I kind of blend in, not just parroting the party line, but listening, receiving." While conventional wisdom might say this approach is insufficiently active, it suits David well and ends up being a big part of his ability to contribute effectively. Today, he pursues this style with ease.

A lot of what David didn't like about consulting in 1989 has also changed. He used to worry about his inability to make long-term plans, clients who didn't acknowledge his contributions, extended travel (about 180 days a year) and financial insecurity. Today, his chief dislike is travel. He's still away as much as ever, and though he's worked out ways to bring his wife with him more often, he finds more than ever that he's "pretty grumpy" walking through airports on Sunday evenings.

But he doesn't worry about long-term planning anymore—even though he had his worst year ever as a consultant last year. With his extensive experience, he knew that business would bounce back and it did. Today, he can count on long-term income projections and not become distracted or discouraged by brief shortfalls.

David also is less concerned when his contributions aren't acknowledged. In its place, however, is a similar concern he wishes he could change about consulting: insufficient support from top management at the outset of an engagement.

"The perception is that you're always hired by the CEO. You sit in his office while he smokes a pipe and ponders the future based on the great changes you'll help him bring about. Then he writes a letter that introduces you as 'his boy' and sends you out to do your work," David observes. "But in reality, you're usually hired by a second-or third-level manager and you have to earn the confidence and support of top management by doing great work without a real mandate from them. It makes the job a lot tougher."

Then again, that may be another of consulting's long-term rewards: The knowledge that you can overcome these kinds of obstacles and still achieve positive change.

"I have a feeling you're not going to be happy about letting them talk you into accepting temporary office space."

8

More Ways to Work

Ten years ago, the kinds of self-employment we've covered so far in this book—starting or buying a business, operating a franchise and consulting—would have pretty much covered the waterfront for executive and professional workers. There's always been an "other" category, but it's been small enough to ignore.

No longer; "other" is big business. In fact, it's at least three kinds of big businesses: freelancing, outsourcing and temping/contract staffing. These specialized components of the self-directed workforce are both old and new, and all are growing faster than employment overall.

"I recently ran a three-day seminar for 300 alumni of one of the major graduate business schools—mostly highly successful people in their late 30s or early 40s," says management guru Peter F. Drucker. "Practically every one of them worked for an organization, but barely half as employees. Fewer still expected to spend their entire working lives as employees of an organization."

In his group, Drucker found a 45-year-old metallurgist who left a Fortune 500 corporation to go out on his own. He's now retained by five companies, one of them his former employer. He found a 38-year-old information specialist who works as a "permanent temp" for a variety of state agencies in the Midwest.

There was an executive from an outsourcing firm who described herself as an "itinerant member of top management." There was an engineer on the payroll of a temporary help firm who works as a plant manager for large companies—on three-year contracts.

How many different arrangements are we actually talking about here? Isn't freelancing a lot like consulting, contracting or starting your own business? What's the difference between temping and contracting? Under what circumstances do you call it outsourcing? Answers can vary on these questions, depending on the perspective of the person describing them, as well as on staffing patterns in the particular industry or organization being discussed. Freelancers in one business may be known as consultants in another.

While there's lots of overlap, there also are important distinctions that create a huge range of experiences for skilled candidates in this evolving workforce. In order to review the range of career choices available to self-directed professionals under these banners, let's attach the following definitions to the three categories:

☆ *Freelancing* is work-for-hire by individuals for a variety of clients. Projects typically are small and often include both creative services and execution. Freelancing differs from consulting in that it isn't advice-oriented or recommendation-driven; it's project-focused. Freelancing is a widely used label for services delivered to communications and media-related industries, and pops up at some level in virtually all businesses, sometimes under the label of "independent contracting."

☆ *Temping and contract staffing* include many of the same characteristics, but carry certain distinctions. Instead of working directly for the organization to which you provide services, you're placed and paid by a third-party agency. And while the work can also be project-focused, temping often means performing an on-going function within an organization, including that blend of project and on-going management work called "turn-arounds" or "crisis management." Temping and contract staffing are typically carried out at the client's location. The difference between them is that contract staffing often includes positions that are (more or less) permanent.

☆ *Outsourcing* is all of this conducted on a larger scale. Rather than simply having a temp in to train and help manage a sales staff, for example, the entire department may be "outsourced," or taken over on a contract basis by a third party. This concept is being applied to more and more functions as organizations seek to trim permanent staff, refocus on a core of creative and strategic activities, and contract out as many fulfillment processes and, sometimes, even manufacturing processes as possible.

Within this category is "employee leasing," which actually is synonymous with outsourcing the human resources function.

With that as the playing field in our New Economy, let's take a more detailed look at each area for an idea of what it's really like to be there.

Freelancing

This title does little to dignify truly professional work, and therefore is often used by its practitioners for its self-effacing effect (as a humble platform perhaps for writing or photography). But it's also a useful term for careers made up of lots of little pieces, sometimes in wildly different kinds of work.

Rostislav Eismont of Richmond, NH, is a freelance artist. As the former art director of several leading magazines, including *Harper's Weekly Horizon, Chief Executive* and *Essence,* Rosti now spreads his design skills into several fields, ranging from publications and logos to landscaping and pottery. He's also a painter when time permits.

With pen, computer, shovel, wheel or brush, he employs vision and considers the meaning of design. This combination of his trades reflects his attitude toward work and life: the sense of balance that comes from a variety of complementary pursuits. It lets you know the process of his work is more important to Rosti than a career ladder in any single direction.

Has he made a conscious sacrifice of commercial success by virtue of his diversity of pursuits? "No one chooses to sacrifice success," Rosti notes, "but if the question is, 'Is it more important than making money?' then yes." Therefore, "if any one of them started generating income to the detriment of my ability to do the others, I'm not sure what I would do."

In this way, freelancing becomes a descriptive term for customized, personalized careers of many kinds, assembled from pieces of pure interest by their creators. Requirements for success include traits and abilities very similar to those necessary for successful consulting, says April Kinser, a New York-based counselor to freelancers. Among those are:

1. Being a self-starter who can develop and follow a business plan, set goals, manage time and stick to a schedule of achievement.

2. Being a good communicator who can interact well with all kinds of people, and effectively relate to the wide variety of clients this approach engenders.

3. Knowing how to network and enjoying it. As with all kinds of self-employment, you've got to spend a certain amount of time finding out what people do and how your interests might be compatible.

4. Knowing how to sell. Even if you work alone, you've got to have the ability to sell yourself and close deals. Learn sales skills, preferably from a good teacher.

5. Be ready for handling lots of responsibility, because it's always yours. Every detail of the big picture is for you to determine and execute. You've got to be able to see how each task fits into your goals so you can set priorities effectively and manage your time well.

6. Be prepared to spend more time marketing than you ever imagined, from at least 20 percent to 50 percent or more of your prime work time. It's a constant event, not an occasional annoyance.

While it's fine if you can do all this, one of the great things about freelancing is the freedom to ignore some of these points if you're strong enough in other areas. If you have to be dragged to work but are a great producer and networker once you get

Many people overlook the fact that working for others does not necessarily mean taking a permanent, or even a full-time job. Many of the country's largest companies are becoming much more flexible in their employment activities.

—James C. Cabrera and Charles F. Albrecht, Jr. in
The Lifetime Career Manager

there, then it may be a simple matter of finding a gimmick for getting yourself to work. Maybe you have a friend who'd be willing to make threatening phone calls to you at 9 every Monday morning. Or, if you're a creative genius who hates selling, you may be able to find a good sales vehicle, such as a person or organization that specializes in marketing and sales for freelancers in your field.

Above all other forms of self-directed careers, freelancing requires flexibility: the kind of flexibility that allows you to identify and deal with your own abilities and weaknesses. You'll also need enough flexibility to ride the ups and downs of too much work (and not enough), and to roll with the punches of a variety of personality and business types who are your customers and clients. To the extent that you have this kind of flexibility, you can enjoy the freedom that comes with it by setting your own pace amid a number of pesky, often competing demands.

As with consulting, your most likely route to success is the one for which you've cracked the marketing nut: either you're naturally good at it yourself, or you've devised a way to make it happen for you. Assuming the former, be prepared to spend plenty of time and effort promoting your skills through networking, advertising and cold calls—or probably all three for a while. Once you identify an opportunity, however, you may, if you're willing, be able to offer an organization better rates than they would pay by using an agency.

As always, your best marketing efforts come from doing good work, then keeping yourself visible by asking for timely performance reviews and feedback.

Please note: As a general rule, you should clarify explicitly the ownership or application of any intellectual property you produce (get everything in writing). And your clients must be careful to protect your independent contractor status by making sure you're free of external controls, subject to profit and loss, invest in your own tools and equipment and determine your own hours and fees.

Temping

While temping has been a part of the workforce for many years, only recently has it gained wide-scale acceptance at the executive and professional level. And since all signs point to continued hiring of employees on an as-needed basis at all levels, we can expect this interesting option to continue to grow.

Middle- to senior-level candidates who take on temporary work are known by a variety of names: interim executives, interim managers, flexible executives, contract executives, professional staffers, short-term executives, line consultants, migrant managers, company doctors, portfolio executives—even business commandos.

Temps of all kinds number almost two million daily, or 1.65 percent of the total U.S. workforce, according to the Virginia-based National Association of Temporary Services (NATS). Of the nation's temp payroll of $24.7 billion, 16 percent is in the professional and technical category, NATS says. Milwaukee-based Manpower alone claims to employ more than 600,000 workers (though that's over the course of a year), and *Human Resource Executive* magazine reports that temporary workers account for nearly 15 percent of all new jobs created annually. In field, the field is growing at 10 times the rate of overall employment, *The Wall Street Journal* reports.

Executive-level temping can take a variety of forms:

☆ It can be project-oriented, in which the temp—or a team of temps—undertakes management of a special project. This could involve a variety of disciplines, but is generally a one-time affair.

☆ It can take the form of filling in for a regular line or staff manager while that person is on leave or on special assignment.

☆ In a third scenario, people can be employed on a temporary tryout basis while the organization determines whether the position will become permanent and whether this person is best suited for the job.

Opportunities for executive and professional temps are growing as more organizations undergo restructuring, mergers, expansion, relocation or downsizing, and develop needs for strategic staffing rather than permanent job creation. Most popular to date have been opportunities in finance, human resources and crisis management. The advantages to corporations are obvious: quick availability of people with task-specific skills, payroll cost control, flexible scheduling and the opportunity to try before "buying" permanent staff.

Not everyone sees the field continuing to grow at its current pace, however. "It makes almost no sense," complains Jeffrey Peffer, a professor of organizational behavior at Stanford University's business school in Palo Alto, CA. "It eliminates all the things that would make someone effective in an organization: knowing the people and knowing how to get things done."

Peffer labels temporary management as unworkable and predicts it will fall out of favor, especially if health-care costs decline under pressure from Congress, making it less expensive to employ people full-time. Adds Paul Hawkinson, editor and publisher of *The Fordyce Letter* in St. Louis, a monthly newsletter for recruitment and career-management professionals: "As active as the temp business has been, I believe that it will undergo some dramatic scalebacks as the economy gets back to normal. If the temp firms are saddled with providing a full plate of benefits, equivalent salaries and the like, then add a profit margin, what advantages can they possibly offer to those companies wishing to employ their temp workers? When this parity occurs, it will be just as simple and cost-effective to hire full-timers."

Nevertheless, until a downtown in this field becomes obvious, professionals with niche expertise will have opportunities to command fees that are 20 percent to 40 percent more than what regular staffers earn, while maintaining relatively more autonomy and less involvement in office politics than salaried employees. On the other hand, you'll likely forfeit such standard and fringe benefits as health insurance and paid vacations, as well as full integration into the corporate culture. You also won't receive much recognition for your efforts, and you may not even get to witness the results of your work.

Temporary jobs work best for the independent, adventurous type of manager or executive who enjoys change and challenge, and isn't concerned with long-term job security. Willingness to relocate is also a plus, since placements can range from a few weeks to a year or more. "When gauging the length of an assignment," says Alan Feder, president of Advance Positions Inc. in Marlboro, NJ, "a good rule of thumb is to triple the employer's estimate."

Unfortunately, there's a limit to repeat business in temping: the IRS requires that you may not work as a temp more than 1000 hours a year (125 eight-hour days) for any single client.

To compound the bad news, as an individual dealing with agencies that specialize in interim-executive assignments, the odds of landing employment at any given time can be quite poor. Many agencies maintain databases of 5000 or more names of executives and professionals who are likely to be qualified and available for engagements, making the competition especially fierce. Getting work often involves making yourself known as someone who stands out from the crowd in some special way. Try to identify and convey your key qualities in a brief cover letter accompanying your resume. (See the end of this chapter for a comprehensive list of agencies you can consider approaching.)

Many executive temps feel the best strategy is to register with multiple firms, particularly those that specialize in your industry or function. Art Fasakas of New York City decided to try a different route. While he approached temping with no expectation of landing positions equivalent to his skills, he was still surprised by what he found. His story, which follows, describes temping's many vicissitudes:

> In 1992, I lost my job as a transportation manager for a Japanese trading company and decided to make a career change. I wanted to become a professional photographer, but needed a way to pay the bills during the years it would take to become established. (I've since decided that the writing profession is more up my alley.) There had to be work I could get right away, but I had no idea what it was.
>
> My wife had been a temporary secretary for about six years, so I began considering that as an option. Unfortunately, she said I'd need to know WordPerfect 5.1 at the very least, and I was PC-illiterate. I started to regret the fact that I'd clung to my typewriter through the four-plus years of my last "permanent" job.

Another roadblock soon appeared: All the agencies I called required at least six months' experience as a temp. I had none. My wife solved both problems when she informed me that her agency, Contemporary Personnel, offered software courses. If I completed its WordPerfect training satisfactorily, the agency would allow me to register. So I signed up for the class, turned out to be the only student, and received extra one-on-one attention. I practiced at home and, after several tries, finally passed the agency's test. I became discouraged, though, when I wasn't offered an assignment immediately.

Fortunately, a friend who'd worked for Kelly Services gave me the manager's name there. I passed the agency's WordPerfect test, and the manager relaxed the minimum-experience requirement for me. I also discovered a government program in my state, called Worker Opportunity Reemployment Center, that paid part of my tuition for an EXCEL course at a local college. Soon, placements started rolling in.

However, my difficulties had only just begun. During the summer, I lost several hours' pay each week because the firm where I was working closed early on Fridays and the supervisors adhered strictly to timecards. Also, the company had little patience for new temps; I couldn't seem to learn my duties quickly enough. Plus, even though I appreciated that temping was keeping me off unemployment, I resented being just a clerk. It was hard to adjust to having to make copies, send faxes and answer phones all day.

A prominent newspaper ad led me to try my luck with Vogue Personnel. The day after I registered, the agency gave me an assignment as the substitute for an editorial assistant at book publisher W.W. Norton & Co. I loved the place, and apparently they liked me, too, since my "two-week assignment" lasted nearly three months—the longest temp position I'd held. During my stay, I learned the Macintosh system and met a number of important editors, agents and authors. There was no opportunity for me to stay on, but switching agencies seemed to have paid off nicely.

Later, a Vogue Personnel executive arranged an interview for me with another client. He failed to mention, though, that dictaphone skills were required. After a further misunderstanding, I canceled the appointment—upon which the agency accused me of losing its client and said it wouldn't use me anymore. This after my star performance at Norton! I was quite angry and ripped up Vogue's cards.

Thanks to another friend, I landed at Leafstone Corp. The agency isn't a household word, but it manages some 4000 temps in a range of jobs. The pay rates were lower, but I enjoyed assignments at the Big Six accounting firm Ernst & Young and at Lehrer, McGovern, Bovis, an engineering firm. I also signed on with Cameo Temporaries, which placed me at

Petersen Publishing and at Mark Partners, a financial services firm. Meanwhile, Chex Staffing sent me to Coopers & Lybrand and a host of other companies.

I'd become obsessed with adding agencies to my stable. This sometimes led to practical and ethical dilemmas, and often to confusion. One morning at Bankers Trust, I realized I'd forgotten which agency I was representing. I had no choice but to ask my supervisor to call personnel and find out. Another day, I called Cameo Temporaries and told the employee manager, "Please tell Carol everything is okay." When he replied, "What do you mean everything is okay?" I realized I had the wrong agency. I apologized, hung up and vowed not to slip up this way again.

At times, I've juggled as many as 10 agencies at once, hoping I'd ensure my five working days each week. Yet while I'm on one assignment, I'm unavailable for other agencies. They suspect what I'm doing, and I gradually lose credibility. Sometimes I accept an assignment for, say, two days. Ten minutes later I get a call for a two-week project. Should I cancel the short gig and upset my first agency in order to accept the "better" offer? Will it really be better? I've found that seemingly attractive jobs can turn out to be unpleasant, undesirable and of shorter duration than advertised.

My wife says that if you work for only one agency, they know where you are and keep you working. My way, I'm scattered around town, without allegiance to or loyalty from any single agency. They don't care whether or not I work, and they place me after their dependable temps. Nevertheless, I'm addicted to multiplicity. When I have no assignment, I go through my stack of cards and call the firms. Sometimes the results are unsatisfactory. Some weeks, I've had no jobs and been forced to return to unemployment for awhile.

For most professionals, temping can help them pay the bills and meet people in key positions while working on a new career or waiting for a permanent job to materialize. It can also provide a taste of a particular company or industry. Occasionally, a temp spot becomes permanent. With the right chemistry, it can happen. And, even if it doesn't, at least you're adding to your resume while you search for something better instead of letting an employment gap grow.

Clearly, temping isn't for everyone, and few are able to handle the headaches Fazakas has encountered. Temping takes place in offices without windows, without nameplates and stationery, without longtime buddies asking you to lunch, or being particularly interested in you at all.

"Sometimes the boss is 20 years your junior," notes business writer Mary Kane. "Sometimes you sit at meetings, ignored,

> Temporary work is viewed by many people in a negative way because it does not provide the desired security, benefits or opportunities for advancement. This is a limited view.
>
> —Howard D. Rosenberg in *How to Succeed Without a Career Path*

recalling the days when underlings hung on your every word. And forget about people buttering you up; they don't have to. You're leaving soon."

Yet, if your ego can stand it, temping offers wonderful opportunities to learn and grow. Says Kane, "Some temporary managers who were sure they were overqualified for their assignments have discovered, to their surprise, that they're learning on the job," citing the example of an advertising industry expert who picked up key technical skills working on a marketing project at a manufacturing plant.

Where to Find Interim Firms

In its latest annual roundup on the market for contract and temporary staff, the *National Business Employment Weekly* identifies 140 agencies placing people in executive and professional positions. Those firms include:

Account Ability Now
1149 Bridgewater Place
P.O. Box 1149
Grand Rapids, MI 49501-1149
(616) 235-1149
Julie Henderson, President
Accounting and data processing professionals for assignments primarily in Western Michigan.

Accountants Connection Inc.
32540 Schoolcraft Road, Suite 100
Livonia, MI 48150
(313) 513-7800
Michael J. LaLonde, President

Accounting and financial professionals and executives for assignments primarily in Southeastern Michigan.

Accountants on Call
(Unit of Adia Services Inc.)
535 Fifth Ave., Suite 1200
New York, NY 10017
(212) 682-5900
Donna Kelly, Vice President
Mid- to senior-level accounting and finance professionals for all industries.

Accountemps
(Division of Robert Half International Inc.)
2884 Sand Hill Rd.
Menlo Park, CA 94025
(Contact local Accountemps office)
Interim executives in accounting, finance and information systems nationwide.

Accounting Alternatives
35 Glenlake Parkway, Suite 550
Atlanta, GA 30328
(770) 671-9647
Craig Miller, President
Accounting and finance professionals for Atlanta-area assignments.

Accounting & Bookkeeping Personnel Inc.
1702 E. Highland Ave., Suite 200
Phoenix, AZ 85016
(602) 277-3700
Marybeth Howard, Vice President
Accounting and bookkeeping professionals for metro Phoenix area assignments.

Accounting Partners
500 108th Ave. N.E., Suite 1640
Bellevue, WA 98004
(206) 450-1990
Karin Garvin or Danielle Reha, Staffing Specialists
Accounting and finance professionals for assignments in greater Seattle area.

AccountPros Inc.
152 Bowdoin St.
Boston, MA 02108
(617) 227-1212
Andrew Goodman, Vice President
Accounting, financial, banking, mutual funds, investment and information systems professionals for temporary and permanent assignments nationwide.

Advance Positions Inc.
9 South Main St.
Marlboro, NJ 07746
(908) 577-1122
Alan Feder, President
Managers in transportation, logistics and materials management for national assignments.

AES Temporary Services
(Division of Alaska Executive Search Inc.)
821 N Street, Suite 204
Anchorage, AK 99501
(907) 276-5707
Diane Bachman, Manager
Specialists in all fields, including engineering, medical and accounting, primarily for Alaska assignments.

The Affiliates
1901 Avenue of the Stars, Suite 490
Los Angeles, CA 90067-6006
(310) 557-2666
Sharon Gerber, Temp Manager
Litigation support specialists, paralegal and legal secretaries for Irvine, Palo Alto, Los Angeles and San Francisco, CA, Seattle, Chicago and Washington DC area companies.

AlternaStaff
(Division of Fortune Franchise
 Corp.)
1155 Avenue of the Americas
New York, NY 10036
(800) 886-7839
Susan Azaria Kanrich, Director
Executives, middle managers
 and technical professionals for
 national assignments in all
 industries.

ALTCO Temporary Services
100 Menlo Park
Edison, NJ 08837
(908) 549-6100
Ken Altreuter, President
Technical professionals and
 managers for food, consumer
 packaged goods, pharmaceutical and medical-device companies for assignments east of
 the Mississippi River.

ArchiPro Staff Agency Inc.
420 Lincoln Rd., Suite 309
Miami Beach, FL 33139
(305) 532-5722
Leslie L. Swisher, President
Architecture, interior design,
 engineering and graphic arts
 professionals for assignments
 primarily in Florida.

**Ascher Interim Executive
Services**
(Subsidiary of the Ascher Group)
25 Pompton Ave., Suite 310
Verona, NJ 07044
(201) 239-6116
Susan Ascher, President, or Eliz-
 abeth Ehrgott, Associate
 Director
Executives in all industries and
 functions for national assign-
 ments, with an emphasis on

human resources, finance and
 logistics professionals.

ASG Inc.
2000 Regency Parkway, Suite 355
Cary, NC 27511
(919) 467-0505
Karen Servance, Account
 Executive
             or
1100 Summer St., Second Floor
Stamford, CT 06905
(203) 356-9540
Mike Baker, Account Manager
Data processing, biostatistics,
 clinical research, decision support and market research professionals (M.S. and Ph.D.
 level) for the pharmaceutical,
 banking, finance, insurance
 and packaged goods industries
 nationwide.

Assisting Professionals Inc.
2000 N. Woodward Ave., Suite
 250
Bloomfield Hills, MI 48304
(810) 647-9800
Nancy Black, President, or
 Sharon Carlson, Executive
 Vice President
Upper and executive management in all industries and
 functions for national and
 international assignments.

Attorneys Per Diem Inc.
(A division of AccuStaff Inc.)
16 South Calvert St., Suite 501
Baltimore, MD 21202
(410) 385-5350
Laura Black, President
             or
1001 Connecticut Ave. N.W.,
 Suite 210
Washington, DC 20036

(202) 737-3436
Felice Wagner, Executive
   Director
Temporary and permanent
   placements for attorneys,
   paralegals, law clerks and
   legal secretaries in Baltimore
   or Washington, DC

Bankers On Call
507 Fifth Ave., Suite 601
New York, NY 10017
(212) 490-2233
Stephen Shuman, President
Bank employees at all levels for
   regional assignments.

C. Berger and Co.
327 E. Gundersen Dr.
Carol Stream, IL 60188
(708) 653-1115
Katie Bartholomew, Director of
   Personnel Services
Library and information management professionals primarily for Midwest temporary
   positions.

Business Partners Inc.
1535 N. Dale Mabry Highway
Lutz, FL 33549
(813) 948-1440
Joe Johnson, Director
Leading edge information technology professionals for
   national assignments.

**Cantor Concern Staffing
Options**
330 West 58th St., Suite 216
New York, NY 10019
(212) 333-3000
Peter Bell, Director
Public relations and communications professionals for national
   assignments in all industries.

The Capstone Group LLC
99 Almaden Blvd., Suite 600
San Jose, CA 95113
(408) 292-0770
David Morton, Managing
   Director
Senior executives in finance,
   administration, human
   resources, operations and MIS.

**Career Marketing Associates
Inc.**
7100 East Belleview Ave.,
   Suite 102
Greenwood Village, CO 80111
(303) 779-8890
Pam Tirk, Director of
   Operations
Technical (engineering, computer hardware and software,
   communications, environmental and regulatory) professionals for temporary and contract
   assignments nationwide.

CFO Associates Inc.
1055 Parsippany Blvd., Suite 501
Parsippany, NJ 07054
(201) 628-0061
Anthony Bergen, Managing
   Director
Chief financial officers and con-
   trollers for permanent part-
   time jobs, interim assignments
   and contract work in all industries in the New York metropolitan area.

CN Associates
100 Smith Ranch Road,
   Suite 301
San Rafael, CA 94903
(415) 883-1114
Charles Nicolosi, Principal
Sales, marketing and technical
   executives and professionals in

data communications, telecommunications and software for assignments primarily on the West Coast.

Complimate Inc.
150 West Iowa Ave., Suite 203
Sunnyvale, CA 94086
(408) 773-8994
Attn: Recruiting Department
Computer professionals for
   national assignments.

**Concorde Temporary
Staffing Inc.**
1 North Broadway
White Plains, NY 10601
(914) 428-0700
Richard Greenwald, President
Accounting, finance, banking
   and office support professionals in assignments tri-state
   New York, New Jersey, Connecticut area.

The Consortium
One Times Square
New York, NY 10036
(212) 221-1544
Martin Blaire, Executive Vice
   President
Human resource, computer technical and finance professionals, attorneys and physicians
   for regional and national
   assignments. Emphasis on
   banking, investment banking
   and telecommunications
   industries. Four offices in New
   Jersey; one in Pennsylvania.

Contract Professionals
P.O. Box 2498
New York, NY 10008-2498
(908) 972-4537
Jay S. Sturges, Managing
   Director

Professionals for national
   interim assignments in all
   support areas, including marketing, management, law,
   architecture, human
   resources, financial planning,
   communications and graphics.

**David C. Cooper &
Associates Inc.**
400 Perimeter Center Terrace,
   Suite 950
Atlanta, GA 30346
(404) 395-0014
Barbara L. Douglas, Director,
   Professional Temporaries
Accounting and finance profes-
   sionals for assignments in the
   Atlanta area.

CounselTemps Inc.
1501 Broadway, Suite 601
New York, NY 10036
(212) 398-1101
Richard Treistman, President
Attorneys for temporary assign-
   ments in all specialties in New
   York metropolitan area.

CT Engineering Corp.
2221 Rosecranz Ave., Suite 131
El Segundo, CA 90245
(310) 643-8333
Guy Schepis, President
High-tech professionals (engineers, scientists, computer
   programmers, software devel-
   opers) for temporary assignments in Southern California.

Culver Staffing Resources
P.O. Box 910569
San Diego, CA 92191
(619) 587-7900
Hope Nelson, Vice President
Office administration, customer
   service, sales, management

and production professionals, and chemists for California assignments.

DAK Interim Executive Services
1100 East Hector St., Suite 388
Conshohocken, PA 19428
(610) 834-1100
Daniel Kreuter, President
Professionals and executives in financial services industry for national assignments.

Dahl-Morrow International
12020 Sunrise Valley Dr., Suite 100
Reston, VA 22091
(703) 648-1594
Barbara Steinem, President, or Andy Steinem, Principal
Director-level and more senior executives in all functions for national and international interim assignments.

D.C. Legal Support Inc.
1899 L Street N.W., Suite 500
Washington, DC 20036
(202) 775-8059
Robert S. Hamberger, Co-Owner
Interim assignments for attorneys in the Washington, D.C., area

Dinte Resources Inc.
8300 Greensboro Dr., Suite 880
McLean, VA 22102
(703) 448-3300
Paul Dinte, President
Senior executives in all functions and industries for national assignments.

Dynamic Systems Services Inc.
3800 North Wilke Rd., Suite 485
Arlington Heights, IL 60004
(708) 259-3444

Michael J. Brindise, President
Computer and information systems professionals for temporary positions in the Chicago area.

EMJAY Contract Services Inc.
1824 Portsmouth St.
Houston, TX 77098
(713) 529-5000
Emma Jacobs, President, or Bobby Lowe, Vice President
Computer professionals for nationwide assignments in all industries.

executeam
(Division of Adow Personnel)
36 East Fourth St., Suite 1020
Cincinnati, OH 45202
(513) 721-2369
Jerry Kern, Vice President
Interim placements for executives and professionals in all functions in the Midwest region.

Executive Choice Ltd.
7621 Little Ave., Suite 216
Charlotte, NC 28226
(704) 543-0396
R. Patrick Perkins, President
Professionals and executives in manufacturing, health care and banking for national and overseas assignments.

Executive Extra
(Division of St. Lawrence International)
6432 Baird Ave.
Syracuse, NY 13206
(315) 432-9288 or 4588
Kathi Rodgers, President
Mid- to senior-level executives in manufacturing, operations, sales, finance, marketing and

engineering. National and international placements.

Executive Interim Management Inc.
(Division of Compass Group Ltd.)
401 South Woodward Ave.,
   Suite 460
Birmingham, MI 48009-6613
(810) 647-4494
(810) 540-2944 (number to fax
   directly into resume database)
Peter M. Czamanske, Director
Senior executives for temporary
   assignments primarily in
   automotive and manufacturing industries.

Executive Options Ltd.
910 Skokie Blvd., Suite 210
Northbrook, IL 60062
(708) 291-4322
Kay Gurtin or Andrea Meltzer,
   Managing Partners
Mid- to senior-level professionals
   in most functions and industries for part-time, interim
   and project consulting positions and assignments in the
   Midwest.

Executive Outsourcing International
16528 Calle Pulido, Suite 101
San Diego, CA 92128
(619) 487-0390
John J. Foley, President
Mid- to senior-level managers in
   all functions and industries
   for Southern California
   assignments.

The Executive Source
55 Fifth Ave., 19th Floor
New York, NY 10003
(212) 691-5505
Richard Plazza or Sarah Marks,
   Principals

Senior human resources professionals and executives for
   short- to long-term temporary
   positions. National assignments, but most in the
   Northeast.

Executives Pro Tem
575 West College Ave., Suite
   101-A
Santa Rosa, CA 95401
(707) 542-2172
Dennis Moss, Partner
Senior executives in sales and
   marketing, finance and general management for assignments in Northern California.

Experience-on-Tap Inc.
Executive Commons
175 Strafford Ave., Suite 1
Wayne, PA 19087
(610) 825-7416
Philip A. Cerasoli, President
Experienced mid- to senior-level
   professionals and executives in
   all managerial and operational
   disciplines and all industries
   in the Delaware Valley region.

The Experts
200 Reservoir St., Suite 305
Needham, MA 02194
(617) 449-6700
Al Porter, Vice President of
   Operations
Interim senior managers, including CEO, COO and director
   positions, for East Coast
   companies.

Express Personnel Services
6300 Northwest Expressway
Oklahoma City, OK 73132
(405) 840-5000
Robert Funk, President and
   CEO

Entry to executive-level professionals for medical, engineering, data processing, personnel, accounting and sales positions. National and international assignments. Express, a franchise company, has 250 domestic and foreign offices.

First Choice Personnel
821 17th St., Suite 400
Denver, CO 80202
(303) 297-2020
Jeff Winwood, General Manager
Information systems, accounting and administrative professionals for assignments nationwide.

Flex Execs Management Solutions
98 West 63rd St., Suite 389
Willowbrook, IL 60514
(708) 460-8500
Karen Murphy or Kris Swanson, Partners
Executives at all levels up to CEOs, for functional and management areas, particularly human resources, finance, manufacturing operations and project management, in all industries. Illinois, Midwest and some national assignments.

Flynn, Hannock Inc.
1001 Farmington Ave.
West Hartford, CT 06107-2618
(203) 521-5005
William F. Coleman or Elwin W. Hannock III
Mid- to senior-level executives in human resources, finance and other functions for regional assignments.

Furst Pro's
P.O. Box 5863
Rockford, IL 61125
(815) 229-7820
Kim Keener, Account Manager
Managers and executives in accounting, systems, manufacturing, business operations, engineering and human resources for temporary or project assignments primarily in northern Illinois and southern Wisconsin.

Garfield Associates/APS
1999 East Marlton Pike
Cherry Hill, NJ 08003
(609) 424-6542
Jay Garfield, President
Finance, insurance, pharmaceutical and advertising professionals and executives for national temporary and contract assignments.

Gibson Arnold & Associates Inc.
550 Westcott, Suite 560
Houston, TX 77007
(713) 869-3600
Jennifer Kruse or Judith Sansom, Recruiters
Attorneys and legal professionals for national assignments. Has six other offices in Southwest U.S.

Glass & Associates Inc.
4571 Stephen Circle NW, Suite 130
Canton, OH 44718-0391
(216) 494-3252
Henry Meyer, Managing Director
Crisis managers for turnaround assignments. Serves more as a

consulting than an interim placement firm.

G/P Contract Staffing
1628 East Market St.
York, PA 17403
(717) 846-0000
Sara Lee Patz, President, or
Lauren Moore, Customer
Relations
Engineering, data processing
and administrative management professionals for assignments nationwide.

Hire Intellect Inc.
1810 Water Place, Suite 240
Atlanta, GA 30339
(404) 850-8502
Julie M. Tokar, Professional
Services Coordinator
Mid-level to executive marketing
professionals for assignments
with companies in the
Southeast.

Hospitality Personnel Services
190 East 9th Ave., Suite 190
Denver, CO 80203-2736
Joan Loken, Director of
Operations
Employees and managers for
hotel, resort, restaurant,
catering, institutional and
other hospitality industry
assignments.

The H.R. Group Inc.
102 South Tejon, Suite 1100
Colorado Springs, CO 80903
(719) 578-3321
Mike Boyd, President
Technical professionals and
executives for high-tech
manufacturing and software

development industry assignments nationwide.

Hunt Advisory Services
(Subsidiary of Hunt Ltd.)
21 West 38th St.
New York, NY 10018
(212) 997-2299
Alex Metz, President
Executives in logistics, including
distribution, transportation,
inventory control, warehousing
and customer service, for
national assignments averag-
ing four to five months.

IMCOR
100 Prospect St.
North Tower
Stamford, CT 06901
(800) INTERIM
(203) 975-8000
Attn.: Director of Resources
Senior corporate division and
functional executives for
interim and "try-out" assignments nationwide that may
convert to permanent. Firm
also contracts for industry-
specific consulting, due dili-
gence and crisis management
assignments. Has offices in
Dallas; New York; Los Angeles; and Chicago.

IntelligentManagement Solutions Inc.
6464 South Quebec St.
Englewood, CO 80111
(303) 290-9500
Judith Geist Pugh, Senior Vice-
President
CEOs and other top-level executives for domestic and international entertainment, media
and telecommunications

companies. Branch office in Gulf Breeze, Fla.

InterExec from MRI
(Division of Management
   Recruiters International Inc.)
1127 Euclid Ave.
Cleveland, OH 44115-1638
(800) 875-4000
(216) 696-1122
Thomas Johnston, Director of
   InterExec
Large national recruiter of
   interim, professional, technical
   and managerial talent in all
   industries, all functions,
   domestically and internationally. Contact local Management
   Recruiters or Sales Consultant
   International office.

Interim Services Inc.
2050 Spectrum Blvd.
Fort Lauderdale, FL 33309
(305) 938-7600
Divisions for finance/account-
   ing, health care, legal and
   information technology professionals. Call for location of
   nearest office.

International Purchasing Service
P.O. Box 39209
Detroit, MI 48239
(313) 459-0030
Thomas Kaucic, President
Interim managers in purchasing
   and materials management for
   national assignments.

International Staffing Consultants Inc.
500 Newport Center Drive,
   Suite 300
Newport Beach, CA 92660-7003
(714) 721-7999 (Fax number)

Engineering, construction, oil
   and gas, marine, power, operations and maintenance, computer and human resources
   professionals for temporary
   assignments primarily in
   southern California. Please
   fax resume and cover letter.

Jackson & Coker.
115 Perimeter Center Place,
   Suite 380
Atlanta, GA 30346
(800) 272-2707
Physicians for interim domestic
   and worldwide assignments.
   Call to be listed in candidate
   database.

Joulé Technical Staffing Inc.
1235 Route 1 South
Edison, NJ 08837
(800) 382-0382
Design, drafting, engineering
   and research science lab technicians for temporary and
   project work nationwide.

JRL Executive Recruiters
2700 Rockcreek Parkway,
   Suite 303
North Kansas City, MO 64117
(816) 471-4022
Larry E. Eason, President
Experienced- to senior-level
   engineering, data processing,
   warehousing, logistics, operations and manufacturing professionals and executives for
   office support, design, construction and management
   positions. Temporary, permanent and try-out national and
   foreign assignments.

Just-in-Time Professionals Inc.
1462 East Shipley Ferry Rd.
P.O. Box 6004
Kingsport, TN 37663
(615) 239-8877
Jim Stewart, President
Manufacturing professionals and managers for temporary positions in the Southeast.

KABL Ability Network
1727 State St.
Santa Barbara, CA 93101
(805) 563-2398
Brad Naegle, President
Executives and senior technical professionals for assignments at smaller companies in southern California.

Lisa Kalus & Associates Inc.
26 Broadway, Suite 400
New York, NY 10004
(212) 837-7889
Lisa Kalus, President
Engineering, construction, facilities management and building maintenance professionals and managers for metropolitan New York assignments.

KPA Consulting and Temporary Services; Borrow-A-Banker
150 Broadway, Suite 1802
New York, NY 10038
(212) 964-3640
Len Adams, Executive Vice President
KPA Consulting specializes in support staff, technical specialists and professionals in banking and finance. Borrow-a-Banker specializes in interim senior managers and professionals in banking and finance. Assignments in New York, New Jersey, Connecticut and overseas.

Klivans, Becker & Smith
22700 Shore Center Drive, Suite 250
Cleveland, OH 44123
(216) 261-3777
Kelley McClelland, Director of Resources
Managers and executives in all functions and industries for national assignments.

Jack B. Larsen & Associates Inc.
334 West 8th St.
Erie, PA 16502
(814) 459-3725
Jack B. Larsen, CPC, President
Engineering, manufacturing and other functional professionals and executives for temporary/contract or permanent placement primarily in Ohio, New York and Pennsylvania.

The Lawsmiths
2443 Fillmore St., Suite 319
San Francisco, CA 94115
(415) 929-1090
Bob Webster, President
Temporary attorney placements in California only. Affiliate office in Los Angeles.

Lawstaf Inc.
(Division of AccuStaff Inc.)
1201 W. Peachtree St., NE, Suite 4830
Atlanta, GA 30309
(404) 872-6672
Judith Serio, President
Contract attorneys for assignments nationwide and other legal personnel for placements in Atlanta.

Litchfield & Willis Inc.
3900 Essex Lane, Suite 650
Houston, TX 77027
(713) 439-8200
Bridgette Dewhurst
Professionals and executives in
all functions and industries
for local and national
assignments.

Lowery, Cotter & Associates
2959 Lucerne Dr., S.E.,
Suite 104
Grand Rapids, MI 49546
(616) 949-2252
Bruce Lowery, President
Finance, human resources and
administrative executives for
interim positions with manufacturing and service industries in the Midwest

MB Inc.
Interim Executive Services
505 Fifth Ave.
New York, NY 10017
(212) 661-4937
Alan M. Levine, President
Marketing, sales, finance and
general management execu-
tives for assignments nationwide.

M2 Inc.
433 California St., Suite 901
San Francisco, CA 94104
(415) 391-1038
Marion McGovern, President
Value-added broker of consultants for a range of assignments, including those in
finance, marketing, information technology, human
resources and operations, primarily for Northern California
companies.

Management As Needed Inc.
2625 Butterfield Rd.
Oak Brook, IL 60521
(708) 573-0910
Harry H. Meyer Jr., President
Primarily operations managers
for turnarounds and continuing operations at companies
nationally.

**Management Assistance
Group Inc.**
10 North Main St.
West Hartford, CT 06107
(203) 523-0000
Jack Tracey, President
Mid-management to upper-level
executives and professionals in
all functions, all industries for
national assignments.

Management Solutions Inc.
99 Almaden Blvd., Suite 600
San Jose, CA 95113
(408) 292-6600
Richard Williams, President
Finance and accounting professionals, supervisors and executives for San Francisco Bay
area and Portland, OR,
assignments.

**Marshall Consultants'
Interim Communicators**
360 East 65th St.
New York, NY 10021
(212) 628-8400
Larry Marshall, President
Corporate communications, public relations, advertising,
investor relations and marketing professionals for temporary assignments primarily in
the New York region.

The Marshall Group Interim Executives
1900 East Golf Rd., Suite M100
Schaumburg, IL 60173
(708) 330-0009
Paul Silverman, President
Senior-level managers for
 assignments in all functions
 and industries in the Midwest.

Maximum Management Corp.
420 Lexington Ave., Suite 2016
New York, NY 10170
(212) 867-4646
Melissa Brophy, President, or
 Nancy Shield, Vice President.
Experienced professionals in all
 areas of human resources,
 including recruiting, compensation, benefits, E.E.O., training and development and
 generalists. Primarily New
 York, New Jersey, Connecticut
 and Pennsylvania assign-
 ments.

McDonald, Long & Associates Inc.
670 White Plains Rd.
Scarsdale, NY 10583
(914) 723-5400
William G. Long, President
Professionals and executives in
 all functions and industries,
 with emphasis on corporate
 finance and financial services,
 for assignments in the
 northeast.

Medsearch
(Division of Alaska Executive
 Search)
821 N Street, Suite 204
Anchorage, AK 99501
Al Finneseth, Manager
Physicians and other medical
 specialists for temporary
 arrangements in Alaska.

Merit Resource Group Inc.
7950 Dublin Blvd., Suite 205
Dublin, CA 94568
(510) 828-4700
Christine Vogensen, Resource
 Specialist
Specialists in all human
 resources disciplines for tem-
 porary assignments in the San
 Francisco Bay area.

Moore Employment Services
P.O. Box 3882
Oak Brook, IL 60522-3882
(708) 357-8118
Ellie Moore, President
Human resources, accounting
 and finance professionals for
 Illinois companies.

Mortgage & Financial Personnel Services
5850 Canoga Ave., Suite 400
Woodland Hills, CA 91367
(818) 710-7133
Doris Loper, Regional Manager
Banking, finance, mortgage
 and accounting professionals
 primarily for California
 assignments.

Mortgage Bankers' Consultants
2711 North Haskell Ave., LB6
Dallas, TX 75204
(214) 841-3100
Jennifer Larson, Director of
 Sales
Mortgage banking professionals
 and executives for national
 assignments.

Networking Unlimited of NH Inc.
67 West Surry Rd.
P.O. Box 802
Keene, NH 03431
(603) 357-1918
Denis R. Dubois, President
Pharmacists and pharmacy technicians for temporary positions in Florida. Branch offices in Clearwater and Plantation, Fla.

Newcomb-Desmond & Associates
73 Powhatton Dr.
Milford, OH 45150
(513) 831-9522
Michael J. Desmond, Chief Operating Officer
Professionals and executives in engineering, manufacturing, human resources, sales and marketing, research and development, finance and banking, data processing and manufacturing support for national and international assignments.

The Nielsen Healthcare Group
P.O. Box 3734
St. Louis, MO 63122-0734
(314) 984-0910
Bruce Nielsen, President
Health-care managers and executives for assignments nationwide in hospitals, long-term care and group practices and other health-care facilities.

Noll Human Resource Services
2120 S. 72nd St., Suite 900
Commercial Federal Tower
Omaha, NE 68124
(402) 391-7736
William T. Noll, President
Generalist executive search firm that seeks information services professionals for contract services nationwide.

Paladin Companies Inc.
875 N. Michigan Ave.,
Suite 3218
Chicago, IL 60611
(312) 654-2600
Brian Brandt, Director of Business Development
or
One Market Plaza
Spear Street Tower, 41st Floor
San Francisco, CA 94105
(415) 495-0900
or
270 Madison Ave., Suite 201
New York, NY 10016
(212) 545-7850
Temporary assignments for advertising, marketing, public relations and communications professionals; includes creative specialists.

Parker Page Group
6924 Trouville Esplanade
Miami Beach, FL 33141
(305) 892-2822
Harry Harfenist, President
Executive search firm that also places interim executives and professionals in all functions and industries in national assignments.

Part-Time Professional Placements Inc.
9812 Falls Rd., Suite 114-293
Potomac, MD 20854
(301) 299-7991
Diane Charness, President
Professionals in all functions and industries for permanent

part-time and temporary positions in the Washington, D.C., metro area.

Part Time Resources Inc.
399 East Putnam Ave.
Cos Cob, CT 06807
(203) 629-3255
Nadine Mockler, President
All corporate specialties for flexible work arrangements in tristate New York area.

PPT/Physicians Pro Tem
1000 Abernathy Rd., Suite 1410
Atlanta, GA 30328
(404) 698-0200 ((707) 698-0200 after 12/1/95)
(800) 989-0989
Naomi Medoff, Vice President
Doctors in all specialties for temporary and part-time assignments nationwide.

The Pickwick Group Inc.
36 Washington St., Suite 240
Wellesley Hills, MA 02181
(617) 235-6222
Cecile J. Klavens, President
Executives in all functions and industries for assignments primarily in the Northeast.

Princeton Entrepreneurial Resources Inc.
P.O. Box 2051
Princeton, NJ 08543
(609) 243-0010
Karin Stratmeyer, President
Senior executives in all functional areas for interim assignments lasting three months or more and for transitional projects leading to full-time employment. Works with large, mid-sized and venture capital groups.

The Professional Resource Group Inc.
2121 Academy Circle, Suite 201
Colorado Springs, CO 80909
(719) 597-3360
Jim Goodman
Technical managers and professionals for interim assignments with Colorado high-tech firms.

Professional Resources Group Inc.
1331 50th St., Suite 102
West Des Moines, IA 50266
(515) 222-0248
Tom Hildebrand, President
Professionals in all functions and industries for assignments primarily in the central Iowa region.

ProResource Inc.
1801 E. 9th St., Suite 715
Cleveland, OH 44114
(216) 579-1515
Donna Fair, QA Manager
Middle managers to senior executives in primary business disciplines and all industries for interim assignments in the Northeast and Midwest regions.

PRO TEM, Professional Staffing Services
1001 S.W. Fifth Ave., Suite 1225
Portland, OR 97204
(503) 228-1177
Jo Rymer Culver, President and CEO
Sales and marketing, human resources and technical professionals for assignments primarily in the Northwest.

ProTemp Temporaries Inc.
150 North Wacker Dr.,
    Suite 1020
Chicago, IL 60606
(312) 346-4300
Scott Bruce, Sales Manager
Engineering, technical, account-
    ing and finance professionals
    for assignments in Chicago
    and Midwest.

Protocol Temporary Services
300 N. Lake Ave., Suite 208
Pasadena, CA 91101
Kelly Lucas, Principal
Accounting, finance, MIS and
    computer programming man-
    agers and support staff, and
    medical professionals.

QCI Technical Staffing
4705 Illinois Rd., Suite 113
Ft. Wayne, IN 46804
(219) 436-9797
William E. Quackenbush,
    President
Technical professionals for
    national assignments.

Quickstaff
P.O. Box 8573
Fresno, CA 93747-8573
(209) 261-9566
Cedric Rees, Manager
Accounting, data processing and
    technical professionals for
    assignments in most indus-
    tries in central California.

Reardon Associates
990 Washington St.
Dedham, MA 02126
(617) 329-2660
Donald Tule, President
Human resources,
    finance/accounting, MIS,
    manufacturing and

administrative professionals
for assignments in New
England.

Reflex Services Inc.
Manor Oak Two, Suite 344
1910 Cochran Rd.
Pittsburgh, PA 15220
(412) 341-4448
Thomas C. Kohn, President
Interim executives, managers
    and professionals in all func-
    tions for local and national
    assignments.

Douglas Reiter Co. Inc.
1221 S.W. Yamhill, Suite 301-A
Portland, OR 97205
(503) 228-6916
Douglas Reiter, President and
    CEO
Senior-level interim executives in
    all industries for national and
    international assignments.

Resource Integration Inc.
P.O. Box 4263
Warren, NJ 07059-0263
(908) 647-7789
Sheldon Kurtz, President
Computer and telecommunica-
    tions professionals for national
    assignments.

**Resource Management
Services**
1501 Fourth Ave.
450 Century Square
Seattle, WA 98101
(206) 223-8991
Cynthia Cross, Vice President
Accounting/finance, marketing,
    human resources and techni-
    cal design and support profes-
    sionals for temporary positions
    in the greater Puget Sound
    region.

RHI Consulting
(Division of Robert Half International Inc.)
2884 Sand Hill Rd.
Menlo Park, CA 94025
For nearest location, call (800) 793-5533.
Contract programmers and technical support in all industries nationwide.

Romac International Inc.
Professional Temporaries Division
120 Hyde Park Place, Suite 200
Tampa, FL 33606
(813) 258-8855
Maureen Rorech, President
Accounting, banking, finance, health-care and data-processing professionals and managers for national assignments. Contact nearest Romac office located in 30 U.S. cities.

Russell Staffing Resources—Execuscope Division
120 Montgomery St., 3rd floor
San Francisco, CA 94104
(415) 781-1444
Geoffrey Easton, Division Administrator
Professionals and executives in all functions and industries for assignments primarily in the Bay Area.

Ryan Miller Temporary Accounting Professionals
4601 Wilshire Blvd., Suite 225
Los Angeles, CA 90010
(213) 938-4768
Lee Ryan, President
Accounting, finance, banking, corporate finance and treasury professionals for assignments primarily in the Los Angeles/Orange County area.

Saber-Salisbury and Associates
25505 W. 12 Mile Rd., Suite 4500
Southfield, MI 48034
(810) 354-4680
Debra Saber-Salisbury, President
Healthcare executives and professionals for interim assignments nationwide.

Scott-Wayne Temporaries
100 Charles River Plaza, 4th floor
Boston, MA 02114
(617) 723-7007
Christopher Smith, Vice President
Accounting and finance professionals for Boston-area assignments.

Search Consultants International Inc.
4545 Post Oak Place, Suite 208
Houston, TX 77027
(713) 622-9188
S. Joseph Baker, President, or Steve McAleavy, Director of Contract Placement
Environmental professionals. Also engineers for oil and gas, chemical, petrochemical and independent power industries.

Senior Career Planning & Placement Service
(Division of National Executive Service Corp.)
257 Park Ave. South, 2nd Floor
New York, NY 10010
(212) 529-6660
David Willcox, Managing Director

Nonprofit organization that places retired executives from all functions and industries in part- and full-time assignments.

Sensible Solutions Inc.
239 West Coolidge Ave.
Barrington, IL 60010
(708) 382-0070
Patrick Delaney, Principal
Primarily senior-level executives for assignments with Midwestern companies in all industries.

Shell Accounting Temps
115 Atrium Way, Suite 122
Columbia, SC 29224
(803) 788-6619
John C. Shell III, President
Accounting and finance professionals for temporary assignments primarily in South Carolina.

Special Counsel International
(Division of AccuStaff Inc.)
20 West 55th St.
New York, NY 10019
(800) 659-9456
Temporary attorneys for law firms and corporations nationwide and overseas.

Spectra International
6991 East Camelback, B-305
Scottsdale, AZ 85251
(602) 481-0411
Sybil Goldberg, President
High-tech, finance, accounting, construction, retail and food industry professionals and managers for national assignments.

The Staff Alternative Inc.
700 Canal St.
Stamford, CT 06902
(203) 323-3777
Catherine Majane, President
Assignments for independent consultants and temporary executives in human resources management, marketing/marketing communications, finance, accounting, general management and operations. Prefers telephone calls to mail inquiries.

Strategic Management Partners Inc.
522 Horn Point
Annapolis, MD 21403
(410) 263-9100
John M. Collard, President
Interim senior executives to help stabilize troubled companies or assist in transitions to new markets.

The Temporary Graphic Service
295 Madison Ave., 14th Floor
New York, NY 10017
(212) 683-0165
Deborah Weiner, Owner, or Rebecca Ellington, Manager
Computer graphics, multi-media and website design professionals for temporary assignments in the Tri-state area.

Tenax Corp.
2035 Lincoln Highway
Edison, NJ 08817
(908) 248-1600
J.M. Gregory, CPC, President
Environmental and telecommunications executives and technical professionals for national and international assignments.

Thor Inc.
4201 Wilshire Blvd., Suite 105
Los Angeles, CA 90010
(213) 932-7222
Attention: SSI
Computer technology professionals for assignments primarily
in Southern California,
Atlanta and Phoenix, AZ.

Thornton Resources Inc.
100 Forbes Ave., Suite 1050
Pittsburgh, PA 15222
(412) 364-2111
John Thornton, President
Engineering, banking and medical professionals for assignments primarily in
Mid-Atlantic states.

Topaz Legal Solutions Inc.
383 Northfield Ave.
West Orange, NJ 07052
(201) 669-7300
Ronni Gaines, President
Temporary attorneys for law
firms and corporations
nationwide.

**Vanguard Accounting
Temporary Personnel**
211 E. 43rd St., 21st floor
New York, NY 10017
(212) 986-1400
Steve Matarese
Accountants for temporary positions in the metro New York
area.

**Western Human Resource
Associates**
316 East Flower St.
Phoenix, AZ 85012
(602) 279-5301
Richard A. Fishel, Executive
Vice President
Human resources, finance and
technical professionals

primarily for Arizona
assignments.

West Valley Engineering Inc.
1183 Bordeaux Dr.
Sunnyvale, CA 94089
(408) 744-1420
Michael F. Williams, President
and CEO
Engineering, design, CAD, software, publications and manufacturing specialists for
predominantly northern California assignments.

The Whitaker Companies Inc.
820 Gessner, Suite 1400
Houston, TX 77024
(713) 465-1500
Bruce Whitaker, President
Temporary physicians and medical professionals (physician
assistants, nurse practitioners
and anesthetists, occupational
and physical therapists); information technology consultants
and temporary professionals;
contract engineers in all specialties; and contract finance
and accounting pros.

**Winston Interim
Professionals**
(Division of Winston Staffing
Services)
535 Fifth Ave.
New York, NY 10017-3663
(212) 687-7890
Doug Russell, Vice President
Accounting, data-processing and
human resources professionals
and executives for New York
metropolitan area assign-
ments; banking professionals
and executives for national
assignments.

Interim Placement Firms by Category

General Placement

AES Temporary Services
AlternaStaff
Assisting Professionals Inc.
Culver Staffing Resources
Dahl-Morrow International
Dinte Resources Inc.
executeam
Executive Options Ltd.
Executive Outsourcing
    International
Executives Pro Tem
Experience-On-Tap Inc.
The Experts
Flynn, Hannock Inc.
InterExec from MRI
IMCOR
KABL Ability Network
Klivans, Becker & Smith
Litchfield & Willis Inc.
MB Inc.
Management Assistance Group
    Inc.
The Marshall Group Interim
    Executives
McDonald, Long & Associates
    Inc.
Newcomb-Desmond &
    Associates
Parker Page Group
Part-Time Professional
    Placements Inc.
Part Time Resources Inc.
The Pickwick Group Inc.
Princeton Entrepreneurial
    Resources Inc.
The Professional Resource
    Group Inc.
ProResource Inc.
Reflex Services Inc.
Douglas Reiter Co. Inc.
Russell Staffing Resources—
    Execuscope Division

Senior Career Planning &
    Placement Service
Sensible Solutions Inc.

Accounting/Finance/ Banking

Account Ability Now
Accountants Connection Inc.
Accountants on Call
AccountPros Inc.
Accountemps
Accounting Alternatives
Accounting and Bookkeeping
    Personnel Inc.
Accounting Partners
AES Temporary Services
Ascher Interim Executive
    Services
Bankers On Call
The Capstone Group LLC
CFO Associates Inc.
Concorde Temporary Staffing
    Inc.
The Consortium
Contract Professionals
David C. Cooper & Associates
    Inc.
DAK Interim Executive Services
Executive Choice Ltd.
Executive Extra
Executives Pro Tem
Express Personnel Services
First Choice Personnel
Flex Execs Management
    Solutions
Flynn, Hannock Inc.
Furst Pro's
Garfield Associates/APS
Interim Services Inc.
KPA Consulting & Temporary
    Services/Borrow-a-Banker
Lowery, Cotter & Associates

MB Inc.
M2 Inc.
Management Solutions Inc.
McDonald, Long & Associates Inc.
Moore Employment Services
Mortgage Bankers' Consultants
ProTemp Temporaries Inc.
Protocol Temporary Services
Quickstaff
Reardon Associates
Resource Management Services
Romac International Inc.
Ryan Miller Temporary Accounting Professionals
Scott-Wayne Temporaries
Shell Accounting Temps
Spectra International
The Staff Alternative Inc.
Thornton Resources Inc.
Western Human Resource Associates
The Whitaker Companies Inc.
Winston Interim Professionals

Human Resources

Ascher Interim Executive Services
The Capstone Group LLC
The Consortium
Contract Professionals
The Executive Source
Express Personnel Services
Flex Execs Management Solutions
Flynn, Hannock Inc.
Furst Pro's
International Staffing Consultants Inc.
Lowery, Cotter & Associates
M2 Inc.
Maximum Management Corp.
Merit Resource Group Inc.
Moore Employment Services

PRO TEM, Professional Staffing Services
Reardon Associates
Resource Management Services
The Staff Alternative Inc.
Western Human Resource Associates
Winston Interim Professionals

Computers/High Technology (data processing, information systems)

Account Ability Now
AccountPros Inc.
Accountemps
ASG Inc.
Business Partners Inc.
The Capstone Group LLC
Career Marketing Associates Inc.
CN Associates
Complimate Inc.
The Consortium
CT Engineering Corp.
EMJAY Contract Services Inc.
Express Personnel Services
First Choice Personnel
G/P Contract Staffing
The H.R. Group Inc.
International Staffing Consultants Inc.
Interim Services Inc.
JRL Executive Recruiters
M2 Inc.
Noll Human Resource Services
Protocol Temporary Services
Quickstaff
Reardon Associates
Resource Integration Inc.
RHI Consulting
Romac International Inc.
The Temporary Graphic Service
Tenax Corp.
Thor Inc.
West Valley Engineering Inc.

The Whitaker Companies Inc.
Winston Interim Professionals

Engineering/Technical/ Environmental

AES Temporary Services
ALTCO Temporary Services
Ascher Interim Executive
  Services
Career Marketing Associates
  Inc.
CT Engineering Corp.
Culver Staffing Resources
Executive Extra
Express Personnel Services
Furst Pro's
G/P Contract Staffing
The H.R. Group Inc.
International Staffing
  Consultants Inc.
Joulé Technical Staffing Inc.
JRL Executive Recruiters
Lisa Kalus & Associates Inc.
Jack B. Larsen & Associates Inc.
The Professional Resource Group
  Inc.
PRO TEM, Professional Staffing
  Services
ProTemp Temporaries Inc.
QCI Technical Staffing
Quickstaff
Resource Management Services
Search Consultants
  International Inc.
Spectra International
Tenax Corp.
Thornton Resources Inc.
Western Human Resource
  Associates
The Whitaker Companies Inc.

Manufacturing/Operations

Executive Choice Ltd.
Executive Extra

Executive Interim Management
  Inc.
Flex Execs Management
  Solutions
Furst Pro's
JRL Executive Recruiters
Just-In-Time Professionals Inc.
Jack B. Larsen & Associates Inc.
Reardon Associates
The Staff Alternative Inc.

Health Care (including physicians)

AES Temporary Services
ALTCO Temporary Services
The Consortium
Executive Choice Ltd.
Express Personnel Services
Garfield Associates/APS
Interim Services Inc.
Jackson & Coker
Medsearch
The Nielsen Healthcare Group
PPT/Physicians Pro Tem
Protocol Temporary Services
ROMAC International Inc.
Saber-Salisbury and Associates
Thornton Resources Inc.
The Whitaker Companies Inc.

Legal

The Affiliates
Attorneys Per Diem Inc.
The Consortium
Contract Professionals
CounselTemps Inc.
D.C. Legal Support Inc.
Gibson Arnold & Associates Inc.
Interim Services Inc.
The Lawsmiths
Lawstaf Inc.
Special Counsel International
Topaz Legal Solutions Inc.

Advertising/ Communications/Public Relations

Cantor Concern Staffing
  Options
Contract Professionals
Garfield Associates/APS
Marshall Consutants' Interim
  Communicators
Paladin Companies Inc.
The Staff Alternative Inc.
The Temporary Graphic Service

Sales/Marketing

Culver Staffing Resources
Executive Extra
Executives Pro Tem
Express Personnel Services
Hire Intellect Inc.
MB Inc.
M2 Inc.
PRO TEM, Professional Staffing
  Services
Resource Management Services

Turnarounds

Glass & Associates Inc.
IMCOR Inc.

Management As Needed Inc.
Strategic Management Partners
  Inc.

Other

Advance Positions Inc. (logistics)
ALTCO Temporary Services
  (food)
ArchiPro Staff Agency Inc.
  (architecture)
C. Berger and Co. (library)
Executive Interim Management
  Inc. (automotive)
Hospitality Personnel Services
  (hospitality)
Hunt Advisory Services
  (transportation/logistics)
InterimManagement Solutions
  Inc. (entertainment/media)
International Purchasing
  Service (materials
  management/purchasing)
JRL Executive Recruiters
  (logistics)
Spectra International
  (retail/food)

Contract Assignments

Gerry Calce, a distribution and logistics manager, had been
working for a major Toronto food manufacturer and distributor
for 16 years when the company recently was sold to a new owner.
In the aftermath, he and other top managers were offered severance packages, but they were also asked to continue working
for the company on six-month contracts.

"It's a six-month contract, but it's more like two weeks due
to the termination clause," which requires only two weeks' notice
to end the contract, says Calce. Nevertheless, he says working on

contract is a good transitional move. "I'm looking at both full-time employment and at [consulting work] on a project basis," he says. "This arrangement is giving me time to network and gather resources to see what's available out there."

As companies reorganize and try to minimize the rising costs of benefits, litigation and severance packages, more prefer to employ people on a contract—rather than on a full-time, permanent—basis. "What many employers are doing is taking steps to protect themselves from complication and potential litigation by employees or former employees," explains Peter Daigle, an employment lawyer with Weir and Foulds, a Toronto law firm.

"For employees, working on contract offers advantages as well as potential problems," says Erin Jones, a career consultant and contract-employment expert in Toronto. Whereas full-time employees generally receive a complete benefits package and are expected to work for a company indefinitely, contractors generally receive no benefits and work according to the terms of a written agreement, which states a specific project start and end date.

Karen Scanlan found contract work an excellent way to build new skills and diversify her editing and publishing background. Development Dimensions International, a Toronto provider of human resources programs and services, hired her last year to handle an assessment project for a major company. Scanlan soon found that her experience in making presentations as an editor helped her facilitate sessions effectively. The project, which also involved assessment and interviewing, took off. Identifying your transferable skills as Scanlan did can help you land contract assignments in an industry you'd like to switch into.

It also may lead to a full-time job. "Contract positions increase your chance of being hired permanently and open the door to new opportunities," says Doug Colling, a principal with KPMG Management Consulting's executive search practice in Toronto.

"Another plus of contract work is the sense of freedom it brings," says Jones. After 15 years as a full-time employee, Deb Chessell started her own independent human-resources consulting practice last year. She says she enjoys the time for her family and the revenue that working on contract can offer. The vacations aren't bad, either.

"The work I do dies down in July and August because most clients are on vacation," Chessell says. "So I shut down for six weeks in the summer for my vacation. Just try to find a company that offers that!"

Chessell also likes the fact that the conditions of employment for contractors usually are spelled out clearly, so she can immediately understand her own and co-workers' responsibilities. "I like to have a good idea of what my role will be," she says. "I get all the users in a project together and set contracts with them. I use a flip chart to identify roles. Then all parties know what my role is. I've found that to be an excellent tool."

The Down Side of Contracting

To be sure, contracting can present some serious disadvantages, so it should be approached cautiously. For example, says Jones, while you're focused on completing a project, you may not have time to look for new assignments. To make sure you have enough time to keep marketing yourself, negotiate your schedule carefully from the project's outset. Propose a four-day week with 10-hour workdays, or request flexible hours so you have time during regular business hours to line up other opportunities and interviews.

Calce, for one, is performing company work in his home office on weekends so he can network more during the week. "It gives me more time to make calls and send resumes, but I'm putting in more hours than I previously did," he says. "It's like running your own business. You must do a lot of networking so you have something [else] set up when the contract period is over."

Indeed, life as a contract employee requires an entrepreneurial mindset, so it isn't for everyone. Scanlan warns that, "Anyone who's thinking about contracts must realize that they'll be exchanging security for freedom. Some people can't deal with that. But I can manage my time and choose my hours."

It's also important to consider your family's attitude toward the arrangement. Says Calce, "Family life is important. If it interferes with family life and your spouse doesn't like it, then [contract work] isn't for you."

Succeeding in contract work requires financial savvy as well, Jones explains. After all, you'll need to charge enough for your services to make up for the corporate perks you'll no longer be receiving, but not so much that you price yourself out of the market.

"I haven't been on salary for years," says Karen Brill, a Toronto-based independent training and development consultant who now works exclusively on short- and long-term contracts. "With contracts, you may not get benefits, [but] usually you get more money."

Vacation, health and dental plans, insurance and other traditional benefits can add 25 percent to 35 percent to the cost of an employee's salary, according to many compensation surveys. You must factor in these and other expenses (such as office space, typing, printing, travel and phone calls) when negotiating the compensation portion of a contract.

Additional questions to consider before accepting a contract position are "When I finish this assignment, will I have new marketable skills and experience?" "Will this project move me closer to one of my career goals?" "Will it strengthen my resume?" and "Could the assignment lead to a full-time position?"

"There's risk and, let's face it, contracting is tough," says Brill. "[But] I want to be paid for the work I do. The realization that the contract could end or not be renewed can motivate you to do an excellent job to justify the company's expense. In an office job, it may seem like you're being paid to just put in time. My money's attached to the task and what I do."

Elements of a Contract

Although you may never have done project work during your career, you may have worked under some form of employment contract without realizing it. For example, oral agreements may have been made when you met with a superior to agree on what duties and responsibilities you'd have in a new job. Or, you may have received an informal employment letter that mentioned you'd be given reasonable notice of termination (except in the case of your being fired for cause) as well as other implied terms.

However, you probably didn't give these items much thought if you expected to remain with the company indefinitely.

Before accepting a formal employment contract for project work, however, it's essential to carefully consider and negotiate key clauses to prevent problems and misunderstandings between you and the employer. Daigle, the Toronto attorney, cites eight main areas to consider when reviewing such a contract:

1. *Job description.* This section should clearly state your duties and authority. Expectations of performance and how it will be measured also should be addressed here. This way, misunderstandings can be avoided and there'll be an explicit reference if a breach of contract occurs.

2. *Management rights.* While the company will want to retain certain flexibility and rights, you'll want to restrict as much as possible the employer's ability to arbitrarily change your job duties.

3. *Term of the contract.* If you're to be hired for a fixed period of time, this should be documented in the contract. This section also should list any terms for renewal of the contract.

4. *Compensation.* Your base salary should be stated here, as well as whether and how pay raises will be implemented. Benefits, vacation time, expense accounts, car allowances and insurance-coverage terms also should be specified. Don't assume something will be provided if it's not in writing.

5. *Exclusive service.* Unless otherwise indicated, you'll be expected to work a regular workweek with regular business hours exclusively for the employer in question. As mentioned earlier, you'll probably want to adapt this clause so you can have time to generate other contract work.

6. *Noncompetition/-solicitation clauses.* Here, the employer may seek to keep you from working with a rival or starting a competing company. If you must accept such a provision, be sure to set as short a time limit for

it as possible. This way, your ability to look for new employment isn't unduly restricted.

7. *Confidential information.* In this section, have the employer be as specific as possible in identifying data and secrets that you can't use or disclose. Again, the terms shouldn't unreasonably limit your search for new work.

8. *Termination.* This component of the contract should clearly outline what will constitute cause for dismissal, as well as how much notice you'd be given. It should also state how much notice you'll give the employer if you choose to quit or resign.

Depending on your level and type of position, contracts can become very complicated. Thus, before you sign, it's wise to seek financial and legal counsel. This initial investment is small compared to the cost of potential litigation.

Paying to have an employment-law specialist review your contracts "is money well-spent," says Daigle. "Otherwise, you could sign away your rights."

Indeed, companies often are advised by their lawyers to tell contract employees to get independent legal advice before signing to ensure that the agreement is binding on both sides. Thus, it's worth asking the company whether it will pay for your lawyer to review the document, advises Daigle.

"You'd be surprised to find that many will. It's in their best interest to do so," he says.

Often, you can negotiate with employers to change clauses in the contract you're unhappy with. Even though the company usually has the upper hand in these negotiations, you'll probably be able to make minor adjustments so the agreement is more acceptable. Say the employer insists on a clause stating that you won't join a competitor for six months after a given project is complete. You may be able to arrange full or partial salary continuance for that half-year period.

Calce persuaded his employer to add some provisions to his contract. "I put in that I want to know two weeks prior to expiration of the contract whether or not it'll be renewed and I negotiated an amendment that if I work weekends at their request, there'll be a surcharge," he says. "If new responsibilities are added, a new pay range will have to be negotiated. There's no vacation per se, but I added in statutory holidays and sick time."

Keep in mind that you'll only receive what the market will bear, says Colling, who helps recruit executives for contract positions. To make sure your expectations are realistic, research compensation levels and consulting fees through professional associations and salary surveys.

But don't be afraid to make special requests, particularly if you have a lot to offer. "You may want to put in a bonus clause if you finish a project ahead of schedule or do something unique," says Colling. "You may also want to negotiate first rights to a position should it become full-time."

Outsourcing

Outsourcing is when an organization contracts out a department or function to be operated by a third-party staffing firm, even if the function is carried on off-site. A recent Coopers & Lybrand study found that 65 percent of the fastest-growing U.S. businesses were outsourcing some of their functions.

Outsourcing enables the parent company to concentrate on its core business and eliminate hiring and regulatory concerns. It's a viable alternative to an outright downsizing, and other advantages may include higher quality production and more efficient service.

Although outsourcing is usually handled by established companies, its growing popularity can represent a substantial opportunity for a knowledgeable industry veteran wishing to become an independent contractor (back to freelancing!). Many creative, self-directed employment possibilities are available by applying this concept on an individual basis. Could you perform a necessary function for an existing firm, such as personnel management, purchasing, accounting, advertising, PR or plant maintenance? This also is a way for your former employer to become your first and best client.

Executives at Freeport-McMoran, the New Orleans-based natural resources conglomerate, have discovered this in spades. Here are two examples: Garland Robinette and his staff of 23 in Freeport-McMoran's corporate communications department launched Planit Communications as an independent entity with Freeport as its largest client; and Dr. Jim Miller, vice president of environmental affairs joined with fellow VP Roy Pickren to spin out an engineering and technical support team that became Crescent Technology, and employs 50 former Freeport workers.

Where It's All Going

More variations—and certainly more labels for the basic structures we've covered—are likely to emerge as these fields continue to grow. And prospects are that growth will be substantial.

"Contract employees are growing like rabbits on a hormone diet," says Ralph Palmen, a business developer and trainer for Express Personnel in Oklahoma and a consultant on contract staffing issues. Palmen cites a *Forbes* magazine report forecasting that, by the year 2000, half of America's workforce will be employed on a contract basis. Palmen finds seven reasons for the rapid expansion of the market:

1. *Flexibility.* By using contract employees, companies are learning how to build flexible work teams of highly specialized position players, around a core of company employees who understand how to orchestrate the skills of each person into a highly productive unit. Palmen says no work form offers greater flexibility than contracting, for both employers and workers.

   "The needs of both parties are met in a unique and satisfactory way," Palmen says.

2. *Rising wages.* Contract employee wages are rising faster than wages for all workers since higher productivity and profits available through effective contract staffing allow organizations to pay more per hour.

   "Highly skilled employees who are performing a job well will be better compensated," says Palmen. "It's like a professional baseball team being able to have an offensive and a defensive team. Most baseball teams have players on their minor-league teams who are better offensively or defensively than some of their major-league players. However, the need to field a team of players with both offensive and defensive skills requires a more complete ballplayer who might not be as outstanding in one area. If they could field a team of their best hitters on offense and their best defensive players on defense, you might see a better overall baseball game."

3. *Independent work.* "Today's generation of workers have been raised on the mother's milk of 'do it your way,'" Palmen observes. "No group of workers in history has been given such extensive latitude in the choices they make. They have grown up in unstructured environments where they have worked at their own pace and made their own choices. Many of them have literally raised themselves." So, he says, to expect these people to fit into a structured work group is often beyond their life experiences and something they adjust to only with great difficulty. But a self-directed work plan is something they can relate to.

4. *Worker strategies.* With fewer new workers arriving on the job market since the end of the rising Baby Boom generation, there's a long-range trend afoot toward worker shortages. Until now, these have been avoided by the entry of more women into the job market. Many positions have also been filled by workers who have been less than fully employed, such as minority and disabled workers.

    "As worker shortages accelerate, we find that portable workforces that can be deployed throughout the community have great appeal," Palmen says.

5. *Training needs.* "The challenge of training workers in the future presents a logistical problem because of the specialized equipment and procedures required for short-run manufacturing processes," Palmen asserts. "As large companies are increasingly decentralized and many smaller companies evolve, the need for third-party training and deployment become even more necessary." He predicts the growth of massive training organizations. "These needs can best be filled by organizations that have the capacity to amortize training costs over a large number of work sites."

6. *Government regulations.* Record-keeping in support of mandated government regulations is a significant challenge for businesses of all sizes. "Staffing firms that are better organized to meet this need will get an increased share of the workforce to manage," Palmen predicts.

7. *Workplace complexity.* As work becomes more technical and complex, so grows the need for greater expertise. "Fast-growth companies have found that it's easier to grow when you concentrate on a few key functions," Palmen says. Therefore, more and more companies—including many startups—are outsourcing as many functions as possible, including those related to human resources. Again, staffing firms that develop the skills needed will play an increasing role in recruiting, training and retaining flexible work teams, he observes.

More Routes to Self-Directed Careers

Time to check our progress. What have we learned so far? Where next? In Chapters 1, 2 and 3, we examined what's going on in the New Economy, as best we can tell from what sometimes seems like the eye of a workplace hurricane. That sets the stage for executives to consider alternatives to the 9-to-5, lifetime care of paternalistic employers.

Then we looked carefully at each of the alternatives: starting a business, buying a business, operating a franchise, becoming a consultant, and working as a freelancer, temp or contract staffer.

While we haven't mentioned it yet, there's another significant step in the process toward a self-directed career: getting education or training that would prepare you specifically for entrepreneurism in a particular way. Enrollment in M.B.A. programs is at an all-time high, and there's more out there than ever in the way of specialized training. The growth of the contracted-staffing industry alone has led to a wealth of training and management development instructional programs.

At the same time, many colleges and other educational institutions are offering career counseling and business opportunity-matching services for alumni. See the Appendix, Resources, for details on places to look for appropriate programs that might lead you more firmly into entrepreneurism or some form of a self-directed workstyle.

As a final thought on the spectrum of self-directedness: Perhaps, if your ultimate dream is a great job in the traditional sense, self-employment is an ideal route to the top. Tough as it is, you'll learn unimaginably big and little things that have the potential of taking you to a level you couldn't have reached if you'd climbed the organization from within.

Given all the reasons for and all the forms of self-directed careers, it's about time to hit the ground running. Our final chapter will get you up to speed for day one on your own. Buckle up.

"We'll call you as soon as we've run your fingerprints, completed your background check, and looked over the results of your lie-detector test."

9

Getting Started

Remember your mom's advice: "Begun is half done. A journey of 1000 miles must begin with a single step. He who hesitates is lost. There's no time like the present. Seize the day. Just do it!"

Cliches abound because there's a great deal of powerful truth in the original thought behind them, as well as all its variations and implications.

The power in this thought comes from the importance of its essence: It's about what we're doing right now. If you believe that truth is the doing, and not a destination, then you're aware of the awesome significance of the process of taking action—any action. In fact, making the most of the moment is so important to our personal and professional success that we have to be careful not to let it freeze us into inaction.

Any golfer who's felt the terror of a means-everything two-foot putt can attest to the power of the moment and its ability to short-circuit even simple, intended physical behavior. Fritz Perls said that humans are the only animals capable of getting in their own way.

In the realm of work and careers, the bigger and more important the challenge, the more difficult it can be to begin. We're often unwilling to take that first step. Is it that we fear failure? Sometimes we entertain that first big step, flirt with it, but remain afraid to commit to it. Sometimes this is true not only for important challenges, but also for little ones. For many reasons, we can get into deeply unproductive habits of avoiding decisions and commitments. In addition, it can become a lonely battle to overcome this behavior when we find others around us who suffer from the same inertia (even if for different reasons)—and may even revel in finding others who share their shortcomings.

When things get this bad for me, I try to think about one of my favorite movies, "What About Bob?"—the one where hopelessly neurotic Bill Murray learns to take "baby steps" and enjoys success beyond his wildest dreams. Knowing I could never be as bad off as he was, I can begin to put my challenges in perspective by thinking about the smallest, most easily achievable things I could do to advance my quest. Then I make a list of them and pick one off the top.

In that spirit, this chapter is about the details of being in business—not all of them—but enough to provide you with a few possibilities for baby steps.

Often, the easiest way to make an "initial" move is to note that it may already have happened and that, with a quick look back, you find you're already well down the road. By now you've probably given a great deal of thought to how you plan to self-direct your career, and those thoughts have likely prompted plenty of brainstorming and fact-gathering along one of the paths discussed in this book. You've probably got at least the rudiments of a home office going and have a business plan of sorts. Maybe you've already been in business but are reading this because you know you didn't think of everything the first time around.

No one does. So here among the details are a few high points about business basics and work space, technology, finances, time management, the psychology of self-employment, your health, your management style, negotiating—even a few reminders on good business manners. Although we're talking details, they're details shared by all kinds of individually instigated businesses.

Discover the SBA

There's no more cost-effective way to get up to speed with all the basics of self-employment than taking an introductory course in small business management through your local Small

Business Administration office. I did this more than a year before I went on my own—well before I had any real intentions of being self-employed, but just as a way to get myself thinking about what it would be like.

These courses are such a good deal you really can't go wrong: Mine was just $75 for five evening-long classes (one a week), plus practically unlimited opportunities to get special help from my instructor and the guests he brought to speak to our class. Further, I became acquainted with a dozen other local people in various stages of the search for self-directed careers, heard their stories, compared my own experiences and gained lots of confidence in my ability to be successful.

A good introductory course in small-business management covers strategy (have you developed a business idea that's good for you, and where do you want to go with it?), market analysis (is there a market for your idea?), marketing (how will you reach your market?) and finance (how to write a business plan, develop budgets and cash-flow charts and find financing). Further, the SBA is well-equipped to lead you toward additional sources of information or help you solve problems specific to your enterprise. Don't overlook this wonderful, comprehensive resource that's subsidized by your tax dollars.

You Name It

What are you going to call your business? Has it been obvious from the beginning or does it seem like you'll never settle on exactly the right signature? Now's the time to cast it in print. You may recall, in Chapter 7 on consulting, that we discussed not being too generic, grandiose or cute. Here, in case you're still struggling with this one, are some words of advice from home-business gurus Paul and Sarah Edwards:

1. Make a long list of words that describe what you want your business to reflect. Think of adjectives, time, place, uses, feelings, features, humorous aspects of what you do, images you have about the business, results you produce and products you offer.

2. Piece the words together. Play with them. Consider phonetically pleasing combinations, puns and acronym possibilities.

3. Review your creations in terms of what you know about your potential customers. Are they traditional, New Age, alternative? High-tech or low brow? Do your customers come to you for expertise or support? Are they at the top, middle or bottom of their field?

   "It's this kind of soft information that enables you to come up with a name with some pizzazz," the Edwardses say.

4. Select the best names you've created and list them on a sheet of paper. Play with them in your computer, using different type faces and arrangements of letters. Then ask 25 customers or prospects to look over the list and tell you which company they'd be most inclined to contact and why.

5. Make sure your name meets most of the following criteria:

   ☆ Easily identifies what you do.

   ☆ Stands out from the competition.

   ☆ Is readily remembered.

   ☆ Is neither too short nor too long.

   ☆ Is simple to spell and pronounce.

Once you've got something you and your customers agree is on target, you can start worrying about whether you're able to use it and whether you want to take action to protect it.

This process begins with a look through the Yellow Pages in all of your potential markets (see the appendix of resources about on-line versions if yours is a wide-ranging market). Then get clearance from your state's Secretary of State's office (or other agencies they'll suggest), and check with your county court for records of informal "doing business as (DBA)" activities that may have preceded yours.

You'll know before even checking with these sources whether your name is likely to have had any precursors, past or present. By now you know your competition well. So one good question is whether you even need to register it for $50, or whatever they charge in your state. Probably you do, at least if the name of your company is anything beyond your own name. In my case, it wasn't. I'm in business simply as David A. Lord and haven't found a need to protect that further, given a substantial history at my current address and the specialized nature of my

> In creating, the only hard thing is to begin.
>
> —James Russell Lowell

work. But I'm an exception here. Most businesses—anything beyond your own name—should at least seek state registration to prevent others from creating any confusion in the market (protection is limited in some states).

For a few hundred dollars or more in legal fees, you can go further—nationally or internationally. A trademark or patent attorney can advise you of others using a name that's exactly the same, or very similar. If, instead, everything looks good, you can apply for a trademark or service mark registration from the federal government (see the Appendix, Resources) if you intend to market outside your state. While that application is in progress, you can begin marking your brand name (if you want to) with a TM or SM symbol next to it. Later, when it's been approved and registered, you can use a circled R—®.

What Kind of Company Is This?

Speaking of professional help, you'll want to consult your accountant on the kind of structure that best suits your business and personal circumstances. Briefly, your choices include:

Sole Proprietorship

This is the easiest to establish since it requires no documentation. You just pay personal income taxes on all your business's income (after whatever deductions you and your accountant agree on) and pay those taxes on a quarterly estimated basis. That's about it, and it's how many people start. Eventually, you may want to move into another structure as the business grows, for either of two reasons: because in other structures you can gain personal protection against liability for your business's actions (or neglect); or because you want to create something that can outlast your personal involvement.

Partnership

If you're one of two or more principals getting a business going, you'll have to consider this (or incorporation). It's like being a sole proprietor, except that there's an additional partnership agreement that defines the relationship of shared ownership. Liability-wise, this is a tough one because all partners are liable for the actions of all others.

A common bit of advice to those entering a partnership agreement is to include a plan for dissolving the partnership if and when it becomes necessary under all imaginable circumstances. The unthinkable is more likely than you think! But before the unthinkable, you can enjoy most of the simplicity of sole proprietorship as a group. You will file tax returns for the partnership even though it will pay no taxes. Instead, you pay personal taxes on the income from your ownership share. Life can get complicated in partnerships, however, even without disagreement. There's great flexibility in determining ownership, allocation and distribution of profits, and capital contributions that affect all of those—which also means there's potential for great complexity (red tape and headaches).

Corporation

When you incorporate, you give birth to a being capable of acting independently of its parents (shareholders) whose liability is generally limited to the corporation's assets. A corporation can sell shares of itself in order to raise capital and can be sold in its entirety to new owners. You can be either a C (regular) corporation, which retains its profits and losses except for what's distributed among shareholders as dividends. Or, as a small business, you can become a Subchapter S corporation, in which profits and losses flow directly to shareholders, with the corporation paying no taxes.

Many more considerations develop when tax laws are applied to your particular situation, so I'll stop here and suggest that you consult your accountant for a careful look at your

> Gardens are not made by singing, "Oh, how beautiful," and sitting in the shade.
>
> —Rudyard Kipling

plans. And if you find you don't have to incorporate, all the better. It brings with it a great deal of time-consuming and potentially expensive overhead.

William Stolze, author of *Start Up: An Entrepreneur's Guide to Launching and Managing a New Business* (Hawthorne, NJ: Career Press, 1994), relates his own experience, "I once had a small software business that I formed as a hobby and made the mistake of incorporating too soon. It cost me about $500 to form the corporation, about $1000 a year in franchise tax and legal and accounting fees, and, finally, about $1000 to terminate the corporation." Don't get into it unless the reasons are clear and convincing.

Limited Liability Company

Here's a new twist that offers the flexibility of a partnership in income and profit distribution, plus the protection against liability of a corporation. State laws governing LLCs vary. Check them out.

Insurance

Most of the liability concerns of a sole proprietor or partner can be taken care of with a good insurance policy. Types of policies vary greatly depending on the kind of business you're in, so ask a trusted insurance agent. In addition to protecting your personal assets against business-related claims, you'll want to consider insurance on business equipment, inventory and documents, as well as liability for injuries occurring on your company's premises, or other liabilities your work may create.

Health insurance will apparently continue to be a key hurdle in self-employment for the foreseeable future. For many small businesses (mine included), it's the single largest monthly bill to pay. While as an employee you probably enjoyed coverage that included all or almost all doctor and hospital fees, as an independent seeking to cover yourself and your family as you launch a new enterprise, your approach will shift. Because of the high cost of full coverage, you'll likely wind up opting for coverage that offers a lower basic premium but has a high deductible, which means you pay for all kinds of routine care as it occurs and are covered only for major illnesses or injuries.

If an equitable system of portable health coverage were ever adopted in the United States, it would be a huge boon to entrepreneurism. Stay tuned to your options and, if you're covered now under COBRA (the option to continue, for up to 18 months at your own expense, coverage provided by your previous employer), you should be planning to get out of it and into a new program while you're healthy. Don't wait until your COBRA eligibility expires. You'll also want to look at disability and/or term life insurance coverage now that your business depends so heavily on your personal ability to be there.

Home Work and Your Work

I raised the idea of working at home in Chapter 3 because I feel it makes so much sense, it may be worth shaping your business around, rather than shaping your life around your work in another locale. Even someone thinking of opening a retail store can consider other ways to serve customers that could make working at home viable. But clearly, working at home isn't for everyone or all businesses.

Your home may simply not be suitable, for example, for reasons of location, available space, family considerations or whatever. Above all, don't locate at home only because it's less expensive. If all other signs point to leasing business quarters, go for it. There's almost nothing more important to the success of your business than your personal comfort at work, since you're going to be spending a huge amount of time there! And if location away from home is key to reaching your customers, seek the best location available and make its cost an immovable, cornerstone item in your business plan.

If your home has room for corporate headquarters and is compatible with your business in at least a few other ways, you're golden. You don't have to go to work every Monday morning just to cover the rent. You've just moved hundreds or thousands of dollars every month straight to the bottom line.

Let's conduct a compatibility check. What are the key practical considerations of basing your business at home? In doing so, let's imagine we're setting up an office that's the home office of a very small company—just you, or no more than another part-time employee or two—or, it could be your home satellite office for a larger enterprise based elsewhere. (Remember my advice in Chapter 3: You've really got to have some kind of office at home anyway, because being self-directed isn't something that's turned on and off at 9 and 5 everyday. So it's all just a matter of degree: How wonderful will your office at home be?)

1. *Will you be able to work regular hours at home?*

This seems to be everyone's chief concern. I wondered about it myself and have answered the question dozens of times since starting out. Well, the right answer might not be yes. Says Madeline Bailey, owner of Quail Creek Computing in Austin, Texas, and an adviser to small businesses, "Do not, I repeat, do not try to keep regular working hours. Why did you bother to work at home in the first place if not to control your own schedule?"

What a refreshing point of view! And she's right, of course. One great thing about working at home is the opportunity to put in your time when you're most ready, willing and able to do so—and that doesn't necessarily happen on a 9 to 5 schedule. My most productive hours are between 6 AM and 9 AM, when I can count on solid creative time before business-hours calls start interrupting or redirecting my day. Also very valuable: the odd hours of reading and record-keeping I can put in during the evening, or on rainy-day weekends, or whenever.

By getting things done when opportunities arise—sometimes even in little bits of time—I prepare myself for other opportunities (including personal and family pursuits) that present themselves during "regular" working hours.

2. *How do you avoid all the distractions at home?*

Again, the answer for me is to question the question: Why would I want to avoid *all* the distractions? Don't I enjoy being at home? True, it's important to be able to create privacy and quiet at key times. My office has a door. But I also love playing with my kids when the spirit moves us, and being around to make a meal, mow the lawn or what have you.

When people ask, "How do you get anything done?" I say, "It's easy because I love my work." If I didn't love my work, that would be a problem, because yes, there are lots of distractions and I enjoy a lot of them! Fortunately, because I enjoy my work at least as much as everything else that goes on around here, I have no trouble putting in enough hours to get my work done. To me, that approach makes working at home an achievable balance rather than an impossible conflict. If, on the other hand, your work is tough and you resent any distractions, you're asking for trouble by setting up at home. You really can't screen them all out.

That said, there are some obvious detours to avoid:

☆ *The refrigerator.* How easy it is to decide that a little smackeral right now would be just the thing to go with this chapter I'm writing! . . . . Okay, I'm back, with a glass of water. For all those moments—tense, thoughtful, frustrated, undecided—when something *else* to nibble on would be great, I try to settle (at least some of the time) for a big glass of New Hampshire well water. Keep a good supply around at all times.

☆ *Other people.* Maybe this is too broad a category. Some people—your spouse, your children and parents—will always have priority over your work when they need you. On the other hand, you have: close friends with too much time on their hands; acquaintances with idle thoughts; volunteer organizers pitching your opportunity to help the community; distant friends and relatives wondering what you're up to; and parents of your kids' friends who were hoping you wouldn't mind doing the driving today because, well, you work at home anyway, don't you?

These folks may need a gentle reminder now and then that you indeed have to work as many hours as they do, even if you're not making a public display of heading off to the salt mines daily (anymore). Otherwise, the rumor will continue to spread that your vague ramblings about being in business for yourself are just a polite cover for the massive inheritance that came your way last year—so they can take advantage of your every waking hour.

☆ *Yourself.* (Excuse me. Just a few more minutes on this crossword puzzle and I'll get back to telling you what I was going to say here. . . . Okay, I'm back.) Healthy curiosity about the world can take on frightening dimensions when you're unleashed with a world of multimedia to explore every day, a houseful of great little projects there never used to be enough time for, the opportunity to stay in shape with a good long walk or workout morning and afternoon, the occasional business meeting on the golf course, those great books you've been waiting all your life to actually read, and so on. Remind yourself that even such constructive play needs to take a back seat to the work you're doing that buys the groceries.

☆ *Your big ideas.* This route to nowhere isn't specific to home-office workers. Anyone can fall on their face chasing a bogus business opportunity. Allot time for brainstorming, but be rigorous about the true potential of each project before you begin to spend large amounts of your only unique asset: your time.

That's about it: If you can stay away from just these four minor diversions—the refrigerator, other people, yourself and your big ideas—you'll have no trouble working at home.

3. *Can you serve your customers well in a home office?*

Now that some 16 million Americans work from home, your potential clients and customers are beginning to get comfortable with the idea that perhaps some people actually do conduct professional-quality businesses from home. More and more tools are available to help make this possible for you (such as great phone systems and services).

The real question is, do you want or need to go to the extent of disguising the fact that your office is at home? I hope not, because I can't really recommend including such a basic deception in your dealings with customers and clients. Maybe it's your intention to let customers in on the secret as soon as you've had a chance to make a first impression on them, free of any anti-home-office bias on their part. Well, if you really feel it's necessary, here are some tips, including a few uncovered recently by *Wall Street Journal* reporter Katia Brener:

☆ Hire a hidden typist. David Young, a communications consultant in Township, PA, types "mbs" at the bottom of his letters, as if they were his secretary's initials. In fact, they stand for "make-believe secretary."

☆ Put the family behind a glass wall. Mike Pitts, an advertising consultant in Manhattan Beach, CA, keeps family noises out of his office background (without losing all contact with his family) with a set of French doors leading to his office. The doors are always closed, but children or visitors can see whether Dad would mind being interrupted without actually disturbing him.

☆ Use your tools well. If you want to invest in state-of-the-art computer and communications equipment, record a message that sounds just like the digital robot inside your telephone, or send out a flyer made up of the hokiest cookie-cutter graphics imaginable that scream, "I FOUND THIS ON PAGE ONE OF THE MANUAL," go ahead. But with a little creativity, personalization and professional help if you need it, you can present a with-it, dignified face and ear to the world. Make sure you look and sound as good as your gear allows.

☆ Give your address the best possible positioning. It's not really worth moving from Broken Bones Trail to State Street in order to give your home-based start-up stationery the right ring. So if your street address is hopelessly suburban-sounding or just plain ugly, use a post office box (at least until you have to disclose your street address for courier service). Many mail-box franchises offer suite addresses if that approach suits your fancy.

☆ Reach out to meet someone. To spare your family the agony of appearing well-behaved, and to avoid the likelihood that you'll be under the kitchen sink when your influential guests arrive, schedule meetings at comfortable public rooms. One of our local banks will loan office space as well as money. You could even consider this new wrinkle on the commercial real-estate scene: "corporate identity settings."

In Fairfax, VA, InterOffice Management offers rentals of offices and conference rooms, along with a listing in the building's lobby, a proper address there and a variety of support services,

It is the greatest of all mistakes to do nothing because you can do only a little. Do what you can.

—Sydney Smith

for as little as a few hours a month so you can make the right impression on key business-meeting occasions.

On the other hand, wouldn't you rather be up-front about your home office and put your energy into delivering such outstanding products or services that no one will care where you work? Of course.

4. *Can you handle the solitude?*

This last measure of whether your business is suited for home-basing is the most personal and subjective, and can even lead to surprising confessionals. Humorist John Buskin, based at home in New York, offers these reflections on his 10 years as a house-worker:

> Often I'd fall to my knees, sobbing in isolation, offering up insane acts of charity or contrition in return for a phoned summons to a business lunch. I talked to myself incessantly. I sang as well, at a passionately high volume, opting for various selections from an eclectic repertoire that included the spirited, zippy Trini Lopez version of "If I Had a Hammer"; the giddy instrumental, "Holiday for Strings"; and the soulful, introspective "I'm a Girl Watcher."
>
> When checks arrived on time, I'd ape-walk through the house, cackling maniacally. When they didn't, I'd shriek with paranoid visions of salivating office dingoes shredding my work, taking credit for it or, worse, performing it aloud in a Dumb Guy persona to an assemblage of guffawing suits. Countless times—as when my wife would appear at my workroom door offering up an assortment of vise grips and brightly recounting the convoluted tale of a crotchety plumbing aperture, usually after the preamble "On your next break . . ."—I was a hair's breadth from homicide.

I sincerely hope your experience is just as exciting.

These, then, are the four main areas in which to look for compatibility between your work and your home:

☆ Can you put in productive hours there?
☆ Can you avoid becoming hopelessly distracted?
☆ Can you seem businesslike and serve customers well?
☆ Can you handle the isolation?

You won't really know the answers to these queries until you try. I certainly didn't. After 18 years in busy offices, I was sure I'd want to put on a tie every day, drive off to a place where someone else took out the trash, and be downtown, even if my space was small. But, honestly, my business didn't require that I be there. I found I was just as smart in blue jeans. My clients weren't going to care (being in New Hampshire already set me far enough away from their world, so whether I worked at home wasn't going to be an issue). So, still not knowing whether I'd be comfortable and productive, I decided to give it a try. So far, I'm delighted. You might be surprised, too.

Technology

It's the last half of the last decade of the 20th century, and computer technology is changing everything. That's especially true for the self-employed lone eagle seeking a niche in an information-based, global economy. As recently as the late 1980s, surface mail and telephones were the main means of business communication, with faxes just a glimmer in the general business public's eye. Now faxes are standard operating equipment around the world and we're moving into a digital age of instant multimedia global connections.

How will this affect your basic office setup for a small business or otherwise self-directed career as we race toward 2000? It means there'll be many choices to make, systems to establish and learning curves to ride. The technology world is becoming a maze of so many paths it requires especially clear-headed, goal-driven planning to assure that it works for you rather than you for it.

Consider it a positive. There's certainly no shortage of equipment and services to meet your needs. Therefore, stay focused on your needs. For most of us, they'll include the following items.

A Personal Computer

You probably have one already. If not, get going, and don't worry: They're easier to use than ever. Exactly what you need in the way of hardware to run a small business begins with what you're using your computer for now, and what your new information and communication needs will do to change what you need.

When one thinks carefully about why certain people who are competent, well-educated, energetic and well-supported with good tools fail, it is often the red thread of superficiality that does them in. They never get seriously and accountably involved in their work.

—Max Depree in *Leadership Is an Art*

For starters, if your office will be at home, do you want or need to incorporate personal and family uses into your number-one PC? Perhaps not, if you have children. If you can afford it, a separate computer for the kids will not only give them freedom to use it even when you're working, but will remove all risk that the virus-laden disk your son brought home from school today will eat your work tonight.

Before launching my business, I owned a basic 386, 25 megahertz processor with 4 megabytes of memory and 80 megabytes of disk space, plus a decent color monitor—the kind of thing everybody bought in 1991.

For many small businesses, this may be plenty of machine—even though most computer "experts" will tell you to have much more. If all you need is word processing, modest financial-tracking and spreadsheet software, you can get by nicely on something much less than the Pentium systems suggested below. While much of the business world is geared toward PCs, and Windows continues to make the PC world more MAC-like, most people without computer experience still find MACs easier to get to know. In my case, I felt an investment in a Pentium-driven machine would power my practice for a long time and I wanted a second PC that would be used exclusively for family entertainment.

If you want the biggest and fastest desktop equipment available, and can spend upwards of $2000, consider these latest recommendations from Walter S. Mossberg, Personal Technology columnist for *The Wall Street Journal:*

The new operating systems—Windows 95 and Apple's Copland— are requiring more muscular machines. For Windows, you should get at least a Pentium chip running at 75 megahertz; if you can afford it, go for 100 megahertz or more. For Copland, you'll want at least a PowerPC chip running at 75 MHz.

Nothing is more important to a satisfying computer experience than having enough memory (RAM). Don't buy anything less than 8 megabytes of RAM, while 16 is recommended for running large programs with complex graphics.

Disk storage should be at least 750 megabytes, and 1 gigabyte (1,000 megabytes) or more is better. This used to sound like an impossibly large amount (remember my old 386 has 80 megabytes). But programs are growing in size as quickly as the prices of hard disks are falling, so it makes sense to buy plenty.

Your monitor should have a dot-pitch rating of .28 or less (the lower the better) and be noninterlaced (less flickering). Consider a 17-inch screen (easier on the eyes). You'll want your computer to have at least 1 megabyte of video memory (VRAM), and two is better. Make sure it can display 65,000 or more colors.

Good sound is a given with Macs. For Windows, get a built-in system compatible with the SoundBlaster card, with stereo speakers.

You'll want a CD-ROM drive (quadruple speed, or 4X) whether you think you do now or not. This will soon be the main vehicle for a great deal of software.

Finally, you'll need a modem for electronic communication and on-line research. Get one that can send and receive data at 28,800 BPS, which is quickly becoming the standard.

Are brand names important? "Unless you're a techie, don't buy a superstore's unknown house brand, or a no-name computer from a little local shop," Mossberg advises. "Stick with established names that offer good warranties and service plans, such as Compaq, Apple, IBM, Hewlett-Packard and Dell. Gateway 2000 and Packard-Bell are generally okay, but their customer service has been weaker than average in the past. Both claim to be improving on that score," he says.

Software

If you buy a hardware package that includes the features described above, it will likely come with software, some of which will be essential, some entertaining and even useful, and some entirely unnecessary. But for the basic tasks you'll need your computer for—word processing, accounting and perhaps a spreadsheet—don't let what might come with your hardware package be the last word. The best programs aren't likely to be the ones they give away.

Nevertheless, you'll likely find in your hardware package, in addition to a Windows operating system, integrated software packages such as Microsoft Works, which will give you word-processing, record-keeping and spreadsheet capabilities all in one program and may meet your needs. A step up from there are the "suites" of more powerful individual programs, including Lotus SmartSuite and Microsoft Office (about $500 to $700).

The key, as always, is deciding what kinds of programs are most important to you. For me, word processing is tops, yet my needs are modest: I still use WordPerfect 5.1, which does the job just fine. You may want a newer, Windows-based version of WordPerfect or Microsoft Word, which are leaders in both IBM and Mac circles. Also popular for IBM compatibles is Lotus Ami Pro.

Spreadsheets, which are key to any kind of analysis you'll be doing, are led by Lotus 1-2-3, Microsoft Excel and Borland's Quattro-Pro. You can pay anywhere from $50 to $400 for them.

How big do you have to be to need an accounting package? Not very. As soon as you're writing 25 or 30 checks a month and filling in a 13-column ledger, you'll want to investigate the features of one of the leading small business accounting packages. My accountant's own recommendation, which I've seen confirmed in several reviews, is that Quickbooks 3.1 (including payroll) is as good, easy and trouble-free as they get. I've also seen and heard good things about One-Write Plus and—for more sophisticated operations—Peachtree. To me, it made sense to go with my accountant's recommendation, to minimize any disagreements we might have over my record-keeping. Ask yours.

Printer

You probably want to go laser here, but if your needs for good-looking printed materials are limited, you could get by with a portable ink-jet unit for around $200. If you're doing anything beyond the occasional letter, though, you'll appreciate the professional appearance and graphics capabilities of a good laser printer, for which you can spend up to $1000 or more ($1500 and up for color). But keep an eye on ink-jet printers; terrific advancements are being made in their capabilities. Within five years, forecasters say, we'll be buying color ink-jet printers with resolution of 1200 dots per inch for about $200.

Fax Machine

Plain paper is the only way to go here. Forget that curly old photopaper you have to slice up and iron. Also, be sure to get a fax machine with memory to safeguard faxes received when you're out of paper or your printing cartridge has just given up.

Photocopier

This is one tool I haven't sprung for yet, but probably will soon. So far, though, I've been amazed at how little I've missed that big beauty we had at work (the old days!). Maybe I used to make a lot of unnecessary copies—one for each file, one for everybody in the office, and so on. Now, I'll make one copy of something I really need on the fax machine, or stop at a friend's office on the way to the post office for a more substantial copying project. Otherwise, I simply settle for having just one copy of a lot of things and find it's no big deal to operate that way. Also, auto-mated record-keeping certainly cuts down on needs here; if I need a copy of anything, I can print it on demand rather than making copies "just in case I ever need this."

Meanwhile, if you haven't yet bought a fax machine or printer, take a good look at an integrated machine, such as the Hewlett-Packard OfficeJet (about $700). This is an all-in-one plain paper fax (with memory), photocopier (that enlarges and reduces) and printer. It makes a lot of sense for a small office.

Phones and Phone Services

You should have at least one phone line just for business, but from there the choices open up to all kinds of personal needs and preferences. Assuming you won't have a secretary answering your business line, an initial choice depends on whether you want to be interrupted by call waiting (so as not to miss incoming calls while talking to someone). Do you want people simply to get a busy signal, or do you want a machine to take messages on a second line?

For me, sending out a busy signal wasn't an option. I want to be more responsive to my clients than that. But the next choice—whether to use call waiting or take messages on a second line—is tough. Many people prefer to know immediately who else is calling, but I dislike having to interrupt a conversation to say, "Excuse me, another call, be right back." So I use a second line with an answering machine or, to be more specific, a two-line integrated phone and answering machine. In fact, to be even more specific, I prefer the more realistic sound quality of tape-recorded messages to the robotic tones of digitized recorders, so I like the Panasonic Easa-Phone KX-T2740. With it, I can record two outgoing messages on tape. One says I'm on the other line or away from my desk for a few minutes; the other is for after hours or longer absences.

I just push a button when I enter and leave the office to put the appropriate message on. My main phone line, when busy, rolls calls over to the second number, which the machine answers for messages (I don't give out this number, to avoid any confusion). I also use the second line as my modem line, which means I have to watch it when I'm on-line and on the phone simultaneously (rare), since incoming callers will then get a busy signal. Finally, I have a third line just for the fax machine.

At first I shared the fax and backup phone on one line and kept the modem line separate; my phone and fax machine could handle incoming calls, whether voice or fax, appropriately. But, I found this set-up to be troublesome: Manual faxers had to press a special code to activate the signal in my fax machine. I gave the fax machine its own line and find it's much smoother to share the modem line.

Also, make sure your main phone has a speakerphone feature, not because it's professional to talk on one (unless you have two people in the room who need to participate), but for all those hours on hold for customer service and for hands-free redialing of busy numbers. In fact, I dial every call on speakerphone, then pick up when I get through. Finally, go for the sound quality of a corded phone, but keep a portable plugged into the same line. That way, you can carry it around the house or yard so you don't miss calls. You'll be spending $300 or more for two such phones, but what equipment is more important to your business?

There are many other phone features to pursue according to your needs: call forwarding, voice messaging through the phone company, toll-free numbers and cellular phones. Consider your needs.

One more phone tip before moving on to other kinds of communication: Do you know how easy it is to create a phone bill that lists your long-distance calls by client or project for purposes of reimbursement? I often find that when I mention doing this, and how much time it saves me when the phone bill comes, many people are surprised that this is available. Here's how it works: Instead of dialing 1 before the area code, dial 0 (like a credit-card call), then punch a 3-digit number you've assigned to the client to which you're attributing the call. When your phone bill arrives, your calls will be categorized by client, and subtotaled for record-keeping convenience. Although this requires a few seconds in dialing each call, it saves hours of trying to figure out which calls go to which accounts. By the way, it's free. Get details from your long-distance provider.

E-mail

PC-based electronic mail is often more convenient, faster and cheaper than phone or fax, and is rapidly becoming the preferred medium for business and personal information exchange. It's only a matter of time before most documents and data will be routinely digitized and transmitted through the invisible phone net, computer-to-computer, never touching paper or awaiting mechanical delivery. Such convenience will soon become the expected norm.

An easy way for independents to establish an electronic identity is through one of the major network services, such as CompuServe, America Online, Prodigy, Delphi or Microsoft Network. For a few dollars per month, you get your own mailbox in cyberspace and push-button messaging from your modem-equipped desktop or portable computer. Or, ready or not, you can buy or lease a hand-held cordless cellular, satellite-relayed Personal Digital Assistant (PDA). For even less money (about $1 per hour), you can get hooked up to a local Internet access provider and get e-mail through them.

Once you've got an electronic address, get it printed on your business card and stationery, mention it to a few friends, and you'll start receiving e-mail. Soon, you'll be in the habit of checking your e-mail once or more a day, and finding along the way that it's so easy to write notes to people this way that you're communicating more than ever. Just keep it to productive business relationships!

In doing so, though, you'll find the medium is less formal and more conversational than letter writing. You'll get familiar with some of the unique conventions of e-mail, such as copying and "pasting" essentials of your addressee's previous message verbatim (usually in quotes) as a reference for your reply.

Regardless of how you feel about e-mailing, its popularity bodes well for the self-employed, since it puts self-directed solos on equal terms with those networked within (and outside) Fortune 500 corporations.

More On-Line

E-mail is just one aspect of electronic communication. On-line, a whole universe of information, organizations, services and talent awaits you, ready to be tapped for your professional advantage. There are thousands of publications, entire discipline-specific libraries, huge searchable databases, indexed directories, up-to-date reference sources, downloadable programs and graphics, professional forums and special interest groups at your disposal. You can participate in informal real-time "chats" and interactive guest "appearances" by nationally known authorities in an infinite range of disciplines. There's hardly a topic or task, question or concern that cannot be addressed on-line quickly, inexpensively and (usually) reliably.

CompuServe alone—perhaps the best all-around information service for small businesses and independent professionals—offers a Working from Home Forum, several Entrepreneur's Small Business Forums and a directory of Government Publications with information on numerous business topics. (See Resources.)

In addition, you may want to connect directly to some of the hundreds of private, state and federal agency special-interest, computer-based bulletin board systems (BBS) available, often for free. For example, the Small Business Administration maintains a toll-free BBS loaded with valuable information on start-up and self-employment. (See Resources.)

Providing the main thoroughfare on this journey is the Internet itself. With 25 to 30 million people now having access to the Internet (and growing exponentially), you can't afford not to be Internet-aware. After all, today's new breed of college graduates have been cruising through cyberspace since high school. You're either wired or retired!

Advances in technology, plummeting hardware prices, user-friendly graphical software and the increasing popularity and numbers of on-line services are together rapidly expanding the scope of the Internet to include advertising, sales, public relations, interactive marketing, consumer activism, education and entertainment. You can order products and services, book trips, pay bills, do your banking, file taxes, contact mass media, trade stocks, find clients and customers and access international resources and markets, literally at the touch of a button.

Opportunities for individual entrepreneurs and new and small companies are vast; perhaps even more so than for large, established (slower, less innovative) corporations.

If you're new to the Net, the easiest way to connect and get around is through one of the commercial services, such as AOL, CompuServe, Delphi or MSN. They offer guidance and provide easy access to the Internet, in addition to their regular in-house services. Less expensive (and less helpful) are local Internet-access services that don't include as much fancy packaging but get you where you're probably going anyway—onto the Internet or the World Wide Web.

The Web is the greatest single reason for the Internet's current transformation into a mainstream medium. Together with simple point-and-click programs designed for it (such as Mosaic and NetScape), the Web allows instant, effortless "go-to" navigation among countless attractive, full-color electronic environments throughout the world. This intoxicating freedom of movement has created an unprecedented boom in Internet usage. In just three years, the number of Web sites has risen from 100 to more than 10,000, and about 60,000 are expected online by this year. Web users totaled about two million in 1995 and are expected to soar to 22 million by 2000, predicts Forester Research in Cambridge, MA.

Most Web sites are promotional in nature, the Web being the only sector of the Internet where advertising is considered acceptable. With a simple Web site-design manual (or a qualified consultant), you can put your logo, products, services, news, questionnaires and accompanying imagery on your own "home page," and invite one and all to drop in anytime, from anywhere. Even sounds and moving images can be included for the growing number of multimedia-equipped users. Costs range from $100 to $1000 per month.

The necessary software for WWW "browsing" and home-page construction is available free for the downloading, or in inexpensive commercial versions complete with manuals. The major online services also offer direct access to the Web.

Tools and Intimacy

Before leaving our section on technology, I want to mention an attitude about your business tools that will help assure your success in a self-directed career. It's the attitude of intimacy: knowing your equipment, as well as the nuts and bolts of your business, very well. In discussing intimacy in *Leadership Is an Art* (New York: Doubleday, 1989), Max DePree says:

> Those of you who have had real experience with machinery, equipment and even buildings know that they have personalities of their own. Intimacy with a job leads one to understand that when training people to do a job, one needs to teach not only the skill of the job but the art of it as well. And the art of it always has to do with the personality of both the operator and the machine. Intimacy is the experience of ownership. This often arises out of difficulty, questions, exasperation, or even survival.

So why complain, as an entrepreneur, that you have to fix your own paper jams, make sense of computer manuals that don't, open all the mail, pay all the bills and keep records of 25-cent phone calls? Why complain about a process that involves you in the details that make your business tick? Instead, you can gain entire new levels of appreciation and respect for your work and, guess what, for yourself. It's called pride of ownership.

Here's a great example of the value of intimacy: In my town, a company called Harrisville Designs makes looms for hand weavers. But based on years of experience in helping their customers get started in weaving, the company doesn't sell looms already put together. It sells only kits. Before learning to weave, customers must first assemble their loom. Only then do they learn how it really works and gain the amount of intimacy necessary to make it work well. It's the same with computers and other office equipment. Allot plenty of time for really getting acquainted with your system. Then, you'll truly own your business and, perhaps, begin not to resent being involved in the details.

Taxes

We covered most of the basics of finance in Chapter 4. If you took the advice there, you've figured out a way to get started in your dream form of self-employment without going into debt (at least not deeply). All you have to worry about now are making bank deposits and keeping track of bills, taxes and, if necessary, payroll. A simple accounting program such as Quickbooks can handle all of this. Here are three noteworthy points on taxes:

☆ *Record-keeping for tax purposes will keep you busy.* If you've been on someone else's payroll for years and never dealt with having other kinds of income or related expenses, you've got a few things to learn. Fortunately, while it's still no fun to hand over all that money to various levels of government, the procedures aren't all that onerous, assuming you have the help of a competent accountant when needed. Here's one caution, however: Don't get caught wildly underestimating (or failing to address) your quarterly federal income tax payments. More than a few well-intentioned businesspeople have slipped here.

☆ *What about home office deductions?* It's always a popular question and likely to remain so. A 1993 Supreme Court ruling severely limited the home-office deduction, and although IRS rules issued since then seem to leave more opportunities to qualify, it's not clear sailing. The deal is: You have to show not only that your office is your headquarters, but also that it's where you provide your services.

The Supreme Court disallowed the home office deduction of an anesthesiologist because the court said his most important work was done outside his office, at hospitals, even though he had no offices there. This seems to leave the status of many independents in question. Here are four examples of how the IRS feels:

1. A self-employed author spends 30 to 35 hours a week in his home office, and 10 to 15 hours elsewhere doing research, meeting with publishers and attending promotional events. The IRS says he qualifies because the "essence" of his work is done at home.

2. A self-employed retailer of costume jewelry spends 25 hours a week handling orders and doing office work at home, and 15 hours a week selling at craft shows and consignment shops. In a close call, the IRS says okay, because her selling activities are at such a variety of other places.

3. A teacher spends 25 hours a week at school, where he shares a small office, and 30 to 35 hours a week working at home. Because the "essence" of his job is at school, the IRS says no home office deduction.

4. A self-employed plumber spends 40 hours a week at customers' homes and offices, and 10 hours a week in his home office, where he has a full-time employee doing office work that supports his practice. No dice, says the IRS: the "essence" of his work is elsewhere.

    Talk to your accountant and keep your eye on Congress. Rules and interpretations can change anytime.

☆ *Can I deduct my business equipment all at once?* During the first year on your own, when you've got no track record on which to estimate your taxes, you may be wondering if you'll have the flexibility of writing off a big chunk of your equipment in order to minimize a sudden tax problem. The answer is a qualified yes. A special allowance on expenses lets you deduct up to $17,500 of qualifying equipment costs in any one year, instead of depreciating those items over several years. Ask your accountant for details.

It's About Time

"I just don't have enough time to do everything!" From all indications, this is the single most common complaint among independent business people. "If I only had more time, I could get more clients, answer all the mail, do the books, write a killer proposal, clean up the office, upgrade my equipment, maintain the database, take some courses, hang out with the kids and take a vacation. If you felt pressed for time in a regular company job, wait until you try running your own operation!

The old business adage says time is money, but in many ways it's even more precious, because although you can spend time (wisely or foolishly), you can never acquire one second more than your fixed allotment, which is exactly the same for everyone (nobody has more time than you!).

Technically speaking, it's impossible to "gain time," "save time" or even "manage time." But you can act efficiently, and that makes all the difference. Time cannot be modified, but behavior can. The key is to unlearn old, dysfunctional habits and replace them with productive ones.

The first step is goal-setting. Ask yourself: What do I really want? Your long-term goals are your rationale for being in business and working hard. They might be financial, such as a comfortable retirement nest egg, ample medical coverage, college tuition for the kids or the freedom to travel. Or they might be more altruistic or intangible.

To succeed, you'll need to know yourself well enough to be certain that your stated aims are in line with your true calling in life. This is the issue we addressed in the early chapters, yet it never goes away and is reflected in the many details of your daily activities. Keep your long-range goals in mind.

Your intermediate goals should begin to address the question, "How do I get there?" These are measurable accomplishments you want to complete over the coming weeks, months and perhaps years to realize your dreams. They might include raising capital, getting significant exposure in your field, building a viable client base, or even selling the business at a large profit. These objectives may be ambitious, but make sure they're also realistic and attainable according to your abilities, or you'll surely crash and burn long before approaching them.

Seneca, the Roman philosopher, said, "When a man does not know what harbor he is making for, no wind is the right wind."

Short-term goals are the ongoing jobs that constitute your everyday work. You define them by dividing up your larger objectives into smaller, action-oriented tasks that can be placed on your agenda, along with all the other obligations and details of running a business. This is where skillful planning is essential. Good planning eliminates indecision and actually increases your flexibility.

First, make a list of all the items requiring your attention. Prioritize, using triage, putting the most urgent business first, postponing others and eliminating all unnecessary time-wasters. (Americans spend eight months of their lives opening junk mail and a year searching for misplaced objects, asserts Michael Fortino, president of Priority Management in Pittsburgh.) What's left becomes your daily "to do" list of immediate physical tasks, such as gathering information, entering data, composing reports, making presentations, reading important mail, making calls, attending meetings, brainstorming and traveling.

This daily action list is what marketing consultant and author Jeffrey Feinman calls "the single most effective time-management tool." Use it to budget blocks of time for each job, setting practical deadlines you can meet. Avoid overloading your calendar, a classic cause of job stress. Allow some free time every day for mental rests, spontaneous impulses and unforeseen events. Remember, you don't have to become a slave to the clock to be time-efficient. Be flexible. The trick is to find your optimal productivity zone, somewhere between laziness and compulsiveness, between boredom and panic. And lest you fear that you're leaning too far in one direction or the other, make necessary adjustments and then remember, as Feinman notes, "Successful people rarely spend more than a minute regretting even big mistakes."

Procrastination is the first (or maybe last) big obstacle to productivity. This self-sabotaging behavior inevitably leads to anxiety, panic and despair. It stems from self-doubt, indecision, worry and regret, which are negative emotions you can't afford. The antidotes are certainty, self-confidence, focused concentration, positive enthusiasm and action.

Counteract your fear of the unknown with information and knowledge. Ask for advice and study the successes of others. Identify and eliminate distractions and time-wasting behaviors and their negative reinforcements, such as snacking, idle socializing or chronic day-dreaming. If you can't tackle a big job, begin with small steps. When in doubt, do anything but nothing!

Never allow yourself to imagine worst-case scenarios. This is a paralyzing mental habit. Instead, visualize in detail your ideal desired behaviors and their positive outcomes. Picture your success. Be specific. See yourself calm, clear and effective. Repeat positive affirmations, such as "I'm completely capable and in control." Then put it in writing.

Our experience of time is subjective. Naturally, the more tasks and appointments on our schedule, the more pressure we feel. But what's not so obvious is that our time-sense is also relative to our prevailing mindset. When you're on a close deadline, time is the enemy. But if your long-awaited vacation starts next week, then this week's days can't go fast enough. Our relationship to time is also a function of our habits, beliefs, values and expectations. If you find yourself constantly racing the clock and begrudging the inexorable passage of time, something is fundamentally askew in your approach, which is most often the only thing within your power to change.

Tips for the Time-Conscious

☆ *Keep on task.* Do one thing at a time. Whenever possible, complete a job before going on to the next. Reward yourself for accomplished assignments. Save easy little jobs for last.

☆ *Speed read.* Learn how to skim text for the essentials. Discard junk mail immediately.

☆ *Handle materials and documents once.* Act on it when it's in your hand. File it once and forever.

☆ *Practice systematic decision making.* Weigh and itemize the benefits and liabilities of each option. Take enough time to be sure of your choice, then stick with it.

☆ *Be organized.* Have a place for everything and keep it there. Use lots of shelving, table surfaces, drawers and labeled bins. You should be able to locate anything in your office instantly. The most work-conducive environments are clean, uncluttered and ergonomically laid-out. A wrap-around desk and rolling office chair enhance your economy of movement. Also important are good lighting and privacy.

☆ *Outside of your office seek early appointments (they're less likely to run late) and group appointments when you can.* Offer to meet nearby people in their offices so you can better control the length of the visit.

☆ *Practice the fine art of creative waiting.* When someone puts you on hold, when you're waiting for a meeting, standing in line at ticket counters or held up in traffic, use these opportunities to read, write, plan and mentally rehearse. Don't kill time, fill it! Do portable work at hotels, in lobbies and at airports. Make commuting and flying time productive with instructional or motivational tapes.

☆ *Skip lunch.* Unless it's an important positive reward, try working right through lunch time occasionally. Have some fruit juice or yogurt at your desk and just keep going. Most of us eat far more than we need for nourishment in the course of a day. Overeating slows you down. You may be pleasantly surprised at how much energy you acquire from emptying and resting your digestive organs.

☆ *Make the most of time-saving technologies.* Fax broadcasting, automated e-mail and software key-stroke short-cuts (called macros and boilerplates) are time savers. If you're on the road much of the time, consider a portable electronic PDA (Personal Digital Assistant) with phone book, calendar, spreadsheet, editor, and so on. Some models include pagers, cellular fax and other special communications features.

☆ *Enlist your right brain.* Balance the analytical and intellectual side with artistic and holistic approaches. Your imagination, intuition, sense of humor—even your dreams—can be valuable allies. Integrate work and play. Practice meditation. You'll be happier, healthier and more effective.

☆ *Have a day's-end ritual.* Tidy up. Throw away as much as possible. Put away everything else. Make tomorrow's "to do" and "call" lists. Take pride in a day's work well done, and mentally and physically release all leftover tension. Leave your work and all business concerns in the office, and deliberately shift to family, recreation and personal living modes.

Save Time on the Phone

Consider how much of your day is spent on the phone and you'll know where you can become much more efficient. For example, ask yourself before each call, "Is this call really necessary?" Many aren't. Don't let yourself become too lazy to realize you could skip the next call without harm.

When a call is necessary, prepare for it. Decide what you want to cover and how long you plan to talk. Then you'll know when to end it.

Screen your calls. Using voice mail allows you to determine who to talk with and when. Keep your conversations focused on business.

Make and return calls in groups. Then you can move on to another project with fewer interruptions. Dial on the speakerphone until you get through, and have something to do in case you get put on hold, such as opening and reading mail or skimming magazines.

Leave action messages. Instead of saying simply, "Call me back," see if you can leave a message that tells the person the step to take next, perhaps avoiding the need for a callback.

Finally, practice what I call "preventive dialing"—a great way to manage your time as well as maximize your impact. That is, call first. (Isn't it always the painfully fundamental stuff that ends up being so important?) As you take inventory of your "to-dos" at each day's outset, ask yourself the question, "What calls, if any, am I worried about receiving today? Look over your list of works in progress and think about who might be wondering what you're up to. Call the person immediately. It works like magic. Something about the simple act of calling first improves the likelihood that the other person will say, "You know, I'm glad you called, because I've been thinking about an even easier and better way we could get that accomplished."

At worst, you've chased a cloud that was quietly hanging out near your day. You can rest assured that person won't be calling to lay any sort of guilt on you. At best, you've earned a break or a bonus. And either way, you've reinforced the impression that you're alert, responsive and well-organized, which is worth more in marketing value than money can buy.

Your Mental Health

Time management techniques lead us into the greater world of the psychology of self-employment. Working solo is in many ways analogous to cross-country running: You're mostly alone, sometimes questioning your endurance and occasionally feeling lost.

A sense of proportion and balance helps. Sometimes your toughest competition is yourself. The following are some typical obstacles to watch out for:

☆ *Isolation.* Many self-employed people try to do everything, all by themselves, all the time, going way beyond what we described earlier as establishing intimacy. This may seem to be a cost-effective labor policy, but it doesn't work so well for your psycho-spiritual needs. Sooner or later, we all need feedback, contact and support. Are you preserving and nurturing important relationships, or neglecting your friends and family? Do you feel misunderstood and underappreciated? Do you have healthy emotional outlets? If not, you may be over-isolating yourself, and needing to reconnect.

☆ *Confused priorities.* Do you protect your health as avidly as you would your business? Are you a high-strung Type A workaholic? Has it been months since you've played, laughed, read a good book, enjoyed sex or felt your connection to nature? If you demand perfection—either of yourself or others—and find yourself cursing the clock, eating on the run, using coffee like a drug and losing sleep, then you're at risk for heart disease, depression and burnout. If you don't take steps to change your attitude, relax your schedule and delegate responsibility, you'll be headed for disaster. It sounds obvious, but remember, you're no good to anyone in a hospital. Your most important business is your health.

☆ *Stress.* Staying at home comes with its own stresses. Perhaps you've eliminated all problems with bosses, but are encountering friction with your spouse, kids or the IRS. Bear in mind one of the classic definitions of job-related stress: high responsibility and low control. As an independent agent, you should be careful of the tendency to accept all the headaches and forget the cure.

The start-up phase and first year of self-employment is the time of highest risk from too much change and challenge. It will be essential to learn how to prioritize, accept compromise and pace yourself. You may even benefit from short-term professional counseling with a qualified psychotherapist or career counselor. Don't be too proud to ask for help.

Coping and Conquering

Your stress is defined not so much by what happens to you, as by how you respond to what happens. Here's a stress-management checklist to help you make the best choices:

> ☆ *Identify your stress triggers and reaction styles.* What (or who) "gets" to you? How do you typically react to difficult people and situations?
>
> ☆ *Observe your emotions.* Do you get angry a lot? Are you easily hurt? Do you want to fight or flee? Can you be more objective?
>
> ☆ *Practice desensitizing.* Mentally rehearse coping under pressure. Gradually expose yourself to stressful situations, under control, and build up your tolerance over time.
>
> ☆ *Practice relaxation techniques.* Move, stretch, breathe, relax. Try meditation or self-hypnosis. Play soothing music. Get a massage.

Body Time

Everything in nature occurs in cycles. Like the seasons and the tides, the body (which is 90% fluid) has its own ebbs and flows. Our daily bio-chemical changes act like an internal clock, regulating our hormone levels, digestive secretions and even brain functions. These circadian rhythms, in turn, affect one's energy levels, moods and even thoughts. Circadian rhythms account for why we perform various activities better at different times of the day. Chronobiologists have concluded (and most office managers, writers and analysts will agree) that the morning is best for concentrated thinking.

Late afternoon seems to be best for physical exercise, when coordination and reaction times are at their peak. In between— the traditional siesta time—we experience a slump in energy. It's best not to schedule important meetings then. Schedule light information acquisition rather than heavy production. If you can't take a nap, you can still minimize your drowsiness by eating lightly, avoiding fats and high protein foods for lunch. There's wisdom in the tradition of supper after sundown.

> For tribal man, space was the uncontrollable mystery. For technological man, it is time that occupies the same role.
>
> —Marshall McLuhan

In the evening, our senses are at their peak, making it a good time to absorb new information, but also to enjoy dining and entertainment. An evening "constitutional" and only moderate eating before bedtime will help insure a good night's sleep, so you can get up and begin all over again!

Nature's Way

There are other healthy steps you can take to modulate the impact of bodily energy fluctuations. After concentrated mental activity, take a stretching and deep breathing break. When your creativity wanes, walk away from your work and do something else. You'll be all the more effective after pausing and recharging. Regular mild exercise is one of the best ways to keep your body functioning normally.

Natural sunlight and fresh air can help overcome fatigue and depression. Go easy on sugar, chocolate, caffeine, alcohol and tobacco. They wreck havoc on your metabolism. And don't attempt to restore the balance with stimulants and sleeping pills. Take natural alternative high-energy snacks, such as dates, raisins, dried apricots and sunflower seeds. Peppermint tea makes a good healthful stimulant, while chamomile will relax you. And vitamins C and B are good anti-stress supplements.

One's mental state has a lot to do with physical feelings. It helps to have some exciting activities to look forward to after a hard day's labor or a long work-week. It's called "re-creation." Hobbies, sports and socializing can make a big difference in your energy levels and outlook. Boredom is actually a kind of stress, so build some variety and novelty into your schedule. It's important to our minds, bodies and souls. And whether you're feeling weak and low, high and hyper, just remember that it's nature's way to insure that everything changes.

Micro-Ecology

As your own landlord, you'll want to put some extra thought into the environmental and ergonomic considerations of the place in which you're spending most of your waking hours. Never underestimate the importance to your mental, physical and financial health of such factors as fresh air, good lighting, noise control, comfortable furniture and well-designed personal computer equipment.

Becoming your own employee means you'll be assuming more of the routine labor that otherwise might have been handled by office assistants, and you're bound to become more sensitive to ergonomics (body mechanics). Poorly designed tools used repeatedly can result in pain and injury. The most common example is Carpel Tunnel Syndrome: nerve and joint damage to the wrist and thumb from too many hours at the keyboard. Wrist rests, ergonomically-designed keyboards and periodic self-massage can help prevent this serious condition.

To avoid neck and shoulder strain, computer screens should be positioned at eye level, and arm rests should be high enough to place your forearms parallel with the floor. Low back pain sufferers might get relief from lumbar supports and "back chairs" with knee rests. And everyone can benefit from stretching occasionally during the workday.

The atmosphere in an office can be polluted by fumes from photocopiers, synthetic carpeting, dust-filled heating ducts and bacteria in air conditioners. In addition, well-insulated homes in certain regions should be tested for radon. The remedy may be as simple as opening a window, but a minimal investment in fans, filters, humidifiers or ionizers goes a long way towards purifying indoor air. Also effective as low-tech "air conditioners" are live plants. They remove accumulated carbon dioxide and give back fresh oxygen. Plants also lend a positive psychological effect.

To avoid eye strain, lighting should be shaded or indirect. Natural light prevents vitamin D deficiency and Seasonal Affective Disorder, so open up those curtains and let the sun shine in. Full-spectrum lights can also help. And make sure your fixtures don't hum and buzz. The noise can get on your nerves and become a real stress factor.

Color, too, has psychological effects, as hospital and prison designers well know. Studies show that rooms with pale green walls are calming. Yellow is exciting. Even pleasing art work can subtly improve the mood in an office. For a relaxing, conducive work environment, avoid visual clutter.

Noisy office machines such as printers and plotters should be isolated or covered, and phones turned down. Padded room dividers effectively muffle ambient noise, as can strategically-placed potted plants. Gentle instrumental music can also be an effective balancing factor in your office sonic environment.

On-the-Job Exercises

Attention, desk jockeys and chair-persons: It's time to get up and take a break. Stretching is a very healthy alternative to coffee and cigarettes and can be done right at the desk, in a lounge area or outdoors. Stretching, deep breathing and relaxation exercises are highly recommended antidotes to tension and fatigue. And a brisk walk after lunch will help overcome afternoon sluggishness. Here are some other simple self-care stress-busters you can build right into your daily work routine.

- ☆ *Neck and shoulder rolls.* To relieve neck tension, bend your head all the way down forward and roll it in slow motion, first clockwise, then counterclockwise in 360-degree rotation. For tight shoulders, shrug them up to your ears, then drop suddenly. Do slow, wide shoulder rolls, pulling the scapular blades together and apart.

- ☆ *Iso-flexing and progressive muscle release.* This technique releases overall muscle tension and promotes good circulation to the extremities. While inhaling, curl in the toes and both feet, then release the tension and exhale at the same time. Then tighten your toes, feet and calf muscles on the next inhalation. Again, release your breath and muscles simultaneously. Next time, add your knees, thighs and buttocks. Continue and repeat this flexing up through your whole body, learning to release muscle tension completely, at will, on each out-breath.

Feel the positive effects. Practice this systematic flexing and releasing several times a day, or when you notice the need. As with all these exercises, the more you practice, the more reliable and profound the results become.

☆ *Forward flop.* This is a passive inversion that relieves neck strain and back aches, and brings an infusion of fresh blood to the brain. Sitting in your chair, bend forward and hang your head and arms between your knees. Exhaling, allow the neck to release, and let the stretch travel down your back. If it's comfortable, stay down for 30 seconds or more. Get up slowly, supporting yourself with your arms, not your back muscles.

☆ *Reach and breathe.* Reach overhead as high as you can, inhaling. Then look up and fall back against the chair, draping your upper spine over it, and spreading your arms diagonally out behind you like an eagle in flight. Exhaling, drop your arms and deliberately make a sound that expresses the release you feel. Relax.

☆ *Deep breathing.* Blow out through your mouth and puff out all your air. Inhale deeply through the nostrils, expanding the abdomen and rib cage and lifting your shoulders. Pull in as much air as possible. Hold briefly, then release suddenly and relax completely. Repeat three times, then rest and feel your breath settle down into a quiet, automatic rhythm.

☆ *Twist a bit.* First twist left by crossing your right hand over to the left side of the chair, next to your leg, with your left hand on the chair-back. Inhale and draw yourself up tall. Exhale and look over your left shoulder as far as you can, pulling the trunk of your body around. Rotate into the position firmly with upper body strength, but let go in the lower back muscles, allowing the spine to twist. Hold for a moment, then release. Repeat to the right side by placing your left hand on the right side of the chair, and your right hand behind you. Remember to lift with an inhalation, and pull your body into the twist on the exhalation.

☆ *Self-massage.* Keyboard users should massage their own hands several times per day, and everyone would do well to get a neck rub occasionally, even if it's from themselves! It's easy, free and therapeutic. Work on your aching muscles with the same care that you would a loved one. Probe as deep as you can, without pain. You'll also find it refreshing to stimulate your head with a rigorous massage. Use your fingers to rub the scalp and your knuckles to knock the skull. It feels great! And don't forget to give your feet a good massage treatment, too.

☆ *Eye palming.* This is particularly useful for people who sit at computer terminals, wear glasses or get head-aches. Rub your palms together tightly and vigorously until they're heated by the friction. Sit back and cover your eyes with your warm palms. Breathe slowly and deeply, relaxing your eyes. Imagine a healing color com-ing from your hands, through your eyes and into your brain. Feel the soothing effects. Use this method to re-lieve eye strain and related headaches.

☆ *Mini-meditation.* You can learn how to relax your body and calm your mind through simple focusing tech-niques. Studies show that just sensing your breath or heartbeat calms the nervous system and lowers blood pressure. You can clear your mind by focusing on a single healing image, comforting phrase or soothing sensation.

☆ *Balance.* Sit comfortably upright and tune into your sense of balance. Balance your body from front to back, then side to side. Coming to rest, bring your attention down to your gravitational center, which is in your belly. Keep sensing this area until you feel your sense of balance contributing to your overall well-being.

☆ *Focus.* Feel your breathing, and imagine that it's be-coming very calm. You can use self-relaxation phrases, such as, "My breathing feels calm and slow." Do the same with your heartbeat. It works!

☆ *Visualize.* Picture yourself in a favorite natural envi-ronment. Recall it with all your senses. Imagine beauti-ful rainbows of light permeating and healing you. Rest still and silent for a few moments. Enjoy the refreshing pause in your otherwise busy life.

Many large organizations, looking at the big picture as well as the bottom line, are promoting worker health through prevention programs, fitness training, stress reduction classes and yoga and meditation training. As a self-employed loner, you'll have to take the initiative and create your own incentives for self-care and wellness. In the long run, managing your health is as crucial (and rewarding) as managing your finances. (It may even be easier.) True success comes from achieving both personal and professional excellence, something that's really worth working for!

Some Closing Thoughts

With a self-directed career so well-planned, first steps taken, new work space well-equipped and made comfortable, finances and other priorities in order, your schedule under control, head on straight and body in shape, you're ready for the real world.

Yet all of this brings you only to the brink of being in business—in terms of closing that first deal. So I want to spend a few moments encouraging you to consider the importance of negotiating well, in whatever line of business you've chosen. Despite all your expertise and preparation, your business doesn't really exist at all until you've "closed" with your first customer. And while your business will undoubtedly have to endure an occasional bad deal, you can't afford to make a habit of it. At the moment of truth, you have to be able to optimize the value of your product or service, or else all your other work will be diminished.

Paul A. Hawkinson, editor and publisher of *The Fordyce Letter* in St. Louis, a newsletter targeting for the recruitment industry, spoke recently on this subject with a great deal of insight. Negotiating skills are highly transferable from business to business, and although he's a specialist in the kinds of deals that bring talent to organizations, what Paul says will apply well to your business. Some highlights:

☆ We have come to believe the most negotiations are adverse in nature, because those are the ones brought to our attention through the media. But it really isn't so.

☆ Don't negotiate if you're uncomfortable doing so in a particular situation, if negotiating won't meet your needs, and if the expenditure of time and psychic energy is more than the benefits that will be received as a result of the encounter.

☆ If you truly believe you're engaged in an honorable and useful profession, you'll win, because you inherently possess power, the ultimate key to negotiating success.

☆ The more information you have about the financial situation, priorities, deadlines, costs, real needs and organizational pressures, the better you can bargain.

☆ An excellent way to elicit information is the "I need your help" maneuver. "Help me to understand how we can better serve you" is a great strategy to use. People love to help. You don't play stupid, but you don't come off as a know-it-all either. The "help me" process leads the client to believe he has the power position, but as a benevolently helpful person, he weakens his position with every bit of information he imparts.

This approach ultimately leads the two of you to the same side of the fictitious bargaining table, jointly trying to solve the problem rather than adversarially trying to decide who'll get the best of whom. It's hard for collaborators to squabble over insignificant items (such as fees, guarantees, etc.) because you're in this thing together, exactly where you ought to be.

☆ Almost anything that's the product of a negotiation has to be negotiable, including the terms of most of these agreements. Don't buy into the nonsensical rebuttal that, "Our legal people won't approve of any changes." I used to tell people who use this tawdry terminology that our agreement with the Federal Trade Commission precluded us from making any changes in our pre-approved fee schedule. That, of course, was a lie, but then so is what you're being told by the other side.

☆ Negotiating requires a certain amount of risk-taking and you must be willing to accept the risks, including the risk that you may have to walk away. But also recognize that the world is full of bargain-hunters. Still others will throw roadblocks in your way to see how you handle them.

☆ Indicate that you care, but not enough to lower your standards. That's a powerful negotiation tool.

I'm going to close with a bit of advice from Jan Yager, a leading Connecticut-based writer on the subject of business behavior. These thoughts are borrowed from her book, *Business Protocol* (New York: John Wiley, 1991). As we know, the way you act with people—which is where the all-important negotiating process really begins—is your most important business development tool of all.

1. Being courteous, polite and pleasant will take you far in the business world, just as being critical, negative or maudlin will hamper your success.

2. Saying "please" and "thank you" should be part of your everyday behavior in the business world unless it's a life-or-death situation, such as a physician saying "Get me another pint of blood."

3. Avoid criticizing anyone—subordinate, co-worker, superior, client or customer—especially in the presence of others.

4. You're judged by the following up of your actions, not just your initial contacts. If you call someone, follow up to see if whatever you talked about has been accomplished. If someone writes to you, follow up with an answer. And always return phone calls.

5. Beware of being silent merely because you feel uncomfortable rejecting someone. You're rejecting the project or situation, not the person. Remember that the person you're afraid to say "no" to today, who now sees you as impolite, might be the person you want to say "yes" to next month, or in 10 years. People never forget impoliteness.

6. Consider including a note or letter with everything you send. Even a simple "For your information" will often suffice.

7. Don't assume that because someone calls you through a referral that your services are presold. You still have to work hard, perhaps even harder, to live up to their expectations.

8. Keep all of your promises.

Appendix

Resources

There's an overwhelming amount of information about career development and entrepreneurism available today—in print, on-line and on audiotape, videotape, CD-ROM and software. I'm sure I've only scratched the surface in nearly a year's research for this book. Not long ago, I visited a Border's multimedia/bookstore and found about 150 square feet of shelves filled with career books—hundreds of titles touching on subjects I've addressed in this book. Since superbookstores are sprouting up almost everywhere, you should have no trouble finding the additional resources you'll need.

I've included a sampling of what I consider to be solid resources you might want to review as you pursue a particular path. By the way, I'd be interested in your nominations for consideration in future editions of this book. Please send your comments to: David A. Lord, P.O. Box 111, Harrisville, NH 03450.

Small Business Administration
(800) 8ASK-SBA
Answer Desk (800) 827-5722 or (202) 205-7701

The national clearinghouse for finance, investment, procurement and development information and assistance, with regional offices nationally. Free "Home-Based Business Start-Up Guide," plus 13,000 experienced volunteers offering entrepreneurial and management assistance. A resource not to be ignored.

Books

The New Individualists—The Generation After the Organization Man
Paul Leinberger and Bruce Tucker
HarperCollins, 1991.

Even though careers and the economy have changed greatly in just the few years since this was written, it remains an insightful look at why Baby Boomers are the way they are and what they think about their work.

Growing a Business
Paul Hawken
Simon & Schuster, 1986

Timeless, practical wisdom with wide applicability.

Do What You Love, the Money Will Follow
Marsha Sinetar
Dell, 1987

A pioneering, valuable treatment.

Love Your Work and Success Will Follow
Arlene Hirsch
John Wiley & Sons, 1996

Insightful with many topical case studies.

The Tao of Pooh
Benjamin Hoff
Penquin, 1982

The what? Teachings of a Great Master of Wisdom as reflected in the eloquently simple characters of Winnie the Pooh—for a measure of spiritual excitement that all entrepreneurs must possess in some form.

Leadership Is an Art
Max DePree
Dell, 1989

Again, for an enlightened view of how we work.

JobShift: How to Prosper in a Workplace Without Jobs
William Bridges Ph.D.
Addison-Wesley, 1994

The prophet of the end of jobs sets the stage for our new attitude toward work.

Build Your Own Rainbow
Barrie Hopson and Mike Scally
Pfeiffer & Co., 1993

Forty exercises to help you establish a new beginning.

*Make Your Own Breaks: Become an Entrepreneur & Create
Your Own Future*
Jim Lang
DBM Publishing, 1994

Very accessible, down-to-earth look at going out on your own.

Country Careers
Jerry Germer
John Wiley & Sons, 1993

Lots of info and insight for the budding entrepreneur whose dream
includes relocating to rural parts unknown.

Career Anchors
Edgar H. Schein
Pfeiffer & Co., 1993

"Process consulting" guru's advice for executives.

Breakaway Careers
Bill Radin
Career Press, 1994

Lively, informative and on-target advice for would-be home-office
independents.

Zen and the Art of Making a Living
Laurence G. Boldt
Penguin, 1994

A comprehensive, 600-page "life's work" assessment and development
manual. Covers self-discovery and quality of life issues to practical
guidance about starting and running a business. Plenty of exercises
and worksheets. Laced with inspirational and whimsical quotes.

We Are All Self-Employed
Cliff Hakim
Berrett-Koehler Publications, 1994

A thoughtful and informative portrait of our new attitude toward
work.

Mid-Career Entrepreneur
Joseph R. Mancuso
Enterprise/Dearborn, 1993

If you enjoyed Mancuso's quizzes in this book, you'll love the full
treatment he gives to the subject.

Nobody Gets Rich Working for Somebody Else: An Entrepreneur's Guide
Roger Fritz
Crisp Publications, 1993

An inexpensive, quick overview of the basics.

The Start Up Guide: A One-Year Plan for Entrepreneurs
David H. Bangs, Jr.
Upstart Publishing, 1994

How to Leave Your Job and Buy a Business of Your Own
C.D. Peterson
McGraw-Hill, 1992

Good sections on finding, valuing and financing a business.

Buying a Business: Tips for the First-Time Buyer
Ronald J. McGregor
Crisp Publications, 1993

Operating a Really Small Business
Betty Bivins
Crisp Publications, 1992

Publications

National Business Employment Weekly
Dow Jones & Co.
(800) JOB-HUNT

Leading career-guidance and job-search publication which includes frequent coverage of and special reports on entrepreneurism and small business issues.

ReCareering Newsletter
Publications Plus
(708) 735-1981

A bimonthly idea and resource guide to second career and relocation planning.

Career Savvy
Developing Executives, Inc.
(810) 615-1811

A monthly newsletter that reports on new resources of note, including those dealing with entrepreneurism.

Kennedy's Career Strategist
Career Strategies
(708) 251-1661

A monthly roundup of job-hunting trends and guidance.

Entrepreneur
(800) 274-6229

The first and still best magazine on the subject.

Inc. The Magazine for Growing Companies
(800) 234-0999

Especially valuable once you're no longer small, or if you're buying a business.

Inc. Business Resources
(800) 468-0800, ext. 5299

The magazine's bookstore arm, with dozens of titles on entrepreneurism and how to build specific skills.

Your Company: The Magazine for Small Business Owners
(212) 522-3263

Time Inc's publication for entrepreneurs.

Guides

Winning with Small Business
American Success Institute
(800) 585-1300

A study course that provides a gentle entry for timid entrepreneurs.

The Whole Work Catalog
The New Careers Center
(303) 447-1087

A sourcebook on home-office, self-employment, "green" and alternative careers.

The Entrepreneur's Bookshelf
(310) 202-0293

An annotated list of books about choosing the right business, networking, negotiating, financing, marketing, etc.

The Small Business Development Catalog
Entrepreneur Group
(800) 421-2300

Lists 150 business guides for sale.

Self-Employment Survival Letter
(708) 717-0488

A 28-page quarterly with anecdotes, tips and resources for modest home businesses.

Small Business Institute Director's Association
(903) 451-9339

"A forum for the test of theory" on small business management; publishes the Journal of Small Business Strategy.

On-line Resources

Small Business Administration On-Line
SBA BBSs http://www.sbaonline.sba.gov
(800) 859-4636 (2400 baud)
(800) 697-4636 (9600 baud)

Lots of free information on start-up and development, financial services, franchising, patents and trademarks, tax regulations, government contracts and lots more. Downloadable software for accounting, record-keeping, forms, contact databases and inventory management. Plus "gateway" to other federal agency BBSs.

America Online
(800) 827-6364

The Entrepreneur Zone (keyword: ezone) offers a thoroughly inviting range of small business services and information, plus connections to American Express ExpressNet small business classifieds, commercial publications, Web & Internet resources.

Home Office Computing (keyword: hoc)
Up-to-the-minute on-line version of the popular magazine.

Microsoft Network
Mainstream Entrepreneur Center
(Find it through the Business & Finance Directory, Mainstream Resource Center)

Full plate of resources on being in business for yourself.

CompuServe Information Service
(800) 848-8990
or (800) 848-8199
Working from Home Forum (go:work)
Entrepreneur's Small Business Forums (go:usen, smallbiz or ebf)
Directory of Government Publications (go:gpo)

These forums offer information on accounting, advertising, computers, copyrights and patents, customer relations, direct mail, family finance, health care and insurance, inventions, legal issues, leasing and marketing questions. Each professional forum has its own library of files, message center and "virtual community" with unlimited resources to share.

MCI Small Business Center
http://www.mci.com/smallbiz

Business Resource Center
(formerly the Small Business Help Center)
http:/www.kciLink.com/brc/

Good-looking, well maintained Canadian Web site. Enthusiastic source of info, ideas, reviews for the newly self-employed. Links to other resources.

Smallbiznet: The Ed Lowe Small Business Network
http://www/loew.org/

Bulletin board, bookstore and clipping library for entrepreneurs.

Cyberpreneurs Guide to the Internet
http://asa.ugl.lib.umich.edu/chdocs/cyberpreneur/Cyber.html

Resources for entrepreneurial uses of the Internet.

Entrepreneur NET
http://www.cyberzine.org/html/Entrepreneur/enetpage2.html

Sites of interest to entrepreneurs, including links to related home pages, finance and tax information, commercial sites, newsgroups and links to most of the major search engines on the web. In addition, ENET also contains ads and offers space to those wanting to advertise at a low cost.

Entrepreneurs on the Web
URL: http://sashimi.wwa.com/~notime/eotw/EOTW.html

A collection of pointers to useful resources, both Business Information Resources and Goods and Services. Well-maintained.

A-ha! Monthly
http://sashimi.wwa.com/~notime/eotw/bus–info–sources/idea–assoc.html

Monthly publication of The IDEA Association (303) 978-0335, "a support group for people starting new businesses."

GNN Personal Finance Center
http://nearnet.gnn.com/gnn/meta/finance/index.html

Global Entrepreneur Network
http://www.entrepreneurs.net/

"The Virtual Community for Entrepreneurs." A worldwide membership organization for entrepreneurs, providing resources, tools and platforms to establish an effective presence on the Net.

Small Business Advancement National Center
http:// http://wwwsbanet.uca.edu/

Comprehensive information and support "to promote the entrepreneurial spirit." Well-designed Web site and a searchable database filled with information pertaining to many aspects of small business and entrepreneurship.

Biz Plan Builder
Jian Tools for Sales, Inc.
(800) 346-5426

The original business-plan software, with a full selection of computerized templates. Plug in your specifics and it generates a professional business plan you can take to the bank.

The Business Plan Toolkit
Palo Alto Software
(800) 229-7526

Another software program with which to develop a business plan.

Big Dreams
http://www.wimsey.com/~duncans/BigDreams/index.html

Despite its grand name, this is a modest but well-conceived free monthly online newsletter of inspiration and practical advice on starting a new business.

Venture Connect
http://www.texel.com/home/mehes/vencon.html

A mating service for ideas and capital. Money-seekers and investors post notices seeking counterparts.

Associations

American Institute of Small Business
7515 Wayzata Blvd., Suite 201
Minneapolis, MN 55426
(800) 328-2906

National Association for the Self-Employed
2121 Precinct Line Rd.
Hurst, TX 76054
(800) 232-NASE
(610) 647-3733
E-mail: shelderfer@softlock.com

Membership organization with a wide-range of benefits: Group insurance, legal advice, tax info, publications, travel discounts, long-distance phone services, 800# access to small-business consultants, plus advocacy with state and federal legislators.

National Association of Women Business Owners
1413 K Street NW, Suite 637
Washington, DC 20005
(301) 608-2590

Leadership training, lobbying, international trade and financial support for nearly 7,000 members. Offers a variety of information resources and publishes Enterprising Women magazine.

National Foundation for Women Business Owners
1100 Wayne Ave., Suite 830
Silver Spring, MD 20910-5603
(301) 495-4975

Research and education arm of NAWBO.

National Federation of Independent Business
600 Maryland Ave. SW, Suite 700
Washington, DC 20024
(800) NFIB-NOW

National Minority Supplier Development Council
1412 Broadway, 11th Floor
New York, NY 10018
(212) 944-2430

Builds business relationships between corporate purchasers and minority-owned business members.

Franchising Resources

Buying Your First Franchise
Dr. Rebecca Luhn
Crisp Publications, 1992

A quick overview of the topic.

Directory of Franchising Opportunities
LaVerne Ludden
Career Research & Testing, 1994

A handbook for entrepreneur/franchise investors with the sources for public/private aid.

Tips and Traps When Buying a Franchise
McGraw Hill, 1994

More solid info on what to look for.

International Franchise Association
1350 New York Ave., NW
Washington, DC 20005
(202) 628-8000

Consulting

Kennedy Publications
(800) 531-0007

Leading independent source of information on the management consulting, executive search and corporate outplacement professions. Publishes The Directory of Management Consultants, The Directory of Executive Recruiters, The Directory of Outplacement Firms, Consultants News, Executive Recruiter News and Special Reports in all three fields.

Jumping the Job Track: Security, Satisfaction and Success as an Independent Consultant
Peter C. Brown
Crown Trade Paperbacks, 1994

Million-Dollar Consulting: The Professional's Guide to Growing a Practice
Alan Weiss
McGraw-Hill, 1992

How to Become a Successful Consultant in Your Own Field
Hubert Bermont
Bermont Books, 1992

Getting New Clients
Richard A. Connor, Jr. and Jeffrey P. Davidson
John Wiley & Sons, 1993

The Consultant's Calling
Geoffrey M. Bellman
Jossey-Bass, 1990

The 10 Hottest Consulting Practices
Ron Tepper
John Wiley & Sons, 1995

Writing Winning Business Proposals
Richard C. Freed, Shervin Freed and Joe Romano
McGraw-Hill, 1995

*Selling Your Services: Proven Strategies for Getting Clients to Hire
You or Your Firm*
Robert W. Bly
Henry Holt & Co., 1994

Practical guide for execs and managers going into consulting.

The Professional Consultant
(503) 224-8834
A monthly newsletter of advice for consultants.

National Directory of Consultants & Consulting Firms
http://sashimi.wwa.com/~notime/eotw/bus–info–sources/consult.html

Freelancing, Temping and Contract Staffing

The Portable Executive
John A. Thompson
Simon & Schuster, 1995

Chairman of pioneering executive temporary placement firm describes the market and how you might become a part of it.

Directory of Executive Temporary Placement Firms
Kennedy Publications, 1995

Comprehensive listing of agencies placing executives and professionals in temporary positions in the United States and Europe.

National Association of Temporary and Staffing Services
119 S. Saint Asaph St.
Alexandria, VA 22314-3119
(703) 549-6287

Contract Employees: Six New Staffing Strategies to Increase Your Profits
Ralph Palmen
National Video Profiles Inc.
(800) 323-7995

Home-Based Businesses

Homemade Money
Barbara Brabec (self-published)
(708) 717-0488

Practical tips for a wide range of home businesses. Ten years worth of hard-earned experience in 325 pages.

Working from Home
Paul and Sarah Edwards
Putnam Publishing, 1990

The gamut of issues, from self-assessment to zoning.

The Best Home Businesses for the '90s
Paul & Sarah Edwards
Jeremy P. Tarcher, 1991

Analyzes types of home work for earning potential and skill requirements.

The Joy of Working from Home—Making a Life While Making a Living
Jeff Berner
Berrett-Koehler Publications, 1994

How to set-up and organize your home office. Motivational and practical tips. Includes marketing, tax and health issues. Good resource listings by chapter.

Success Working from Home
Jeff Berner
P.O. Box 244
Dillon Beach, CA 94929

Bimonthly newsletter that combines facts and opinions, plus guest experts and established home-business examples.

Home Office Computing
(800) 228-7812

Excellent monthly magazine offering coverage of the increasingly important link between technology and home business. HOC maintains a presence on all the major on-line services.

Home Business Review: The Educational Source for Home-Based Businesses
(800) 460-2458
http://www.tab.com/Home.Business/

A high-quality monthly newsletter.

Home-Based Business News
(503) 246-3452

Bimonthly newsletter for the new home-business person about taxes, marketing, consulting services, technology and the law.

The Kern Report: Trends & Issues in Home-Based Business & Telecommuting
P.O. Box 14850
Chicago, IL 60614

Eight-page quarterly that covers government policy issues, trends, profiles and resources for home-based livelihood.

Home Business Line
American Home Business Association
397 Post Rd.
Darien, CT 06820

Monthly eight-page comprehensive newsletter.

American Association of Home-Based Business
P.O. Box 10023
Rockville, MD 20849
(800) 447-9710 or (301) 963-9153
76655.1560@compuserve.com

American Home Business Association
4505 South Wasatch Blvd.
Salt Lake City, UT 84124
(801) 273-5455

Association for Electronic Cottages
677 Canyon Drive
Sierra Madre, CA 91024

International Association of Home-Based Businesses
P.O. Box 4841442
Denver, CO 80248-1442
(800) 414-2422
73523.2506@compuserve.com

National Alliance of Homebased Businesswomen
P.O. Box 306
Midland Park, NJ 07432

Marketing and Technology

153 Ideas for Totally No-Cost Marketing
Peter Silver
Marketing Communications Report
P.O. Box 2152
South Miami, FL 33243-2152

Checklist of creative and practical tips for getting customers.

Secrets of Successful Direct Mail
Richard V. Benson
NTC Publishing, 1993

Insights and secrets from a successful direct-mail veteran.

Advertising on the Internet FAQ
http://sashimi.wwa.com/~notime/eotw/ad–faq.html

T.A.B. Net
http://www.tab.com
E-mail: tomb@tab.com
Economical Web page publishing/display and Internet servicing.

Doing Business on the Internet
Mary J. Cronin
Van Nostrand Reinhold, 1994

The Mosaic Handbook
Dale Dougherty & Richard Koman
O'Reilly & Associates, Inc.
Sebastopol, CA 1994
(800) 998-9938

The Wall Street Journal's Personal Technology Column
Walter S. Mossberg
http://ptech.wsj.com

Internet in a Box
Spry Communications
(800) 557-9614, ext. 213
E-mail: iboxinfo213@spry.com

The first and best-known home Internet connection kit.

Health and Time Management

Time Well Spent
Larry Tobin
Beyond Words Publishing, 1989
(800) 284-9673

Daily self-reminders about stress reduction and office efficiency.

Zap! How Your Computer Can Hurt You
Don Sellers
Peachpit Press, 1994
(800) 283-9444

Self-care at the keyboard: How to prevent carpel tunnel syndrome, eyestrain, back & neck pain, etc.

Finances

Finding Money for Your Small Business
Max Fallek
(800) 328-2906

Internal Revenue Service
(800) 829-3676
Tax Guide for Small Business (Publication 334)
Self-Employment Tax (Publication 533)
Free Tax Services (Publication 910)

Taxing Time
http://inept.scubed.com:8001/tax/tax.html

Easy Financials for Your Home-Based Business
Norm Ray
Payve Productions
(800) 852-4890

Index

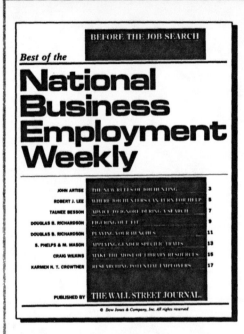

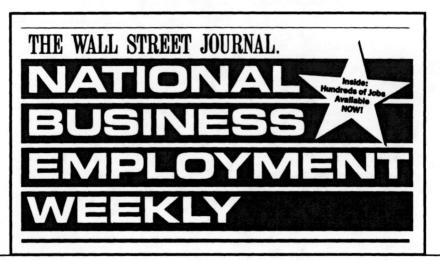

LaVergne, TN USA
13 January 2010
169734LV00006B/8/A